For Reference

Not to be taken from this room

The Atlas of Birds

MIKE UNWIN

W9-BYG-520

The Atlas of Birds

DIVERSITY, BEHAVIOR, AND CONSERVATION

MIKE UNWIN

PRINCETON UNIVERSITY PRESS

PRINCETON AND OXFORD

Published in the United States, Canada, the Philippine Islands, and Puerto Rico by
Princeton University Press, 41 William Street, Princeton, New Jersey 08540
nathist.press.princeton.edu

Produced for Princeton University Press by
Myriad Editions
Brighton, UK
www.MyriadEditions.com

Copyright © Myriad Editions Limited 2011

Requests for permission to reproduce material from this work
should be sent to Myriad Editions Limited.

All rights reserved
The moral rights of the author have been asserted

Library of Congress Control Number: 2011920367
ISBN: 978-0-691-14949-3

Edited and coordinated by Jannet King and Candida Lacey
Designed by Isabelle Lewis and Corinne Pearlman
Maps and graphics created by Isabelle Lewis

Printed on paper produced from sustainable sources.
Printed and bound in Hong Kong through Lion Production
under the supervision of Bob Cassels, The Hanway Press, London.

This book has been composed in
Baskerville Old Face, Stempel Garamond, and Myriad Pro

1 3 5 7 9 10 8 6 4 2

This book is sold subject to the condition that it shall not by way of trade or otherwise,
be lent, re-sold, hired out, or otherwise circulated without the publisher's prior consent
in any form of binding or cover other than that in which it is published and without a
similar condition including this condition being imposed on the subsequent purchaser.

Front cover photograph credits (top to bottom, left to right): Green Honeycreeper
(*Chlorophanes spiza*), Northern Range, Trinidad. Photographer: Kevin Schafer/
Photoshot; Green-headed tanager (*Tangara seledon*), Brazil. Photographer: Mike Lane/
Photoshot; European bee-eater (*Merops apiaster*) calling, Lleida, Catalonia, Spain.
Photographer: Jordi Bas Casas/Photoshot; Painted bunting (*Passerina ciris*) male, perched
in granjeno bush, Texas, USA. Photographer: Larry Ditto/Photoshot; Robin (*Erithacus
rubecula*), Spain. Photographer: Jordi Bas Casas/Photoshot; Hoopoe (*Upupa epops*),
Lleida, Catalonia, Spain. Photographer: Jordi Bas Casas/Photoshot

Contents

Ref
598

A World of Birds

By the time you've read to the bottom of this page – wherever in the world you are – you will probably have seen or heard a bird. Perhaps sparrows bickering at your garden feeders, gulls mewling overhead or pigeons on the office windowsill. Maybe even a caged budgie in the very room where you're sitting.

If a real flesh-and-blood bird eludes you, there will doubtless be one represented on a greetings card, stamp, or book cover. Or you could check your kitchen for eggs.

Few creatures are more ubiquitous than birds. This is not surprising. First, there are a lot of them: around 10,000 species, give or take a few contested ones. Indeed, compared with some 5,500 species of mammal, 8,200 species of reptile, and 6,300 species of amphibian, this makes birds comfortably the most diverse of all terrestrial vertebrate classes.

Second, birds are unmissable. Most of those mammals are small and nocturnal, while the majority of reptiles and amphibians are hidden away under rocks or leaf litter. Birds, by contrast, are noisy, colourful, and conspicuously present in every sphere of our daily lives, from shopping trips to ocean crossings. Try totting up how many wild mammals you see in the course of a day. Then do the same with birds.

The upshot is that we know a great deal about birds. They have been the subject of more published literature than any other faunal group, and have inspired our understanding of everything from evolution (Darwin's finches) to animal migration (ringing swallows). Today, birds are often the touchstone by which we monitor threats to our natural environment, be it pesticides in the food web or the impact of deforestation. The canary in the coalmine is, in this respect, an apt metaphor. This atlas aims to illuminate our understanding of birds in terms of geography. It looks at their biology, their conservation status, and their importance to both humankind and the wider environment, in a global context.

First it considers where birds are found. There is no habitat on Earth, including the most hostile deserts, mountaintops, and ice-caps, that does not have its own avifauna. However, the patterns of bird distribution have a significant bearing on our understanding of biodiversity and conservation. For example, the richest bird habitat by sheer number of species is lowland tropical forest. And this is the very habitat that is currently most threatened by human development.

It is a truism that birds know no political boundaries. Where birds live is determined by the wider landscapes to which they have adapted over millennia, not by arbitrary lines on a map. And yet it is often on a national level that threats to birds arise and action is taken. Thus, knowing which countries have the most species is important – as is mapping the distribution of endangered and endemic species. Invariably, areas that are important for endemic birds are hotspots for endemism in general, and so indicate priority areas for biodiversity conservation. BirdLife International has identified more than 10,000 Important Bird Areas (IBAs) around the world. This atlas considers each continent in turn, both in terms of its overall diversity and its IBAs.

No consideration of where birds live, however, would be complete without understanding how they live. From simple reptilian beginnings, birds have evolved an astonishing variety of forms, behaviours, and lifestyles. Indeed, it is this variety of adaptations – their evolutionary versatility – that explains why birds, as a class, have been able to occupy virtually every ecological niche available. This atlas illustrates all key facets of bird biology in a global context, from the tools and techniques with which birds find food, to the costumes and performances with which they attract a mate.

Looking at bird biology and behaviour is also crucial to tackling the threats that birds face. Studies of migration, for instance – both the astonishing journeys of individual birds and the great flyways along which entire populations traverse the globe – have revealed how birds that may be secure in one part of their range are severely threatened in another. Similarly, we need to understand the colonial nesting behaviour of seabirds before we can appreciate just how this most threatened group is affected by changes to the world's oceans.

An atlas also provides the best way to illustrate the many hazards that birds face. Humankind has had a catastrophic impact on birdlife. At least 150 species are known to have died out in the last 500 years as a result of human influence, and today around one in eight species is classified as endangered.

Some of this can be explained by direct persecution – the hunting of the passenger pigeon to extinction over just a few years in the late 19th century being a classic example. The targeting of particular prized species for trade, notably parrots, pheasants, and birds of prey, has also had a severe impact.

But the biggest threats to birds come from the many ways in which human development has damaged and modified the places where they live. This atlas maps each major threat, including deforestation, agriculture, the divisive sprawl of infrastructure, and the insidious pollution of the oceans. It reveals how the invasive alien species that have accompanied us around the globe have devastated many bird populations – especially island species, whose evolutionary isolation has ill equipped them to resist these invaders. And it looks at climate change, the most pressing threat of the 21st century, examining how the distribution of many species is set to change as global warming influences sea level, plant communities, and other vital components of their habitats.

BirdLife International, and its international network of partner organizations, is at the heart of efforts to address these threats and secure the future of birds. Conservation strategies range from intensive programmes that target individual species, such as the well-publicized projects to save the Kakapo and the Californian Condor, to local community action that safeguards or restores key sites and habitats. Education is especially important, particularly among communities in the developing world, where many of the world's most bird-rich – and threatened – habitats are found.

One big advantage of the conspicuous nature of birds is that our understanding of their decline, and of many of the threats they face, does not require volumes of scientific data. It is there for all to see – in, for instance, the disappearance of once common species from farmland, or the distressing sight of oiled seabirds on beaches. Thus, the public interest in birds, and

willingness to act in securing their welfare, plays an important part in their conservation. Wide support for organizations such as the RSPB (UK) and Audubon (USA) gives bird conservation more clout in the political arena, influencing the adoption of legislation and conventions that help safeguard birds. Meanwhile "citizen science" schemes, such as the RSPB's Big Garden Birdwatch or Audubon's Great Backyard Bird Count, allow ordinary people to contribute valuable data, while the popularity of birdwatching as a pastime gives communities all over the world a very real economic incentive for protecting their birdlife.

We need birds. Consider how much they have given us already. As a source of food, few animals on the planet have proved more important than the junglefowl – whose domesticated descendant, the farmyard chicken, is reared in its billions to provide meat and eggs around the globe. Then there are the less tangible but no less significant gifts of companionship, pleasure, and spiritual wellbeing that arise from the way in which birds have permeated our culture. And on an environmental level, birds provide many of the basic biological services, from pest-control to pollination, that keep our environment functioning healthily.

But bird conservation is not about birds alone. Today, BirdLife International and other conservation bodies emphasize that by protecting birds we are protecting the wider biodiversity of the habitats in which they occur. Indeed, studies have illustrated just how many other organisms benefit from bird conservation. Our species is one such organism. Preserving the planet's biodiversity is in our own interests, as it ensures the healthy functioning of the biosphere on which we, too, depend. And we could do worse than start with birds.

Mike Unwin
Brighton, February 2011

Acknowledgements

I am grateful to BirdLife International, who kindly supplied many of the maps used in this atlas, and whose State of the World's Birds was both an inspiring and invaluable source of reference. In particular, I would like to thank Adrian Long, both for his advice in the early stages and – along with Dr Lincoln Fishpool – for his rigorous checking of material as we were rushing to press.

I am also grateful to Danaë Sheehan (RSPB), Nigel Redman (BirdQuest), Robert Cardell (BirdLife Malta), and Rössing Uranium, Namibia for their generous donation of images from their respective projects.

I would like to thank all the Myriad team: Candida Lacey, for her faith in me; Corinne Pearlman, for her formative early input; Isabelle Lewis for her sterling maps and design work; and, especially, Jannet King, for her editorial energies, excellent ideas, and indefatigable pursuit of every detail I overlooked.

Above all, I am deeply indebted to all the many scientists, conservationists and volunteers around the world who have dedicated their lives to making the world a better place for birds. They have, in the process, also made it a better place for me.

Finally, thanks – as ever – to my family, for all their support and patience.

Photo Credits

The author and publishers would like to thank the following for the use of their photographs.

FLPA *www.flpa.co.uk*
6 Hen Harrier: Christian Hütter/Imagebroker; 8 Jamaican Tody: Neil Bowman; Resplendent Quetzal: Thomas Marent; Greater Rhea: Jurgen & Christine Sohns; 15 Confuciusornis: Bert Muller/FN/Minden; Brahminy Starling: Harri Taavetti; 17 Magnificent Frigatebird: David Hosking; 18 Northern Bobwhite: S & D & K Maslowski; 19 Eurasian Sparrowhawk: John Watkins; Long-tailed Widow: Chris & Tilde Stuart; 23 Snow Bunting (summer): Gerard Schouten/Minden Pictures; 24 Long-wattled Umbrellabird: Murray Cooper; 25 Sulawesi Red-knobbed Hornbill: Mark Jones/Minden Pictures; 29 Blue-bellied Roller: Bill Baston; 32 Crab Plover: Neil Bowman; 33 Red-crowned Cranes: Stephen Belcher/Minden Pictures; 34 Shoebill: Jurgen & Christine Sohns; 35 White-necked Picathartes: Frank W Lane; 37 Jamaican Tody: Neil Bowman; Resplendent Quetzal: Thomas Marent; Greater Rhea: Jurgen & Christine Sohns; 39 Southern Royal Albatrosses: Frans Lanting; 40 Gentoo Penguins: Hiroya Minakuchi/Minden Pictures; 44 Red-winged Tinamou: Mike Lane; 48 Hamerkop: Hugh Lansdown; 49 Sunbittern: Edward Myles; African Openbill Stork: Koos Delport; 52 Peregrine Falcon: Konrad Wothe/Minden Pictures; 53 Harpy eagle: Tui De Roy/Minden Pictures; Honey Buzzard: David Hosking; Hobby: Roger Tidman; Black-winged Kite: Neil Bowman; Secretary Bird: Elliott Neep; Osprey: Scott Linstead; African Fish Eagle: Tim Fitzharris/Minden Pictures; White-backed Vultures: Pete Oxford/Minden Pictures; 55 Fischer's Turaco : Jurgen & Christine Sohns; Hoatzin: Flip De Nooyer; 56 Tawny Frogmouth: Gerry Ellis/Minden Pictures; 57 Crested Treeswift: Bill Baston; Sword-billed Hummingbird: Tui De Roy; 59 Speckled Mousebird: John Karmali; Southern Yellow-billed Hornbill: Gerard Lacz; 60 South Island Wren: Geoff Moon; 61 Black-and-red Broadbills: Neil Bowman; Superb Lyrebird: Frans Lanting; 64 Magnificent Frigatebirds: David Hosking; 65 Peregrine Falcon: Konrad Wothe/Minden Pictures; Ruppell's Vulture: Ingo Arndt/Minden Pictures]; 67 Hyacinth Macaw: Frans Lanting; 68 Sword-billed Hummingbird: Tui De Roy; 69 Bearded Vulture: Nigel Dennis; Black Heron: Neil Bowman; 70 Woodpecker Finch:; 71 Kiwi: Tui De Roy; Oilbird: Krystyna Szulecka; 73 Satin Bowerbird: Konrad Wothe; 75 Malleefowl: Eric Woods; 77 Red-and-green Macaws: Frans Lanting; 78 Bird ringer with Ural Owl: David Hosking; 80 Pallas's Leaf Warbler: Roger Tidman; 81 Eleanora's Falcon: Konrad Wothe; 82 Wallcreeper: Mike Lane; 86 Kerala: Parameswaran Pillai Karunakaran; 87 Traditional trapper: Ariadne Van Zandbergen; 87 Martha the Passenger Pigeon: S & D & K Maslowski; 89 Guano collectors: Tui De Roy/Minden Pictures/; 90 Papua New Guinea headdress: Patricio Robles Gil/ Minden Pictures; 92 Osprey eggs: Frans Lanting; 93 Arabian Babbler: Mike Lane; 95 Arctic Tern: Winfried Wisniewski/Minden Pictures; Quelea: Jurgen & Christine Sohns; 97 Red-and-green Macaws: Frans Lanting; 101 Spix's Macaw: Claus Meyer; 102 Yellow-eared Parrots: Murray Cooper/Minden Pictures; 103 Asian Crested Ibis: Mitsuaki Iwago; Spoon-billed Sandpiper: Chris Schenk/FN/Minden; 105 Little Bustard : Malcolm Schuyl; 107 Demoiselle Cranes: Winfried Wisniewski/Minden Pictures; Barn Owl: Richard Du Toit/Minden Pictures; Emu: Mark Sisson; 108 Hen Harrier: Christian Hütter/ Imagebroker; Common Quail: Sunset; 109 Hong Kong bird market: ImageBroker/Imagebroker; Red-vented Cockatoo: Gerard Lacz; Lilac-crowned Parrot: Jurgen & Christine Sohns; 110 House Sparrow: Mark Newman; 111 Galápagos Petrel: Tui De Roy/Minden Pictures; Cyanide notice: Colin Monteath/Minden Pictures; 112 Northern Gannet: Steve Trewhella; 113 Laysan Albatross: Rebecca Hosking; Common Guillemot: Roger Tidman; Common Goldeneye: Mark Newman; 115 Sooty Shearwater: Terry Whittaker; Common Cuckoo: Marcel Van Kammen; 118 RSPB: David Hosking; Red-fronted Macaw : Tom and Pam Gardner; 119 Spot-breasted Plover: Ariadne Van Zandbergen; Eastern Imperial Eagle: David Hosking; 121 Thames Estuary: Robert Canis; 123 Crested Ibis: Xi Zhinong/Minden Pictures; Black Robin : Geoff Moon; White-rumped Vultures: John Holmes; 125 Caribou: Ingo Arndt/Minden Pictures; Skylark: Hugh Clark; Marbled Teal: Alan Parker; 127 Sokoke Scops Owl: Neil Bowman ; Nepalese villagers: Broker/Imagebroker.

iStockphotos *www.istockphoto.com*
1 Red-tailed Tropicbird: Dennis Maloney; 5 Blue-footed Booby: Burt Johnson; 7 Collared Dove: Iain Cartwright; 9 Malachite Kingfisher: Johan Swanepoel; 12 Peafowl feather: Adrian Costea; 14 Large Ground-Finch: Michael Stubblefield; Small Tree-Finch: Kristian Larsen; Common Swift: Andrew Howe; Hummingbird: Richard Rodvold; 15 Archaeopteryx: Bob Ainsworth; Southern Cassowary: Craig Dingle; 16 White Pelican: Igor Kovalenko; 17 Ostrich: John Carnemolla; Mallard: Tammy Wolfe; Black-crowned Night-heron: Robert Blanchard; 18 King Vulture: Steffen Foerster; 19 Common Eider nest: janol; Great Crested Grebe: Kevin Browne; Asian Fairy Bluebird: Neal McClimon; 20 Emperor Penguins: Armin Rose; Roseate Spoonbill: Rob Hill; Adelie Penguins: Christian Wilkinson; European Bee-eater: Nikolay Stoilov; Burchell's Sandgrouse: Johan Swanepoel; 25 Great Gray Owl: Saipg; Superb Fairywren: Keiichi Hiki; 27 Weka: Holger Mette; 29 Great Hornbill: TommyIX; 30 Gannets: Alan Crawford; English Partridge: Mark Green; 31 Golden Eagle: alarifoto; Tawny Owl: Andrew Howe; Eurasian Bittern: John Mottram; Eurasian Hoopoe: Iliuta Goean; 32 Black-billed Capercaillie: Mihail Zhukov; Collared Dove: Iain Cartwright; 33 Golden Pheasant: Danish Khan; Bar-headed Geese: Pradeep Kumar; Alpine Chough: Mihail Zhukov; Rhinoceros Hornbill: Sze Fei Wong; 35 Lesser Flamingos: Liz Leyden; Okavango Delta: Peter Malsbury; Cape Vultures and Bearded Vulture: Lukas Maton; 36 Blackburnian Warbler: Paul Tessier; Common Yellowthroat: Larry Hennessy; 37 Andean Cock-of-the-rock: Windzepher; Snowy Owl: Rich Phalin; Andean

Condor: Jakob Leitner; **39** Lesser Bird-of-Paradise: Omar Ariff; Southern Cassowary: Craig Dingle; Takahe: Graeme Knox; Laughing Kookaburra: Keiichi Hiki; New Holland Honeyeater: Gerry Pearce; Galah Cockatoo: Nico Smit; **40** Snowy Sheathbill: Mike Matas; Wandering Albatross: Cassie Tait; King Penguins: Mlenny; **41** Little Auk: Pauline S Mills; Hawaiian Goose: Cay-Uwe Kulzer; Red-tailed Tropicbird: Dennis Maloney; **42** Crested Caracara and Great Egret: Frank Leung; **44** Emu: John Carnemolla; **45** Malachite Kingfisher: Johan Swanepoel; **46** Chachalaca: Frank Leung; Magpie Goose: Charles Gibson; **47** Common Loon: Mike Eikenberry; Western Grebe: Michael Thompson; **48** Lesser Flamingos: Liz Leyden; **49** Great Blue Heron: Damian Kuzdak; Jabiru Stork: Torsten Karock; Roseate Spoonbill: Robert Blanchard; Sacred Ibis: Robert Blanchard; Greater Flamingo: Lori Skelton; **50** Bush Stone-curlew: Craig Dingle; Black-browed Albatross: Richard Sidey; **51** Brown Pelican: Lynn Berreitter; Red-tailed Tropicbird: Dennis Maloney; Rockhopper Penguin: Rich Lindie; **52** Andean Condor: Jakob Leitner; **53** Northern Harrier: Paul Tessier; **54** Wood Pigeon: Andrew Howe; Sulphur-crested Cockatoo: Chrisho; Burchell's Sandgrouse: Johan Swanepoel; **57** Allen's Hummingbird: Richard Rodvold; Rufous Hummingbird: Frank Leung; Stripe-Tailed Hummingbird: John MacIlwinen; **58** Red-and-yellow Barbet: Rob Broek; **59** Elegant Trogon: Frank Leung; **61** Common Cardinal: Steve Byland; Common Redstart: Mikko Hyvärinen; Common Magpie: Nicole Aletta Planken-Kooij; **62** Northern Gannets: Ray Herns; **65** Ruby-throated Hummingbird: Frank Leung; White Storks: earthmandala; Copmmon Swift: Andrew Howe; **66** Blue-footed Booby: Burt Johnson; **67** Nuthatch: Bruce MacQueen; Osprey: Thomas Takacs; Greater Road-runner: Digital Photo Services; African Jacana: Mogens Trolle; Rainbow Lorikeets: Dave Townsend; **69** Clarke's Nutcracker: David Parsons; Crossbill: Vassiliy Vishnevskiy; Black-browed Albatross: Richard Sidey; Toucan: ranplett; **70** Blue Jay: Allan Mueller; **72** Red-necked Phalarope: Dmitry Deshevykh; Bullfinch: Andrew Howe; **73** Sage Grouse: Tom Tietz; Kingfishers: Andy Gehrig; Bluethroat: Vassiliy Vishnevskiy; Peacock: Tony Campbell; **73** Waved Albatrosses: Achim Baqué; **74** Tufted Puffin: Sandra Banister; Burrowing Owl: Missing; **75** Great Tit: Charlie Bishop; Olive-backed Sunbird: Tan Kian Khoon; Killdeer eggs: Bonnie Lee Kellogg; Masked Weaver: Johan Swanepoel; **76** Snow Geese: Frank Pali; **77** Starling flock: Arpad Radoczy; Oxpeckers: Herbert Kratky; Sociable Weavers: Kira Kaplinski; **78** Barn Swallows: Fibena; **79** Sedge Warbler: 12396002; Green Warbler: Dave Sangster; **81** Turkey Vulture: Nancy Nehring; Dunlin: Carsten Madsen; **83** Shelduck: Nikolay Stoilov; **84** Domestic chicken: Andyd; **86** Red Junglefowl: pongpol boonyen; **87** Pheasant shooter: son Lugo; Turkey hunter: Jon Huelskamp; **88** Ostrich: senai aksoy; **89** Snowy Egret: John Pitcher; Rubens engraving: Steven Wynn; Chinese fisherman: Christophe Testi; Lanner Falcon:

Philippa Banks; Budgerigars: Poula Hansen; **91** Bald Eagle: Andy Gehrig; Robin: Andrew Howe; Raven: Ivan Bliznetsov; Goldfinch: Andrew Howe; Crested Partridge stamp: Ray Roper; **92** Barnacle Goose: Andrew Howe; **93** Black-legged Kittiwake: Liz Leyden; Black Woodpecker: Vassiliy Vishnevskiy; Bateleur Eagle: Johan Swanepoel; **94** Whooper Swans: Peter Zwitser; **95** Scarecrow: Erik de Graaf; Millet: Alexey Buhantsov; **96** Ospreys: Norman Bateman; **98** Cassowary warning sign: Wendy Townrow; **101** Moa: Alexander Dam; **104** Rainforest loss: mikadex; **105** Cerrado cultivation: ricardoazoury; Forest fire: Brasil2; **107** Appalachian mining: Christina Richards; Spanish Imperial Eagle: Grafissimo; Lesser Flamingos: Sebastien Burel; White-rumped Vulture: ErickN; **111** American Crow: Nancy Nehrig; Cat: Vassiliy Vishnevskiy; White-headed Duck: Terry Lawrence; Ruddy Duck: Ken Hoehn; **112** Atlantic Puffin: Joe Gough; **114** Cape Longclaw: Alta Oosthuizen; **115** Keel-billed Toucan: Eduardo Mariano Rivero; Emperor Penguins: GentooMultimediaLimited; Pied Butcherbird: Craig Dingle; **116** Blue Tit: Dmitry Maslov; **119** Finland: Samuli Siltanen; Fairy Tern: Terry J Lawrence; Rhinoceros Hornbill: Sze Fei Wong; **122** California Condor stamp: Ray Roper; California Condor: Palle Rasch; **123** Great Bustard: Steven Cooper; **124** Western Meadowlark: Charles Brutlag; **125** Great Bittern: Georgios Alexandris; Sumatran Tiger: Mark R Higgins; **126** Bullock's Oriole: Missing35mm; **127** Birdwatcher: Alexander Kosev; **128** Downy Woodpecker: Tammy Wolfe.

Mike Unwin:

15 Nile Crocodile; **17** Toco Toucan; **19** Greater Potoo; **29** Eider Duck; Mountain Gorilla; **31** Greater Flamingos; **37** Chestnut-eared Aracari; **41** Fulmar; **56** Spotted Eagle Owl; **58** White-fronted Bee-eater; **61** Ovenbird nest; Bokmakierie; **71** Painted Stork; **77** Cattle Egrets; **91** Falcon hieroglyph; African headdress; **97** Ruwenzori Sunbird; **101** Great Auk; **103** Lesser Kestrel; **105** African Spoonbill; **115** Dunlin; **126** Iceland Gull.

Others:

23 Snow Bunting (winter): Gary Trew; **26** Seven-coloured Tanager: NHPA/Harold Palo Jr; **27** Cape Sugarbird: NHPA/Nigel J Dennis; Helmet Vanga: NHPA/Nick Garbutt; Great Philippines Eagle: *www.philippineeagle. org*; **70** African Grey Parrot: Jannet King; **71** Kestrel: Creative Commons; **80** Bird ringing: Creative Commons; **86** Battery chickens: CIWF Compassion in World Farming; **87** St Kilda: The St Kilda Tapes; **88** Pigeons: Bundesarchiv; **95** Feeding the pigeons: Jannet King; **96** Alan and Ruth Davies: Peter Lobo; **97** US birders: George Gentry / National Digital Library; Birdwatching in Georgia: Nigel Redman; **101** Hawaii O'o: Creative Commons; Ivory-billed Woodpecker: Anon; Dodo: Dronte; **106** Cerulean Warbler: Creative Commons; **108** Maltese hunter: Robert Cardell; **109** Blue-fronted Amazons: Fly Free; **121** Birdwatchers: Rossing Uranium, Namibia; **125** RSPB: RSPB;

Part One

INTRODUCTION TO BIRDS

Modern birds can trace their lineage back to the Jurassic Period, some 150 million years ago. Indeed, most scientists now believe that birds represent the only living relatives of the dinosaurs. Since then, on the basic template of a skeleton adapted for flight, evolution has fashioned a cornucopia of variations. The key to this variety has been the feather – an adaptation that was present in birds' Jurassic forebears, and that has evolved a dazzling range of forms and functions in their modern descendants.

Bird Beginnings

Birds' origins have long been a hot topic of debate. Scientists have had to work with relatively meagre pickings from the fossil record, as the lightweight bones of birds are not easily preserved. Nonetheless, there is now enough evidence to link birds firmly to the dinosaurs.

Central to the debate has been *Archaeopteryx lithographica*, the famous "missing link" fossil discovered in 1861 in what is now southern Germany, just two years after the publication of Darwin's *On The Origin of Species*. This crow-sized creature had a reptile's jawbone, teeth, clawed toes, and bony tail. But it also had wings and feathers, which suggested that flight – even if only in short bursts – was important to its survival.

Archaeopteryx, which lived about 150 million years ago, was for a long time seen as the ancestor of modern birds. The truth, however, is now thought to be more complex. This ancient reptile probably represented a parallel lineage in the class Aves, which, like birds, descended from theropod dinosaurs. Theropods had already evolved a number of birdlike features before the advent of birds, including hollow bones, a wishbone, a backward-pointing pelvis, and a three-toed foot. In time, their forelimbs and hands became progressively longer and more flexible, allowing them to make a swift snatching motion – probably in order to catch prey – that was almost identical to the flight stroke of modern birds.

Small Tree-Finch (Camarhynchus parvulus)

Large Ground-Finch (Geospiza magnirostris)

Recent fossil evidence unearthed in China suggests that feathers, too, evolved in theropods before birds. These modified scales may initially have served for warmth or display, but their capacity for providing lift offered distinct advantages to a small predator that leapt from the ground after prey. Soon feathers began evolving more sophisticated adaptations for the demands of flight.

It was during the Cretaceous Period (145 million to 65 million years ago) that birds began to diversify significantly – and this was probably when the subclass Neornithes, which comprises modern birds, evolved. Many new lineages emerged, including the Ichthynornithes, which were gull-like fish-eaters, and the Hesperornithiformes, which adapted so thoroughly to their aquatic niche that, paradoxically, they lost the ability to fly.

By the end of the Cretaceous, the Neornithes had already split into two superorders, determined by the anatomy of their jaws: the Paleognathae, or "old jaws", which today comprises just the flightless ratites and the Latin American tinamous; and the Neognathae, or "new jaws", which comprises all other modern bird orders. Among the latter, the superorder Galloanserae, which includes the Galliformes (game birds) and Anseriformes (waterfowl), was also already established.

Ever since a mass extinction – probably triggered by a meteorite strike – brought down the curtain on the dinosaurs at the end of the Cretaceous Period, the Neognathes have continued to proliferate, dividing into the many orders that we know today. While scientists continue to debate the relationships between these orders, there is now little doubt that modern birds are the only living descendants of the dinosaurs.

The species engine

The Galápagos finches (Geospizinae) are a group of 15 small birds found on the Galápagos Islands that have played a pivotal role in evolutionary theory. It was Charles Darwin's studies of these birds, collected during the voyage of HMS *Beagle* (1831–1836), which crystalized his thoughts on natural selection. Though similar in most respects, the finches differ significantly in their bills, each of which is adapted in size and shape to exploit a specific food source. Some have large bills to break open seeds, others have fine bills to catch insects, and some use their bills like woodpeckers, to check beneath tree bark. All, however, are descended from a single ancestor, one of the first land birds to reach these remote islands. They have since diversified through natural selection to fill roles that are occupied by completely different birds on the South American mainland. This diversification of one species into many, fuelled by newly available ecological niches, is called adaptive radiation.

▼ Growing together, moving apart

Unrelated species may evolve similar outward traits by adapting in similar ways to shared environmental challenges. This is called convergent evolution: the species in question have converged from different backgrounds towards a similar point, usually reflected in their build or behaviour. Swallows and swifts, for instance, both have long narrow wings, forked tails, tiny feet, small bills, wide mouths, and agile flight as adaptations for catching insects on the wing – and indeed these birds are often confused, despite belonging to completely different orders.

Hummingbirds, on the other hand, which *are* related to swifts, have adapted to a very different lifestyle and so are quite different in appearance. This is an example of divergent evolution.

Common Swift
(Apus apus)

Barn Swallow
(Hirundo rustica)

Allen's hummingbird *(Selasphorus sasin)*

Copyright © Myriad Editions

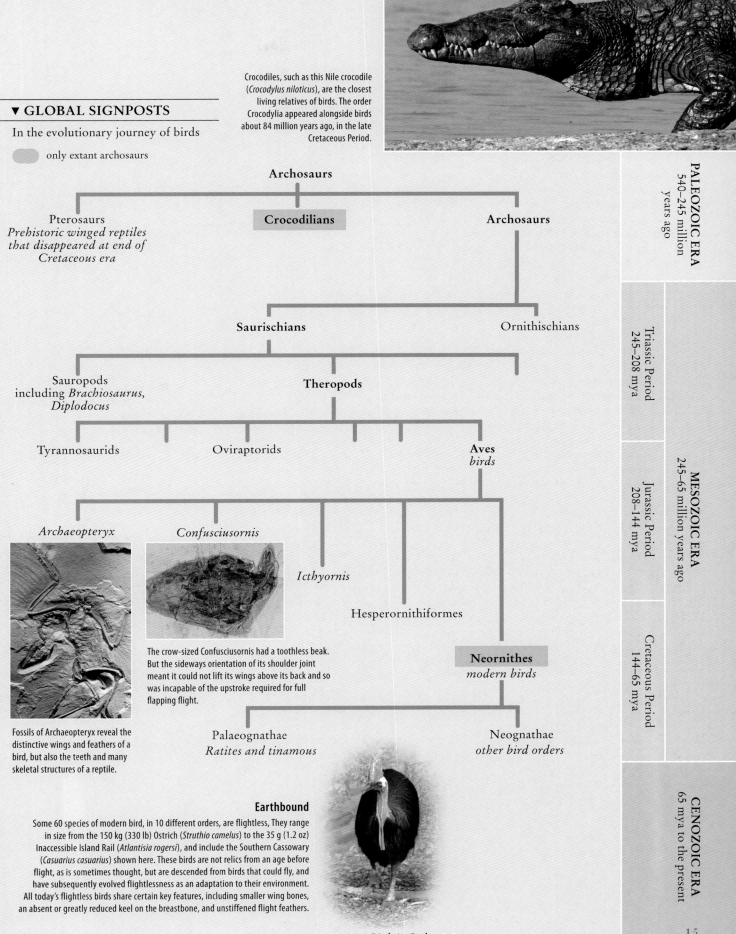

Crocodiles, such as this Nile crocodile (*Crocodylus niloticus*), are the closest living relatives of birds. The order Crocodylia appeared alongside birds about 84 million years ago, in the late Cretaceous Period.

Archosaurs

Pterosaurs
Prehistoric winged reptiles that disappeared at end of Cretaceous era

Crocodilians

Archosaurs

Saurischians

Ornithischians

Sauropods
including *Brachiosaurus*, *Diplodocus*

Theropods

Tyrannosaurids

Oviraptorids

Aves
birds

Archaeopteryx

Confusciusornis

Icthyornis

Hesperornithiformes

Neornithes
modern birds

The crow-sized Confusciusornis had a toothless beak. But the sideways orientation of its shoulder joint meant it could not lift its wings above its back and so was incapable of the upstroke required for full flapping flight.

Fossils of Archaeopteryx reveal the distinctive wings and feathers of a bird, but also the teeth and many skeletal structures of a reptile.

Palaeognathae
Ratites and tinamous

Neognathae
other bird orders

Earthbound

Some 60 species of modern bird, in 10 different orders, are flightless, They range in size from the 150 kg (330 lb) Ostrich (*Struthio camelus*) to the 35 g (1.2 oz) Inaccessible Island Rail (*Atlantisia rogersi*), and include the Southern Cassowary (*Casuarius casuarius*) shown here. These birds are not relics from an age before flight, as is sometimes thought, but are descended from birds that could fly, and have subsequently evolved flightlessness as an adaptation to their environment. All today's flightless birds share certain key features, including smaller wing bones, an absent or greatly reduced keel on the breastbone, and unstiffened flight feathers.

42–61 Birds in Order ▶▶

PALEOZOIC ERA
540–245 million years ago

MESOZOIC ERA
245–65 million years ago

Triassic Period
245–208 mya

Jurassic Period
208–144 mya

Cretaceous Period
144–65 mya

CENOZOIC ERA
65 mya to the present

Fit for Purpose

Many of the traits often considered fundamentally avian – from singing and nest building to flight itself – are also found in some other animals. Among vertebrates, however, birds are defined by the way in which they have evolved for a largely airborne lifestyle. Feathers are just one of their many unique anatomical adaptations.

The most immediately obvious way in which a bird's body is adapted for flight is the modification of its front legs into wings. The humerus (upper arm) is held close to the body and powers the flap. This means the first visible section of the spread wing is the ulna (forearm), the flexible middle joint the wrist, and the outer section the hand. It is this hand that supports and controls the flight feathers, allowing birds their aerial manoeuvrability.

A bird's skeleton must be both light enough to get airborne and strong enough to withstand the exertions of flight. To reduce weight, most larger bones are hollow, with internal struts to keep them from buckling, while many small tail and finger bones have disappeared altogether. A lightweight bill of keratin has replaced heavy jawbones and teeth; instead of chewing, a bird must grind down food in its gizzard – a modification of the gut.

For strength, other bones – including some vertebrae, the pelvic girdle, and the clavicles – are fused, to help brace the skeleton. The enormous, keel-shaped sternum (breastbone), which in mammals is proportionally much smaller and flatter, anchors the massive pectoral muscles that power the wing beats.

Birds' leg bones, unlike their wing bones, are solid. This helps absorb the impact of landing, and supports their entire body weight while on the ground. The "feet" are actually toes – thus the apparently backward-bending "knee" joint is really an ankle, with the real knee concealed among belly feathers. This arrangement provides balance: by holding the powerful upper leg (femur) close to the body, a bird keeps a solid centre of gravity. The lower leg has no fleshy muscles; tendons stretched over the joints operate the toes.

Flight requires prodigious energy, so birds have also developed a super-fast metabolism to fuel their exertions. They feed often, taking mostly high-energy foods such as seeds and insects. Excess energy is stored as fat, with small birds capable of laying this down at astonishing speed.

Special adaptations enhance both respiration and circulation. A bird's heart is four-chambered, like a mammal's, but proportionately larger – especially in smaller birds. When the bird breathes, the air circulates through a number of connected "air sacs" that, in turn, are connected to some of its hollow bones. Thus, the lungs are constantly supplied with oxygen-rich air: two breaths in and out pump it through the entire respiratory system, rather than just the one that mammals need. These breaths are driven not by a diaphragm but by muscular contractions of the ribcage.

Birds have
11 to 25
neck vertebrae
compared with
just 7 in humans.

relation to flight. Despite its size, with a wingspan approaching 2.5 metres (over 8 ft), its skeleton weighs no more than the sum of its feathers.

▼ The beating heart

Hearbeats per minute

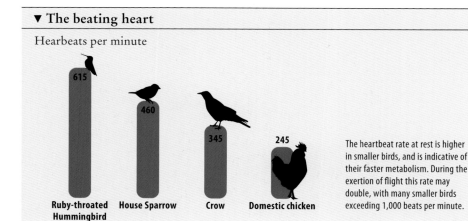

615	460	345	245
Ruby-throated Hummingbird	House Sparrow	Crow	Domestic chicken

The heartbeat rate at rest is higher in smaller birds, and is indicative of their faster metabolism. During the exertion of flight this rate may double, with many smaller birds exceeding 1,000 beats per minute.

Two legs good

The Ostrich (*Struthio camelus*) and other flightless bird species retain the bipedal stance of flying birds. A running ostrich can exceed 70 km/h (43 mph). Like all running birds, it hold its powerful upper legs close to its body, so all that is usually visible to the observer is the lower leg, flexed at the ankle and balanced on the toes.

Cold feet

The feet of this Mallard (*Anas platyrhynchos*) appear highly vulnerable to the freezing conditions. But they are protected by a system known as counter-current heat exchange. The blood vessels leading to and from a bird's legs pass alongside each other, so warm arterial blood leaving the body heats up the cold veinous blood leaving the legs. This prevents frostbite, and enables birds to maintain a constant body temperature of 40° Celsius (104° Fahrenheit).

Automatic locking

A roosting Black-crowned Night-heron (*Nycticorax nycticorax*) perches securely on a branch. An ingenious mechanism prevents birds from losing their grip while asleep. Each toe is connected to a tendon, which stretches tight when the leg is bent and so locks the toes around their perch.

Overloaded

You might imagine that the enormous bill of a Toco Toucan (*Ramphastos toco*) would pose problems in flight. But despite being one-third of the bird's length, this lightweight appendage weighs just one twentieth of its mass. Inside the outer shell is a foam-like honeycomb of air pockets, divided by keratin-fibre struts, which means the bill is both light enough for flight and strong enough for feeding.

Two-part harmony

A Brahminy Starling (*Sturnia pagodarum*) warbles its breeding song. Unlike mammals, which use a larynx in the throat, birds produce their sounds deeper down in an organ called the syrinx, which vibrates when air passes through it. The syrinx is located where the trachea divides into the two bronchial tubes that lead to the lungs. This means most bird vocalizations are effectively composites of two separate sounds – and explains their complexity. Members of the starling family are among the most articulate of all songsters.

Copyright © Myriad Editions

Feathers

Feathers define birds. Having evolved among their reptilian ancestors to provide insulation, these modified scales have since adapted to multiple purposes, from waterproofing to camouflage, display and, of course, flight.

Different feathers have different functions on a bird. Tiny soft feathers, called down, lie against the skin and trap an insulating layer of warm air. More robust "contour feathers" overlap neatly to provide a weatherproof outer shell. The large "flight feathers" in wings and tail provide air resistance and control in flight. Some birds have specialized feathers for other purposes: bristles are stiff, hair-like feathers around the bill of insect-eating birds, which help detect prey, while plumes are modified feathers used by many species in display.

The simple, flexible structure of feathers explains their versatility. Each consists of a central shaft with a row of branches, called barbs, along each side. On contour and flight feathers these barbs attach to one another by tiny hooks, called barbules, to create a sleek resistant surface called a vane. Tiny muscles at each feather's base allow a bird to adjust its plumage as required.

Feathers need constant maintenance. Birds preen with their bill and feet, and spread oil from a gland at the base of the tail to waterproof their plumage. They also take regular baths. Most species moult some or all of their feathers twice a year, to replace those that are worn or damaged. Moult is an energy-intensive activity and so generally takes place after the breeding season.

Outer plumage also provides a colour palette that is vital to a bird's survival in various ways. First, subtle camouflage colouration can help a bird blend into its surroundings. This is especially important to ground-nesting birds, in which females tend to have brown, mottled plumage that makes them hard for predators to spot. Second, colourful or striking plumage serves to enhance courtship and breeding success – and many species sport decorative plumes for this purpose, such as the ear tufts of a grebe, or the wispy train of an egret.

Many species are sexually dimorphic – males generally having brighter plumage than females – with extreme examples including most ducks and game birds. But conspicuous plumage can attract predators as well as mates, so males of many species moult into a more subdued plumage after breeding. Colours also change with age. Birds that mature slowly, such as gulls and eagles, may take several years before acquiring full adult plumage.

An additional and fundamental function of plumage patterns is identification. Signature markings ensure that each species mates only with its own kind. Thus, where similar species share a habitat – for example ducks such as Mallard (*Anas platyrhynchos*) and Northern Shoveler (*Anas clypeata*) – the males' distinct colouration helps prevent mistaken identity.

▼ Three main feather types

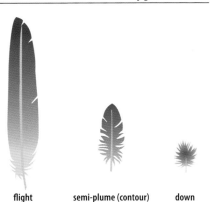

flight   semi-plume (contour)   down

Dusting down
A male Northern Bobwhite (*Colinus virginianus*) takes a dust bath. A number of species use this as an alternative to water. By sifting the dust through their plumage they can dislodge parasites and other impurities.

Skin deep
The King Vulture (*Sarcoramphus papa*) has a largely unfeathered head and neck. This adaptation, common to both Old World and New World vultures, prevents its feathers from becoming soiled with blood when it probes a carcass. Vultures are scrupulously clean birds and bathe daily.

▼ FEATHER FORMS AND FUNCTIONS

Softly, softly

The female Common Eider (*Somateria mollissima*) lines her nest with down plucked from her breast. Eider down is a better insulator than any other known natural material, being exceptionally soft, thick and lightweight. Eiders nest in and around the Arctic and North Atlantic, where for centuries their down has been harvested to use in quilts and other bedding material.

Feather figures

Longest feathers ever recorded: ornamental chicken bred in Japan in 1972, whose tail feathers measured 10 m 59 cm (34 ft 9 in) long.

Longest feathers of any wild bird: the tail feathers of the male Crested Argus Pheasant (*Rheinardia ocellata*), which can reach 173 cm (5 ft 8 in) in length.

Longest wing feathers relative to body length: the trailing inner primaries of the breeding male Pennant-winged Nightjar (*Macrodipteryx vexillarius*), which measure 60 cm (2 ft).

Most feathers: the Tundra Swan (*Cygnus columbianus*) has over 25,200, of which 80% are on its head and neck.

Fewest feathers: the Ruby-throated Hummingbird (*Archilochus colubris*) has 940.

Longest time to develop full breeding plumage: six to nine years for a Wandering Albatross (*Diomedea exulans*).

Head-shaker

The facial adornments of a Great Crested Grebe (*Podiceps cristatus*) are present in both male and female, and are used to enhance their headshaking courtship displays. The ruff and crest are shed in winter, when the bird moults into a plainer plumage.

Wet through

A Eurasian Sparrowhawk (*Accipiter nisus*) takes a bath in a woodland pool. Regular bathing is important for keeping feathers in good condition. Some species will dive into water in flight; others may sit out in a rain shower, or rub their plumage against wet foliage.

Now you see me…

The Greater Potoo (*Nyctibius grandis*), a nocturnal species, uses not only its cryptic plumage, but its posture, to appear almost as a seamless extension of its perch.

Trick of the light

The brilliant blue of an Asian Fairy Bluebird (*Irena puella*) is produced by the refraction of light through tiny prisms in the feather barbs. All blues and greens in birds' plumage are produced in this way. Other plumage colours come from pigmentation within the feather. Melanin, for instance, produces black, brown and chestnut, while minerals called carotenoids produce reds and yellows.

Weighed down

The extravagant tail of the male Long-tailed Widow (*Euplectes progne*) is a highly visible advert to females during his slow, cruising display flight. But it also leaves the bird extremely vulnerable to predators. As soon as the courtship season is over, these long black plumes are moulted and replaced by an anonymous streaky brown plumage like that of females.

Copyright © Myriad Editions

Part Two

EMPEROR PENGUINS (*Aptenodytes forsteri*).

WHERE BIRDS LIVE

Birds have conquered every habitat on earth, including the most hostile deserts and ice-caps. Certain habitats are more productive than others, however, and the regions with the greatest number and variety of birds are those where tropical forest predominates. Each continent has its characteristic avifauna, though many species range all over the world – both by land and sea. Isolated regions have the highest proportion of endemic species. BirdLife International has identified more than 10,000 Important Bird Areas around the globe, which provide a focus for conservation efforts.

Bird Habitats

There is scarcely an inch of the planet that is not home to one bird or another. Alpine Choughs (*Pyrrhocorax graculus*) have been recorded at 8,080 metres (26,500 ft) on Mount Everest, and Emperor Penguins (*Aptenodytes forsteri*) at 550 metres (1,650 ft) beneath the Antarctic Ocean. Birds have adapted to ice-caps and deserts, and crossed oceans to colonize the remotest islands.

The Earth's many habitats – both aquatic and terrestrial – fall into a number of broad ecological zones, called biomes. Each is defined by its plant structures and its prevailing climatic conditions, which reflect latitude, humidity, and elevation. The same biome may go by different names in different parts of the world: temperate grassland, for example, is known as "steppe" in central Asia, "prairie" in North America, and "pampas" in South America.

The richest biome for birds is forest, which is home to nearly three-quarters of all species. Other significant biomes are shrubland, grassland, savanna, inland wetlands, and "artificial", the last of these comprising various urban, agricultural and other landscapes that have been modified by humans. Each biome can, in turn, be subdivided into smaller habitat types. There are numerous types of forest, for example, of which subtropical/tropical lowland moist forest supports the most birds, with over 3,600 species.

Over time, every habitat has acquired an avifauna adapted to its specific conditions. This has resulted in groups sharing similar traits. Rainforest species of many families have especially loud songs in order to broadcast their message through the dense canopy, while grassland birds as diverse as bustards and larks use conspicuous breeding displays to take advantage of the open terrain.

Such specializations mean that many birds are tied to a single biome. In Africa and Madagascar, some 910 species – 42 percent of the regional total – are confined to single biomes. Migrants, however, change biomes with the season, as they follow their food source from one habitat to another. Some of the world's most successful species are generalists that can tolerate many habitats: the Winter Wren (*Troglodytes troglodytes*) is Britain's most numerous bird precisely because it can thrive everywhere, from mountains to suburbia.

Every species uses only part of its chosen habitat to supply its needs. Thus, each habitat can be further subdivided into microhabitats, known as niches. This allows similar species to live close together without competition. On a single European tree, for instance, Blue Tits (*Cyanistes caeruleus*) can search for insects among thinner twigs than the heavier Great Tits (*Parus major*). The diversity of plant life in tropical rainforest offers more niches than any other habitat, and explains why this habitat supports the most birds.

The dependence of birds upon the habitat in which they have evolved has profound implications for conservation, with habitat loss being the single biggest factor behind declining bird populations worldwide.

▼ Forest bird species

Distribution by type of forest

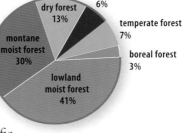

◯ subtropical/tropical

- dry forest 13%
- montane moist forest 30%
- lowland moist forest 41%
- tropical mangrove 6%
- temperate forest 7%
- boreal forest 3%

There are 6,900 forest species compared with 200 in deserts

▼ Sea cliff cities

Multiple niches within each habitat enable different species to co-exist without competition. A sea cliff can support a variety of seabirds by satisfying the differing requirements of each, including shelter, available nest material, access to food, and safety from predators.

Puffins nest in earth burrows as protection from larger, predatory seabirds.

Gannets nest in dense colonies near the top, usually on islands, which have fewer predators.

Kittiwakes build colony nests of mud, grass, and seaweed on narrow ledges.

Guillemots build no nest, and cram into dense colonies on the narrowest, barest ledges

Shags nest in smaller numbers lower down, fashioniong messy nests from seaweed and refuse.

▼ Habitat

Number of bird species supported by each habitat

- forest 6,900
- artificial 2,800
- shrubland 2,400
- grassland 1,400
- wetlands 1,200
- savanna 1,200
- coastal 500
- marine 250
- desert 200

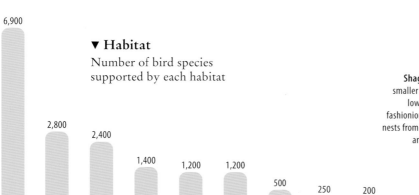

▼ TERRESTRIAL BIOMES

The 18 principal biomes*

- ice-sheet and polar desert
- tundra
- taiga
- temperate broadleaf forest
- temperate steppe
- Mediterranean vegetation
- subtropical rainforest
- monsoon forest
- grass savanna
- tree savanna
- subtropical dry forest
- tropical rainforest
- arid desert
- xeric shrubland
- dry steppe
- semi-arid desert
- alpine tundra
- montane forest

* Different authorities recognize different biomes, but all conform to the same basic pattern.

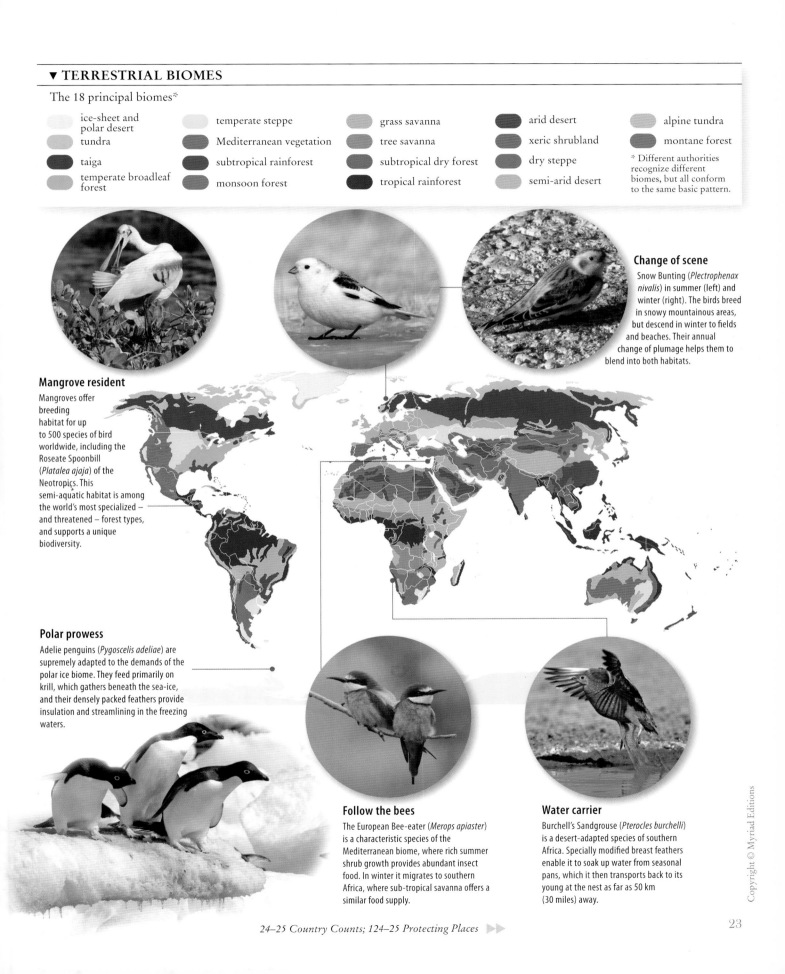

Change of scene
Snow Bunting (*Plectrophenax nivalis*) in summer (left) and winter (right). The birds breed in snowy mountainous areas, but descend in winter to fields and beaches. Their annual change of plumage helps them to blend into both habitats.

Mangrove resident
Mangroves offer breeding habitat for up to 500 species of bird worldwide, including the Roseate Spoonbill (*Platalea ajaja*) of the Neotropics. This semi-aquatic habitat is among the world's most specialized – and threatened – forest types, and supports a unique biodiversity.

Polar prowess
Adelie penguins (*Pygoscelis adeliae*) are supremely adapted to the demands of the polar ice biome. They feed primarily on krill, which gathers beneath the sea-ice, and their densely packed feathers provide insulation and streamlining in the freezing waters.

Follow the bees
The European Bee-eater (*Merops apiaster*) is a characteristic species of the Mediterranean biome, where rich summer shrub growth provides abundant insect food. In winter it migrates to southern Africa, where sub-tropical savanna offers a similar food supply.

Water carrier
Burchell's Sandgrouse (*Pterocles burchelli*) is a desert-adapted species of southern Africa. Specially modified breast feathers enable it to soak up water from seasonal pans, which it then transports back to its young at the nest as far as 50 km (30 miles) away.

24–25 Country Counts; 124–25 Protecting Places ▶▶

Copyright © Myriad Editions

Country Counts

No two countries share the same selection of the world's 10,000 or so species of bird. The number varies by state, from fewer than 50 on some island nations to more than 1,800 in the most bird-rich territories. In each case, several factors are involved.

First, size isn't everything. Russia is more than 60 times the area of Ecuador, yet Ecuador's 1,515 recorded bird species are more than twice Russia's 645. In fact, only one of the world's five largest countries, Brazil, is among the top five by number of bird species.

The explanation lies in habitat. Much of Russia, lying largely at northerly latitudes, comprises vast tracts of taiga and tundra, where biodiversity is limited. Ecuador lies in the Neotropics, the richest of the biogeographical realms. Its modest borders enclose sizeable chunks of the Amazon rainforest and the Andes, both prolific bird habitats.

Other factors include physical barriers, such as oceans and mountain ranges, that prevent birds from expanding their range, and climatic factors, such as rainfall, with high-rainfall areas supporting higher numbers of species. The highest bird diversity is in the tropics, and thus the countries with the greatest species density are all equatorial. Tropical birds also tend to have smaller ranges, so that the composition of species varies more from place to place than it does in temperate or polar regions.

The number of species in any country does not necessarily reflect its total number of birds. Iceland, for instance, is home to only 73 breeding species of bird, but some – such as the Atlantic Puffin (*Fratercula arctica*) occur by the million. And, the number of states in which a particular bird occurs does not necessarily reflect that bird's overall abundance. The 1.5 billion Red-billed Quelea (*Quelea quelea*) are all confined to Sub-Saharan Africa, but represent the world's most numerous species. The Peregrine Falcon (*Falco peregrinus*), by contrast, occurs on every continent bar Antarctica, but its global population is estimated at fewer than 300,000 breeding pairs.

Birds, of course, do not recognize national boundaries. Nonetheless, ascertaining in which countries a species occurs is important in conservation terms, as countries differ dramatically in both culture and resources. This is of particular concern with migrants, whose annual journeys may take them over a number of different countries. It is significant in this respect that the most bird-rich countries are all in the developing world, where conservation may be lower down a list of national priorities. The highest fully developed nation on the list is the USA, at number 23. No European nation makes it into the top 60.

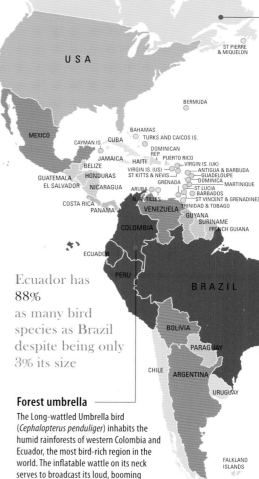

Ecuador has **88%** as many bird species as Brazil despite being only **3%** its size

Forest umbrella

The Long-wattled Umbrella bird (*Cephalopterus penduliger*) inhabits the humid rainforests of western Colombia and Ecuador, the most bird-rich region in the world. The inflatable wattle on its neck serves to broadcast its loud, booming courtship calls through the dense forest canopy.

▼ Biogeographic distribution

Number of land bird species by biogeographic realm

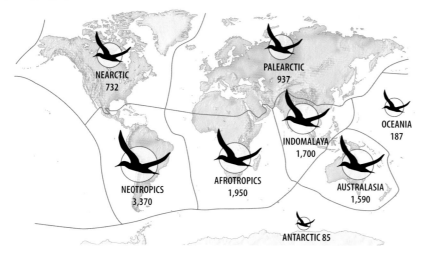

NEARCTIC
732

PALEARCTIC
937

OCEANIA
187

INDOMALAYA
1,700

NEOTROPICS
3,370

AFROTROPICS
1,950

AUSTRALASIA
1,590

ANTARCTIC 85

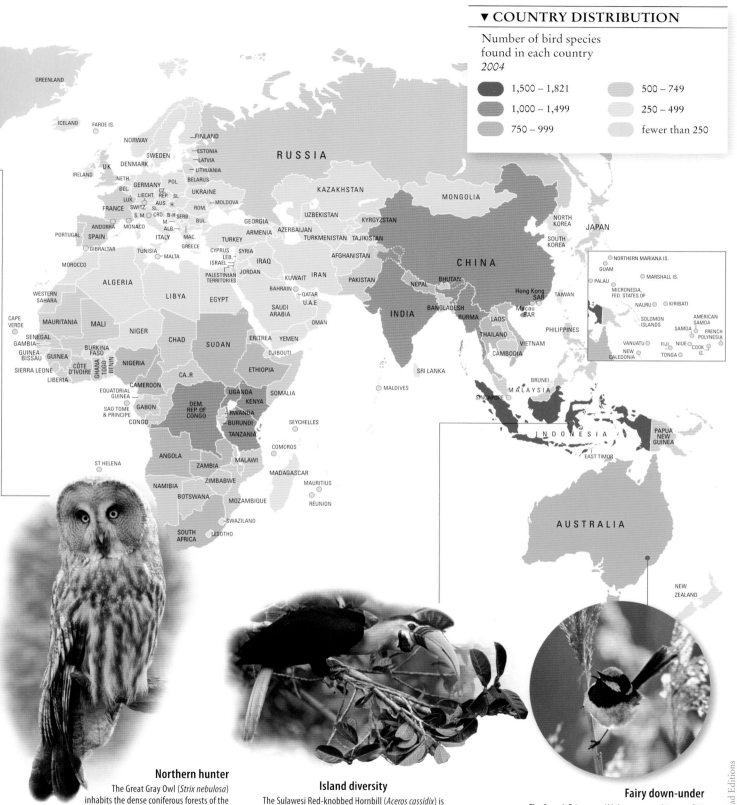

Copyright © Myriad Editions

▼ COUNTRY DISTRIBUTION

Number of bird species
found in each country
2004

1,500 – 1,821	500 – 749
1,000 – 1,499	250 – 499
750 – 999	fewer than 250

Northern hunter

The Great Gray Owl (*Strix nebulosa*)
inhabits the dense coniferous forests of the
taiga, extending across the northern hemisphere
through Russia, Scandinavia and Canada, where it preys on
other birds and small mammals. Harsh winter conditions
explain why this habitat is relatively poor in species diversity.
Even specialists like this must often travel large distances in
search of food.

Island diversity

The Sulawesi Red-knobbed Hornbill (*Aceros cassidix*) is
confined to Sulawesi and its outlying islands, and is one of
several hornbill species that thrive in the fruit-rich
rainforests of Indonesia. The rainforests of the
Indo-Malayan zone support the greatest biodiversity after
the Amazon Basin, and Indonesia has the most bird species
of any country outside South America.

Fairy down-under

The Superb Fairywren (*Malurus cyaneus*) is one of 14
fairywren species in the family Marulidae, which is confined to
Australia and New Guinea. It occurs across a wide range of
habitats, from grassland to forest and suburbia, and is notable
for its unusual pair-bonding behaviour – both partners being
socially monogamous but sexually promiscuous.

Endemic Birds

A species of bird – or indeed any other organism – found in only one place is described as being endemic to that location.

Endemism generally arises when species evolve in a particular suite of environmental conditions, with minimal influence from outside. Consequently, remote oceanic islands often have a high proportion of endemics among their avifauna. Other endemism hotspots include isolated areas of a particular habitat, such as forest, wetland, or mountain, which act as ecological islands. The Wattled Ibis (*Bostrychia carunculata*), for example, is found only in the Ethiopian highlands at altitudes above 1,500 metres (4,920 ft).

Endemism may also arise when the population of a species that was once widespread has been reduced to a single location or habitat. This phenomenon, known as paleoendemism, is becoming increasingly common as human exploitation of natural resources destroys unique habitats to which the survival of specialist species is tied.

Endemic species are especially vulnerable because they have nowhere to go when factors such as habitat loss or competition from alien species threaten their survival. This explains why islands have seen the most recent extinctions. On Hawaii, for instance, at least 45 endemic bird species have become extinct since the arrival of the first humans – with nine of those disappearing in the last 200 years alone (compared with just two in that time for the whole of mainland North America).

BirdLife International has identified 218 Endemic Bird Areas (EBAs) around the world. Each is home to two or more "restricted range" species – those with a range of less than 50,000 square km (19,300 sq miles). EBAs are of particular concern to conservationists, as the presence of endemic birds is generally an indication that much of the other flora and fauna is also unique and thus worthy of particular attention – and, almost certainly, protection.

► Island Endemics

Endemic species as percentage of total *2004*

Madagascar: 111 out of 262
42%

Forest colours

The Atlantic lowland forest of Brazil comprises a completely separate biome from the Amazonian forests to the north and west, and is home to a rich array of endemic fauna and flora. Among over 200 endemic birds are at least ten endemic genera, including such spectacular species as the Seven-coloured Tanager (*Tangara fastuosa*).

▼ Endemic Bird Areas

The 218 EBAs identified by BirdLife International as home to two or more species with a restricted range

- central point within EBA

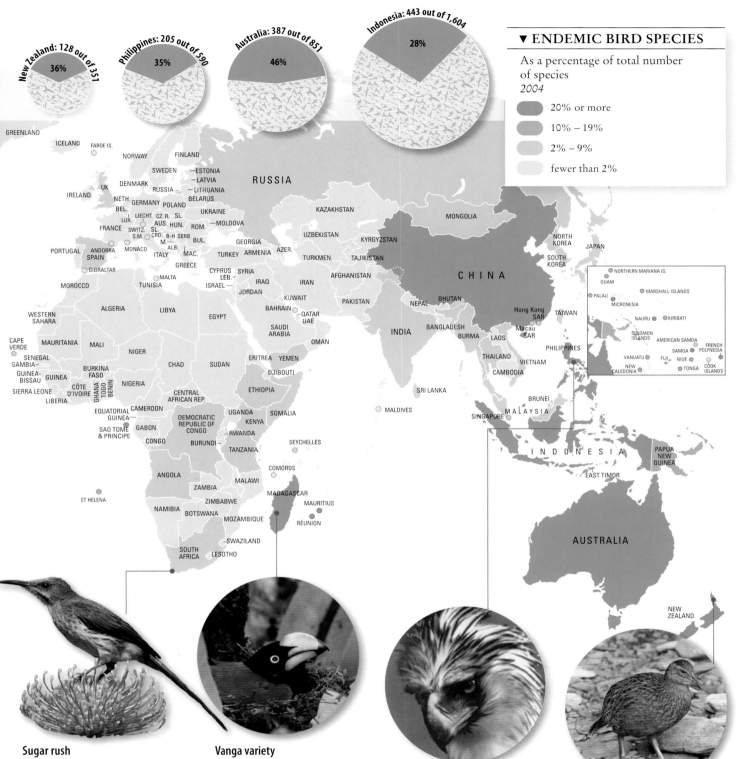

New Zealand: 128 out of 351 — 36%

Philippines: 205 out of 590 — 35%

Australia: 387 out of 851 — 46%

Indonesia: 443 out of 1,604 — 28%

▼ ENDEMIC BIRD SPECIES

As a percentage of total number of species
2004

- 20% or more
- 10% – 19%
- 2% – 9%
- fewer than 2%

Sugar rush

The Cape Sugarbird (*Promerops cafer*) is one of six bird species endemic to the fynbos of South Africa's Cape. This heath-like habitat is proportionally the richest, though by far the smallest, of the world's six floral kingdoms. It comprises a diverse community of endemic flowering shrubs, such as proteas. The Sugarbird uses its long, curved bill to extract nectar from these blooms, thereby playing an important role in the pollination process.

Vanga variety

Madagascar's high degree of endemism reflects its evolutionary history. The island broke away from the Gondwana super-continent some 120 million years ago, allowing many groups of birds to evolve in isolation. Vangas (Vangidae) are an endemic family of small forest-dwellers, whose 22 species exhibit a great variety of adaptations. The formidable bill of the Helmet Vanga (*Euryceros prevostii*) allows it to snap up frogs, spiders and crabs.

Monkey-eater

The Great Philippine Eagle (*Pithecophaga jefferyi*) is one of more than 200 birds endemic to the Philippines. Weighing up to 7 kg (15.5 lb), it is among the world's largest eagles, capable of capturing prey the size of monkeys and palm-civets. Today, fewer than 500 of these impressive birds remain, with the bulk of the population found on the island of Mindanao, where they inhabit mid-montane forest.

Grounded

The Weka (*Gallirallus australis*) is among an amazing 87% of New Zealand's native birds that are endemic to the country. Its flightlessness evolved in the absence of indigenous terrestrial predators. Today, introduced predators such as cats and foxes pose a severe threat to all flightless species.

Copyright © Myriad Editions

Important Bird Areas

Birds are found all over the world, in all habitats. But some locations are more important than others. BirdLife International, together with its partner organizations worldwide, has identified nearly 11,000 sites in some 200 countries and territories as Important Bird Areas, or IBAs. These provide a vital conservation tool both for birds in particular and biodiversity in general.

The number of recognized IBAs is growing annually, as participation in the IBA programme worldwide gathers momentum. At the Nagoya conference on global biodiversity in October 2010, BirdLife unveiled a new map that plotted for the first time the location of over 10,000 IBAs worldwide. This shows that the distribution of IBAs is far from even. Europe's seemingly disproportionately high total of 4,500, for instance, reflects the fact that the European landscape has become highly fragmented by agriculture and development, so that important bird habitats tend to exist in small, scattered pockets. In some countries, by contrast, the process of IBA identification is only now getting off the ground, due to lack of resources, lack of knowledge, or both.

The criteria used to identify IBAs follow an internationally agreed standard. Each site must do one or more of the following: first, hold significant numbers of one or more globally threatened species; second, belong to a set of sites that together hold a suite of restricted-range species or biome-restricted species; and third, support exceptionally large numbers of individuals either at breeding sites, on migration, or in their non-breeding ranges.

Identifying marine IBAs presents additional challenges, particularly with regard to site delimitation. Areas at sea that are being included in the IBA network include seaward extensions to breeding colonies, migration bottlenecks, and sites for concentrations of non-breeding seabirds, both in coastal waters and in the open ocean for pelagic species. Many such areas are vast. Certain countries, including New Zealand, Spain, Portugal, and Estonia have already proposed a number of IBAs on this basis.

In total, the world's terrestrial IBAs occupy around 7 percent of its land area. This may seem a relatively small proportion, but these sites punch above their weight in conservation terms. First, none exists in isolation: IBAs form networks, creating corridors that allow for the movement of birds from one region to another. Second, studies have shown that IBAs are also extremely important for other taxa. Uganda's 30 IBAs, for example, occupy just 8 percent of its land surface, but capture at least 74 percent of the country's 1,247 butterfly species and 82 percent of those of highest conservation concern.

By focusing attention on important areas for birds and other wildlife, IBAs offer a valuable conservation tool. Nonetheless, they do not guarantee protection. Barely a quarter of the world's IBAs enjoy fully protected legal status; in Africa alone, 43 percent receive no recognition at all. Many IBAs around the world are under severe threat from habitat loss and agricultural expansion. BirdLife International and its partners now place increased emphasis on working with local communities, promoting sustainable land-use and poverty-reduction schemes, and involving local people directly in the monitoring and safeguarding of IBAs.

▼ IBAs in Turkey

Importance of IBAs for other fauna and flora

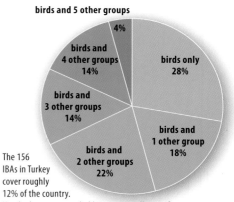

birds and 5 other groups

- birds only 28%
- birds and 1 other group 18%
- birds and 2 other groups 22%
- birds and 3 other groups 14%
- birds and 4 other groups 14%
- 4%

The 156 IBAs in Turkey cover roughly 12% of the country. Nearly three-quarters hold internationally significant populations of at least one other wildlife group, from plants, mammals, reptiles, amphibians, and freshwater fish. Nearly a third are of global or regional importance for three or more different groups, in addition to birds.

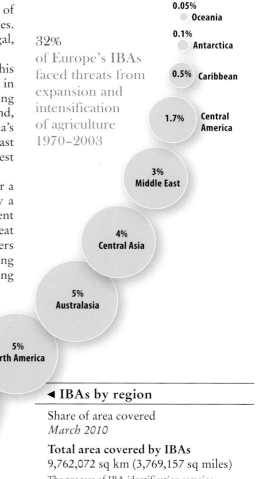

32% of Europe's IBAs faced threats from expansion and intensification of agriculture 1970–2003

- 0.05% Oceania
- 0.1% Antarctica
- 0.5% Caribbean
- 1.7% Central America
- 3% Middle East
- 4% Central Asia
- 5% Australasia
- 5% North America

- 25% Asia
- 23% Africa
- 22% South America
- 12% Europe

◄ IBAs by region

Share of area covered
March 2010

Total area covered by IBAs
9,762,072 sq km (3,769,157 sq miles)

The process of IBA identification remains incomplete in some areas, in particular North America, Australasia, Oceania, and Antarctica

All at sea

The Common Eider (*Somateria mollissima*) is among many species of sea duck that pass through the Baltic region in large numbers outside the breeding season. Latvia and Estonia are among the European countries leading the way in identifying marine areas into which they can extend their IBA programme

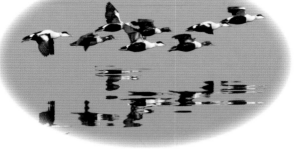

Hornbill haven

A Great Hornbill (*Buceros bicornis*) in an area of lowland forest and wetland in Tây Ninh province, Vietnam, identified as an IBA in 2001 when a survey established the presence of several globally threatened birds and restricted-range species. Local leaders, who had been unaware of the site's biodiversity value, immediately halted development plans. In July 2002, the prime minister declared the area as Lo Go Xa Mat National Park.

▼ BIRDLIFE WORLD IBAS

 Identified by BirdLife International *March 2010*

wholly or partially protected

no or unknown protection

Identification of IBAs in the USA is an on-going process and is being carried out and managed at state level. This map shows only IBAs meeting global criteria and so those classified as state level IBAs are not included.

The Blue-bellied Roller (*Coracias cyanogaster*) is one of 54 bird species confined to the Sudan–Guinea Savanna biome. This vast area of tropical woodland and wooded grassland extends across 22 countries, from Senegal to Eritrea, and lies between the arid Sahel to the north and the Guinea–Congo rainforests to the south. All 54 species are found within the biome's network of 105 IBAs, which occupies just 7% of its total area.

▼ IBAs with biome-restricted species
In Sudan-Guinea Savanna biome and its transition zone with the Guinea-Congo Forests biome

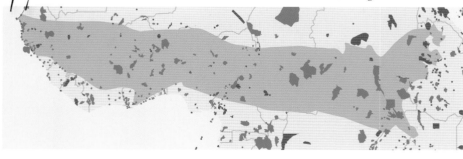

Advantages for apes

Volcanoes National Park in Rwanda's Virunga Mountains has been identified as an IBA. It supports a suite of biome-restricted bird species, many of which are endemic to central Africa's Albertine Rift region. Mountain Gorillas are among numerous other species of conservation concern found within the park's boundaries.

Copyright © Myriad Editions

Europe

Europe, more than anywhere else on Earth, bears a heavy human footprint. The great forests that once covered nearly 90 percent of the continent have been reduced to barely a quarter of that, lost over the centuries to agriculture and development. Nonetheless, a varied avifauna thrives on the habitat mosaic that has supplanted them, with some 700 species finding a regular home on the modified land, and nearly 1,000 recorded in total.

Forest, where it survives, remains the dominant biome across much of Europe. Dense boreal forest extends from northern Asia into the north and east of the continent. South of this, a belt of temperate deciduous forest reaches across to the Atlantic shores – nourished by the Gulf Stream – while further south still the Mediterranean biome is typified by cork oak woodland and low, dry scrub. A tongue of short-grass plains reaches west from central Asia into Hungary, bringing to Europe a taste of the steppes.

The only genuine pockets of wilderness are in the highest mountain ranges, such as the Alps and Pyrenees, and the Arctic tundra of northern Scandinavia and Russia. Here, the alpine conditions support a number of specialist species in summer but very little in winter. Wetlands, by contrast, offer a rich year-round habitat for birds, and among Europe's key avian hotspots are Spain's Coto Doñana, France's Camargue and Romania's Danube Delta.

Coastal habitats are also important, especially large tidal estuaries, such as the Wash in eastern England, which offer vital stopovers for migratory waders and wildfowl. The more inaccessible cliffs and islands, such as those of Western Norway and the Outer Hebrides, support some of the northern hemisphere's most impressive breeding colonies of seabirds.

The fact remains, however, that all Europe's natural habitats have to some extent been modified by human activity. As well as the great tracts of farmland and urban areas, large areas of "forest" are, in reality, monocultural plantations that support a very reduced biodiversity. Even the rugged moorlands of the northern UK are a relic of once extensive forests, felled over the centuries for sheep farming, and this land supports far fewer birds than in its original state.

Birds have proved versatile, however, with many species adapting to agricultural land and urban areas. Some "artificial" habitats, such as reedbeds, heathlands and fishponds – each the product of human intervention – have also developed their own rich avifaunas. There is no turning back the clock, but conservation today focuses on managing these habitats in a way that best protects and restores their biodiversity.

BirdLife International has identified around 4,500 IBAs in Europe – more than any other continent, with 500 in Germany alone (more than Indonesia and Brazil combined). This abundance reflects partly the interest that bird conservation receives in Europe, and partly the fragmented nature of the habitat, which leaves IBAs smaller and more scattered. Either way, there is no cause for complacency, with at least 32 percent of Europe's IBAs currently receiving no legal protection.

Seabird cliffs

Northern Gannets (*Morus bassanus*) crowd onto the steep slopes of the Bass Rock, part of the Firth of Forth Islands IBA in Scotland. This IBA hosts 84,700 pairs of breeding seabirds, including around 40,000 Northern Gannets – nearly 15% of the world population.

Down on the farm

Farmland birds such as the Grey Partridge (*Perdix perdix*) have been in steady decline across Europe for several decades, victims of modern intensive farming practices that deprive them of food and breeding habitat. Farmland birds are now a key focus of conservation action under the EU Birds Directive.

▼ Corncrake conservation

Number of breeding pairs
1998

- 14,000
- 1,000 – 3,200
- 100 – 750
- fewer than 100

NORWAY SWEDEN FINLAND ESTONIA LATVIA LITHUANIA RUSSIA DENMARK UK IRELAND NETH. GERMANY POLAND BELARUS BEL. LIECHT. CZ. REP. SLOVAKIA UKRAINE LUX. AUS. HUNGARY FRANCE SLOVENIA CROATIA ROMANIA YUGOSLAVIA BULGARIA ITALY

At the beginning of the millennium there were 303 IBAs across Europe in which the Corncrake (*Crex crex*) was known to be present. Their combined area of 125,438 square km (48,430 sq miles) supported 28,958 pairs, of which 49 percent were in Russia.

This species breeds in damp, long-grass meadows, and its fortunes are closely tied to farming. In recent decades it has been declining rapidly – by between 20% and 50% in 22 European countries during the 1990s alone – primarily as a result of modern harvesting techniques and drainage. Now listed by BirdLife International as Near Threatened, the Corncrake is the subject of a Single Species Action Plan across Europe, which promotes corncrake-friendly farming as a central strategy.

▼ IMPORTANT BIRD AREAS

Identified by BirdLife International in Europe *March 2010*

wholly or partially protected IBA

IBA with no or unknown protection

Where eagles dare

The Golden Eagle (*Aquila chrysaetos*) is one of Europe's largest predators, capable of killing prey the size of a red fox. Breeding only in the most remote upland regions, each pair requires a territory of around 150 square km (58 sq miles). In winter they descend to lower altitudes in search of food.

Reedbed refuge

Reedbeds are a transitional habitat that provides an important refuge across Europe for wetland wildlife. In Hungary, large reedbeds fringe artificial lakes created for carp fishing, known as fishponds. They support significant breeding populations of threatened waterbirds, such as the Eurasian Bittern (*Botaurus stellaris*), plus large concentrations of migratory waterfowl.

Probing deep

The Eurasian Hoopoe (*Upupa epops*) is a typical species of the Mediterranean, where it nests in tree holes in olive groves and similar open habitats. It uses its long curved bill to probe the ground for insects. The Mediterranean biome is rich in insect-eating species.

French connections

The Camargue is one of Europe's largest and most important wetlands, and one of 277 IBAs in France. A network of freshwater channels, reedbeds and saline lagoons provides habitat for the Greater Flamingo (*Phoenicopterus roseus*), along with a wealth of other waterfowl and aquatic wildlife.

Wood for the trees

The Tawny Owl (*Strix aluco*) is a typical species of deciduous woodland. This habitat, comprising oak and other species, is the dominant forest type across much of central Europe, and supports a rich biodiversity. However, much has been lost to agriculture or modified by woodland management.

Copyright © Myriad Editions

▼ Europe's most bird-rich countries
Number of recorded bird species, including vagrants

557	517	515	501	487
UK	France	Spain	Portugal	Germany

─── Asia & the Middle East ───

A sia is the largest continent, and home to 2,700 species of bird – more than a quarter of the world's total. Its landscapes vary from tropical forest to Arctic tundra and Arabian desert, and include the Himalayas, the greatest of all mountain ranges. It is also home to over half the world's human population, which poses serious challenges for birds.

Two quite separate biogeographical realms meet in the centre of this vast landmass: the Palearctic and the Indo-Malayan. The former, which also comprises North Africa, Europe and the Middle East, is much the larger, but also much the poorer in terms of its avian diversity.

The Palearctic realm extends south from the Arctic Ocean to the Himalayas and the Yangtze river. Ice covered much of the region between two and three million years ago, pushing the vegetation zones south, and much of the bird life in the region has subsequently moved up from southern and eastern Asia. Arctic tundra carpets the highest latitudes. Though virtually bird-free in winter, this inhospitable biome receives a summer invasion of migrants from the south, including great numbers of wildfowl. South of the tundra is a vast belt of boreal forest, known as taiga. Further south still are the central Asian steppes, the deserts of the Middle East, and the Himalayas. Each of these biomes supports a relatively low diversity of bird species but is home to many specialists that have adapted to its challenging conditions.

The Indo-Malayan realm, formerly known as the Oriental realm, lies south of the Himalayas. It extends from India in the west to the islands of Indonesia in the east, where it meets the Australasian realm at the island of Lombok. This tropical and subtropical realm is dominated by forest, from the monsoon forests of India to the lowland rainforests and montane cloudforests of Indonesia.

Biodiversity in South-East Asia's forests is second only to that of South and Central America, and this habitat accounts for nearly three-quarters of all Asia's bird species. Indonesia has the most birds of any country outside South America. Typical families of this region include hornbills, pittas and trogons, while the foothills of the Himalayas host a spectacular array of pheasants. The region's prolific diversity is boosted by its great number of islands, notably in Indonesia and the Philippines, where isolation and productive habitats have fuelled the process of speciation.

Asia's birds, however, are under pressure from the continent's human population of 3.5 billion, with 2.5 billion people in China and India alone. Rampant growth and development have led to wholesale environmental destruction – notably the felling of Indonesia's rainforests – and one in eight species of bird in Asia is now globally threatened. Direct exploitation of birds, both as food and for the cage-bird trade, also takes a heavy toll. BirdLife International has identified 2,295 Important Bird Areas in Asia, which occupy 7.6 percent of the continent's land area, and another 391 in the Middle East.

Northern exposure

The Black-billed Capercaillie (*Tetrao parvirostris*) is a large grouse that breeds in the larch taiga forests of eastern Russia, as well as parts of northern Mongolia and China. It is a sedentary species, tied to the boreal zone. Males fan their tails during the spring courtship display.

Desert shores

A total of 391 IBAs have been identified in the Middle East, covering about 5% of the land area. Over half of these are wetlands, reflecting the great importance of such areas to birds and other wildlife in a region where water resources are scarce. The majority of the world's Crab Plovers (*Dromas ardeola*) breed in the Middle East, excavating their nesting burrows on sandy islands and coastal dunes.

▼ Collared Dove goes west

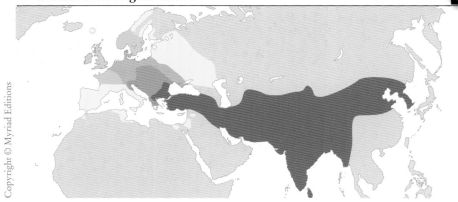

Copyright © Myriad Editions

1930–2010

	1930		1955
	1945		1970		2010

The Eurasian Collared Dove (*Streptopelia decaocto*) has proved over the last century to be one of the great colonizers of the bird world. Its original range was warm temperate and subtropical Asia, from Turkey east to China and south to Sri Lanka. In the 20th century, however, it started spreading west, reaching the UK in 1953, where it bred for the first time in 1956. It has since crossed the Arctic Circle in Norway and reached the Faroe Islands.

◄◄ *22–23 Bird Habitats; 24–25 Country Counts; 28–29 Important Bird Areas*

▼ IMPORTANT BIRD AREAS

IBA Identified by BirdLife International in Asia and the Middle East
March 2010

wholly or partially protected IBA

IBA with no or unknown protection

Revered but endangered

Red-crowned Cranes (*Grus japonensis*) perform a courtship dance on Hokkaido, Japan. This species, also known as the Japanese Crane, is the second rarest crane in the world, and has totemic cultural significance in eastern Asia, where it is seen as a symbol of luck, longevity and fidelity.

Wetland refuge

The Keoladeo National Park is one of 465 IBAs in India. It provides protected status to India's Bharatpur wetlands, which not only support a wealth of breeding birds, but also provide wintering quarters to thousands of migratory waterfowl from further north. The Bar-headed Goose (*Anser indicus*) breeds on the high-altitude Tibetan Plateau, but winters in India, northern Burma and the wetlands of Pakistan.

A wing and a prayer

The Alpine Chough (*Pyrrhocorax graculus*), pictured here in front of Tibetan prayer flags, is a gregarious member of the crow family that occurs in the Himalayas at the highest altitude of any bird in the world.

Hidden colours

The Golden Pheasant (*Chrysolophus pictus*) of western and central China is one of many colourful pheasant species native to the Himalayan foothills. The male's spectacular plumage is generally hidden among the dark undergrowth of the evergreen forests in which it lives.

China's natural environment has suffered widespread degradation, but many areas are still immensely rich in wildlife, including over 1,200 species of bird. In recent decades, the government has declared many hundreds of new protected areas. This provides a major opportunity to ensure the long-term survival of the country's unique biodiversity.

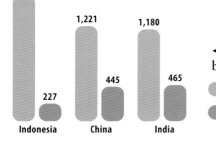

Island variety

The islands of South-East Asia are a prolific centre of bird diversity, with Borneo alone home to more than 630 species, including the Rhinoceros Hornbill (*Buceros rhinoceros*).

◄ Asia's most bird-rich countries

number of bird species recorded

number of IBAs

	Indonesia	China	India
bird species	1,604	1,221	1,180
IBAs	227	445	465

33

Africa

Ever since Aristotle, Africa has been renowned for the wonders of its natural history, and its birdlife is no exception. While the continent as a whole does not boast as many species as South America, it nonetheless supports some of the world's most spectacular wild places, where the avifauna is just one component of a prolific biodiversity.

Africa is the world's second largest continent and, with a surface area of over 30 million square km (11.6 sq miles), represents around one-fifth of the total landmass. Its landscapes fall into three main regions: in the north, the immense Sahara Desert and the arid Sahel; in the centre, the great forests of the Congo basin; and across the east and south, a patchwork of woodland and savanna. Look closer, however, and the picture is more complex. Among the continent's 15 recognized biomes are such unique landscapes as Ethiopia's Afromontane highlands, with their alpine influences, and South Africa's fynbos, with its distinctly Mediterranean flavour.

This tapestry of habitats is home to over 2,400 species of bird in 111 families. Over 1,400 species are endemic to Africa, as are two orders – the mousebirds (Coliiformes) and turacos (Musophagiformes). Among 20 endemic families are the engaging helmetshrikes (Prionopidae) and the bizarre Shoebill (*Balaeniceps rex*), the latter in a family of one. The highest proportion of endemic birds is found in Madagascar, where 111 of the 262 recorded species are found nowhere else. In addition, Africa is a haven for countless million wintering migrants from across Eurasia.

BirdLife International has identified more than 1,230 Important Bird Areas in Africa, which collectively cover around 7 percent of the continent's land area. These range from such biodiversity hotspots as the Albertine Rift in Uganda and Rwanda, home to at least 24 endemics, to vital migration pit-stops, such as the Banc d'Arguin, an area of inter-tidal mud-flats, channels, creeks, and shallow seas in Mauritania.

Despite Africa's great natural riches, its birds are under threat. More than 230 species are classed as globally threatened, between 80 and 90 of them endangered or critically endangered. Although many IBAs fall within or overlap well-known protected areas, such as Tanzania's Serengeti National Park, more than 40 percent still receive no formal recognition. At least half, protected or otherwise, are under direct threat from such factors as agricultural expansion and intensification. While Africa continues to struggle with pressing development issues such as poverty, disease, conflict, and food security, it is hardly surprising that bird conservation does not always take priority.

Faced with such challenges, conservationists are today placing an increased emphasis on working with local communities, involving them more directly in the IBA programmes and contributing to poverty-reduction schemes that help alleviate pressure on protected areas. Meanwhile, a number of ambitious 21st-century initiatives – including the creation of trans-boundary "peace" parks, which establish conservation corridors between nations – aim to protect and restore Africa's biodiversity, including its birds.

▼ IBA protection status

Level of protection of the 100 IBAs holding the greatest number of globally threatened bird species

- ● complete overlap with fully protected area
- ● partially protected
- ● unprotected

▼ Importance of IBA networks

Range of Blue Swallow in relation to IBAs

- non-breeding range
- breeding range
- ● IBAs for non-breeding populations
- ● IBAs for breeding populations

The Shoebill (*Balaeniceps rex*) is endemic to Africa. This bizarre-looking bird, whose scientific name means "king whale-head", stands 1.5 metres (5 ft) tall and uses its enormous clog-shaped bill to capture aquatic prey in the deepest swamps of central Africa, from southern Sudan to Zambia. Today, its population is listed as Vulnerable, with a declining population estimated at between 5,000 and 10,000.

The Blue Swallow (*Hirundo atrocaerulea*) is one of Africa's most threatened species, with an estimated population of no more than 3,000. A network of 34 IBAs has been identified in order to help its conservation: 27 are on its breeding grounds on the montane grasslands of central and southern Africa, while six are on the moist tropical grasslands of the Lake Victoria basin, where it migrates to spend the winter. Together, these sites comprise an area of 20,612 square km (7,958 sq miles) and offer the swallow a cross-continental corridor of protection.

Copyright © Myriad Editions

Identified by BirdLife International in Africa *March 2010*

⬤ wholly or partially protected IBA

⬤ IBA with no or unknown protection

Crossing borders

The threatened White-necked Picathartes (*Picathartes gymnocephalus*) is one of more than 240 forest-dependent bird species to benefit from a new trans-boundary "peace park" established in 2009 by the governments of Liberia and Sierra Leone. This park unites the Gola Forest Reserve in Sierra Leone with the Lofa and Foya Forest Reserves in Liberia to protect one of the largest remaining blocks of intact Upper Guinea forest — one of the world's most biodiverse ecosystems.

In the pink

Lake Nakuru National Park in Kenya was the first national park in Africa to be branded an IBA. Home to more than 450 bird species, it is best known for its population of up to 1.5 million non-breeding Lesser Flamingos (*Phoenicopterus minor*), and is one of just a handful of soda lakes in east and southern Africa where this species finds refuge. Other important wildlife here includes the endangered Black Rhinoceros.

Wetland wonder

Botswana's Okavango Delta, the world's largest inland delta, supports a wealth of water birds, alongside the other wildlife for which the area is internationally celebrated. Here, the Saddle-billed Stork (*Ephippiorhynchus senegalensis*) towers above other herons, storks and egrets. This vast IBA receives Ramsar protection, and also includes a national park and several private reserves. Nonetheless, conservationists fear that a planned hydropower station upstream in Namibia would have a serious impact on its biodiversity and bird life.

Vulture culture

Two endangered Cape Vultures (*Gyps coprotheres*) and an immature Bearded Vulture (*Gypaetus barbatus*) perch high on the great basalt escarpment of South Africa's Giant's Castle Game Reserve. This World Heritage Site forms part of the Natal Drakensberg Park IBA and, with over 200 breeding pairs, is one of the world's strongholds for the Cape Vulture.

1,148	1,103	1,056	1,015	936
Dem Rep Congo	Kenya	Tanzania	Uganda	Cameroon

◀ **Africa's most bird-rich countries**
Number of bird species recorded

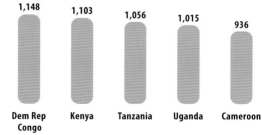

The Americas

The Americas stretch nearly from pole to pole, forming a continental landmass that encompasses many of the earth's greatest topographical extremes and is home to more than 4,500 species of bird – nearly half the world's total.

The two halves of the Americas, however, have a very different avifauna – a fact explained by their evolutionary history. South America split from Africa some 135 million years ago as the prehistoric super-continent of Gondwana broke up. It was not until some three million years ago that it forged its link with North America at the Isthmus of Panama. North America, by contrast, has shared both a continental connection and a recent glaciation history with Europe, the latter explaining the many similar habitats on either side of the north Atlantic today.

North America is the world's third largest continent. Its habitats range from Arctic tundra to the deserts of the southwest, each with a distinct avifauna. Though it has fewer bird species than South America, it makes up for this in sheer abundance, with an estimated 10 billion land birds present at the end of each breeding season. This number falls in winter, however, when the world's greatest mass migratory movement sees approximately 40 percent head south to their tropical wintering grounds.

Bird diversity increases further south towards Central America. Mexico alone is home to more bird species (1,040) than the USA and Canada combined, and typical Central American families such as toucans, motmots and trogons are thought to have originated in South America then extended their range northwards. The Caribbean is of particular interest in conservation terms, with about 25 percent of the islands' 500 or so species being endemic to the region.

South America is less than three-quarters the area of North America, but is home to some three-quarters of the continent's birds – more than 3,200 species. This makes it the most biodiverse region on Earth, and Colombia, Peru, and Brazil are the world's three most bird-rich countries. Of particular interest are the New World sub-oscine passerines, a subdivision of the Passeriformes unique to the Neotropics, with groups such as cotingas, manakins and antbirds showing spectacular diversity.

Other notable bird regions in South America include the Tropical Andes and the Atlantic rainforests of Brazil, both of which harbour numerous endemics. Further south are such avian hotspots as the vast Pantanal wetlands, with its huge gathering of waterbirds, and the Argentinian pampas, home to grassland specialists such as rheas and seriemas.

Sadly, the birds of the world's most bird-rich continent are far from secure. Vast swathes of habitat have been lost to logging, mining, and slash-and-burn agriculture, and today more than 300 species face extinction. BirdLife International has identified more than 2,450 IBAs across South America, and conservation organisations are focusing their attention on these key areas.

Colourful travellers

There are more than 100 species of wood-warbler native to the Americas, many of which breed in the boreal forests of Canada and northern USA and migrate south to winter in Central America. New World wood-warblers (Parulidae) are unrelated to the warblers of the Old World (Sylviidae) and are thought to have evolved in Central America before expanding their range north. Different species gather in large mixed flocks on migration.
Above: Blackburnian Warbler (*Dendroica fusca*)
Left: Common Yellowthroat (*Geothlypis trichas*)

▶ Species diversity in North America

Number of species in areas
of North America

fewer than 45		138 – 176	
45 – 94		177 – 233	
95 – 137		234 – 355	

The diversity of land bird species in North America correlates with latitude. Over the course of a year, more than 350 species of land bird may be found in parts of Mexico, whereas the high Arctic hosts fewer than 45 species. However, this does not reflect abundance, and many of those few Arctic species will occur in very high numbers.

Identified by BirdLife International in The Americas *March 2010*

wholly or partially protected IBA

IBA with no or unknown protection

Arctic hunter

The Snowy Owl (*Bubo scandiacus*) is one of several Arctic species found in North America that have a circumpolar distribution. It breeds on the tundra and moves further south during winter according to the fluctuation of its food supply, chiefly rodents such as lemmings. The owl's largely white plumage is a camouflage adaptation to its snowy environment.

Swamp refuge

The Everglades National Park, at the southern tip of Florida, is the largest subtropical wilderness in the USA and receives over a million tourists a year. It is one of only three locations in the world to share the designations of International Biosphere Reserve, World Heritage Site and Wetland of International Importance. More than 350 species of bird inhabit the mosaic of wetland and marine ecosystems.

Wetland bills

The Pantanal, which spans Bolivia, Brazil, and Paraguay, is the world's largest wetland, covering up to 195,000 square km (75,000 sq miles) in peak flood. It is home to more than 475 species of bird, including the Chestnut-eared Aracari (*Pteroglossus castanotis*), one of at least 38 species in the toucan family (Ramphastidae).

Island endemics

The Jamaican Tody (*Todus todus*) is one of five species in the family Todidae. These diminutive birds are endemic to the Caribbean and exemplify the principle of adaptive radiation, with each species confined to a single island – except on Hispaniola, where there is one species in the highlands and one in the lowlands. Their flattened bills are an adaptation for catching insects.

American ostrich

The flightless Greater Rhea (*Rhea americana*) inhabits the grasslands of South America, from the tropical savannas of Brazil to the Pampas of Argentina. Like its African equivalent, the Ostrich, it has been exploited for use in many products, including feather dusters and leather goods.

Bird of the gods

The Resplendent Quetzal (*Pharomachrus mocinno*) is the largest member of the trogon order (Trogoniformes). This spectacular bird is found in tropical montane forest from southern Mexico to Panama. It features heavily in the indigenous myth and folklore of Central America and was venerated as the snake god Quetzalcoatl by the Aztecs and Mayans.

Peruvian performer

The Andean Cock-of-the-rock (*Rupicola peruvianus*) is one of many colourful members of the cotinga family, indigenous to the Neotropics, and known for the communal courtship display of the males. It inhabits the cloud forests of the tropical Andes, a region that is home to 2,681 species of bird, and is the national bird of Peru.

Wings over the Andes

The Andean Condor (*Vultur gryphus*) is the largest of the New World vultures and uses its 3-metre (10-foot) wingspan to soar effortlessly above the Andes in search of carrion. New World vultures are a fine example of convergent evolution, being completely unrelated to Old World vultures (Accipitridae), despite having independently evolved striking similarities of both appearance and behaviour.

1,860 **1,825** **1,822**

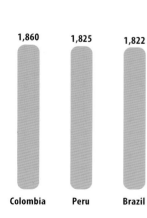

◄ **South America's most bird-rich countries**
Number of bird species recorded

Colombia **Peru** **Brazil**

Copyright © Myriad Editions

Australasia

The continent of Australasia comprises Australia, New Guinea, New Zealand, and the Pacific island groups of Polynesia and Melanesia. This single biogeographic realm is home to at least 1,590 species of bird, including many unique to the region. Only in relatively recent times have people appeared on the scene, but their impact on its birdlife has been profound.

Australia once formed part of the supercontinent Gondwana. About 150 million years ago this huge land mass began to break up, with Australia finally splitting from Antarctica 50 million years ago. Much of the flora and fauna from this Gondwana past has remained relatively unchanged due to Australia's isolation: the native mammals, for instance, are largely marsupials, which on most other continents have been replaced by the placental mammals that evolved later.

The country was once covered with rainforest. But as it has shifted north so it has dried out, leaving a desert interior from which a succession of vegetation zones radiate outwards. These include savanna, woodland, heath, and sclerophyll forest – the last dominated by fire-resistant eucalypts. Rainforest remains only in the northeast, where it still supports the country's greatest biodiversity. The tropical north holds extensive wetlands and mangroves, while saltpans in the arid interior occasionally become seasonal lagoons, attracting numerous breeding waterbirds.

An amazing 45 percent of Australia's 800 bird species are endemic – the highest proportion of any country in the world. Most groups have their evolutionary origins in the Indo-Malayan realm, their ancestors having passed down through the islands of what is now Indonesia. Notable, are the mound-building megapodes, the flightless emu, the nectar-feeding honeyeaters and a rich selection of parrots – including cockatoos and budgerigars.

The heavily forested island of New Guinea, comprising Papua New Guinea and the Indonesian territory of Irian Jaya, has the greatest diversity of birds in Australasia, with at least 720 species recorded in Papua New Guinea alone. Down the island's spine are the rugged and remote Central Highlands. Much remains to be learned about New Guinea's natural history, with new species of fauna and flora being described annually.

New Zealand's long isolation has given rise to one of the world's most unusual avifaunas. With no native terrestrial mammals, a range of species – including the kiwis and Kakapo – have evolved to take their place, many becoming flightless in the process. New Zealand and its offshore islands are also the world's capital of seabirds, with 37 endemic species.

The arrival of humans has had a dramatic impact across much of Australasia. Hunting by the Maori, who arrived on New Zealand 1,000 years ago, accounted for the giant flightless moas. In more recent times the process has been accelerated by the arrival of invasive flora and fauna, from rabbits to cane toads, which have driven many species to the brink of extinction or beyond – either by direct predation, competition, or habitat destruction. In working to conserve what remains, Birds Australia has identified 314 IBAs in Australia. IBAs in New Zealand, New Guinea, and other island groups are still being established.

▼ Australian IBAs

Number of IBAs in each state
2008

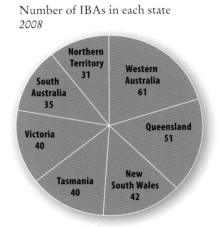

Wallace Line

The islands of Australasia are contiguous with those of South-East Asia, but they belong to two different biogeographic realms, divided by what is known as the Wallace (or Wallace's) Line. Bali and Lombok, just 35 km (22 miles) apart, are either side of this line. To its west, the fauna and flora are part of the Indo-Malayan Realm; to the east they form part of the Australasian realm.

The line is named after Alfred Russel Wallace, a contemporary of Darwin and early evolutionary theorist, who noticed the division between two distinct eco-zones during his travels in the 19th century. It follows a deep oceanic trench that has prevented the movement of most species – even when periods of lower sea-level allowed movement within the island groups on either side.

▼ IMPORTANT BIRD AREAS

Identified by BirdLife International
in Australasia *March 2010*

wholly or partially protected IBA

IBA with no or unknown protection

Pretty Polly

The Galah Cockatoo (*Eolophus roseicapilla*)
also known as the Rose-breasted
Cockatoo, is one of 21 species in the
cockatoo family (Cacatuidae), which is
largely confined to Australasia. These
robust, large-headed parrots are
found in woodland habitats
across much of Australia. This
species is one of the more
common and widespread,
and has adapted well to
suburbia in many areas.

Plumes of paradise

The Lesser
Bird-of-Paradise
(*Paradisaea
minor*) is one of 40
species in the family Paradisaeidae.
Most are confined to New Guinea,
with a few also found in the
Moluccas and eastern Australia.
The spectacular breeding plumes
of the males, used in
communal courtship displays,
have long been collected
for ritual purposes by the
indigenous peoples of
New Guinea.

Rainforest giant

The Southern Cassowary (*Casuarius casuarius*)
inhabits rainforest in northeast Australia and
southern New Guinea, where it plays an important
ecological role in seed dispersal. This flightless bird is
the world's second heaviest, after the ostrich,
weighing up to 85kg (187 lb). The casque on its head
is thought to help amplify its courtship calls. An
important population
survives in the
Daintree IBA in
northern
Queensland.

Nectar specialist

The New Holland
Honeyeater
(*Phylidonyris
novaehollandiae*) is found across southern
Australia and was the first of the country's
bird species to be scientifically described.
Honeyeaters are endemic to Australasia,
with the exception of a single species on
Bali. They feed primarily on nectar, some
species having a brush-tipped tongue for
this purpose, and play an important role in
plant pollination.

Back from the dead

The Takahe (*Porphyrio hochstetteri*) is a
large flightless member of the rail family,
endemic to New Zealand. Once thought
extinct, it was rediscovered in 1948 and
has since been the subject of an intensive
conservation programme, with small
numbers transported to offshore islands,
such as Tiritiri Matangi, that have been
cleared of invasive predators.

Laughing carnivore

The Laughing
Kookaburra (*Dacelo
novaeguineae*) has
achieved iconic status in Australia, thanks to its maniacal call.
Native to eastern areas, though introduced elsewhere, this large
terrestrial kingfisher is one of four kookaburra species. It is
carnivorous, feeding on reptiles, small mammals, large insects
and even other small birds.

Ocean wings

Southern Royal Albatrosses (*Diomedea
epomophora*) flaunt their 3-metre (10 ft)
wingspan during a courtship display at their
breeding colony on the Chatham Islands. New
Zealand's offshore islands are home to more than
half of the world's 22 species of albatross, and all
fall within a network of marine IBAs.

Copyright © Myriad Editions

Antarctica, Oceans & Islands

The world's continents do not account for all birds. Many seabirds spend their lives roaming the high seas, breeding on remote outposts in the Southern and Arctic Oceans. A select few land birds also inhabit oceanic islands, many having evolved in isolation from their continental ancestors.

True pelagic seabirds include the Procellariiformes (shearwaters, petrels, and albatrosses), which are uniquely adapted to life on the ocean wave. Long, narrow wings enable them to glide with minimal effort on updrafts, and their tubular nostrils are adapted to excrete salt from seawater and thus allow them to survive months at sea without fresh water. Outside the breeding season these birds disperse over the world's oceans, tracking converging currents and upwellings for food.

Pelagic birds breed in colonies, generally on islands but also on some continental coasts. Most are found at high latitudes: some, such as auks, in the northern hemisphere, but the great majority, including the penguins and most of the shearwaters and albatrosses, in the southern hemisphere. The island groups of the Sub-Antarctic, such as South Georgia and the South Orkney Islands, are especially important for seabirds. Although the continent of Antarctica is vast, conditions inland are so harsh that most birds are confined to the coast, where the sea provides abundant food. Of the 45 or so species recorded there, 19 breed in the pack-ice that fringes the coast, and the rest mostly on the Antarctic Peninsula.

Ocean record-breakers

Most pelagic bird: Sooty Tern (*Onychoprion fuscatus*) may remain constantly at sea for up to 10 years

Most aquatic bird: most penguins spend 75% of their lives in the sea

Most northerly breeding bird: Ivory Gull (*Pagophila eburnea*) breeds on edge of Arctic pack-ice at 80°N

Most southerly breeding bird: Antarctic Petrel (*Thalassoica antarctica*), recorded at 80°30'S

Fastest swimming bird: Gentoo Penguin (*Pygoscelis papua*) recorded at 36 km/h (22.3 mph)

Longest-submerged bird: Emperor Penguin (*Aptenodytes forsteri*) timed at 18 minutes underwater

In their element

The cold waters of the Southern Ocean teem with krill and other marine life, and penguins, such as these Gentoo Penguins (*Pygoscelis papua*), are supremely adapted to exploit it. Though flightless, they use their wings as flippers to move through the water at great speed and can dive deep below the sea-ice.

Threatened seabirds in the Southern Ocean

The world's highest density of threatened seabirds is in Southern Ocean, but much of this area falls outside national sovereignty, so conservation requires international cooperation – especially for the protection of seabirds against incidental capture by commercial longline fisheries.

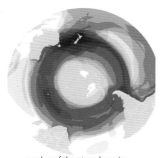

number of threatened species

1   10   20

Ice scavenger

The Snowy Sheathbill (*Chionis alba*) is Antarctica's only permanently land-based bird, and its only species without webbed feet. It is an opportunistic feeder, living around the edge of penguin and other seabird colonies, where it scavenges eggs and dead chicks.

ANTARCTICA

Antarctic Peninsula

South Orkneys Is.

Crozet Island

Southern Ocean

South Georgia

Tristan da Cunha

Tristan da Cunha

The entire world population of the Great Shearwater (*Puffinus gravis*) breeds on four islands in the Tristan da Cunha group. This pelagic seabird is one of the few species that breeds in the southern hemisphere and migrates to the northern. It feeds on fish and squid, and may gather behind fishing boats.

Crowded colonies

King Penguins (*Aptenodytes patagonicus*) are among a number of penguin species that breed on Sub-Antarctic Islands, at the northern reaches of the Antarctic. The largest colony is on Crozet Island, with around 455,000 pairs.

Wanderer

The Wandering Albatross (*Diomedea exulans*) has the greatest wingspan of any bird, reaching 3.5 m (11 ft 6 in) or more, which enables it to spend hours on the wing without flapping. This species ranges for more than 64.7 million square km (25 million sq miles) over the southern oceans, but its breeding range is restricted to just 1,900 square km (730 sq miles) on a handful of Sub-Antarctic islands.

There is no land at the North Pole, and no birds breed on the ice. However, a number of species inhabit Arctic islands, such as Greenland and Svalbard. The northern oceans are also an important refuge for sea duck and other wildfowl, which breed on the coasts and tundra, then disperse across the sea for much of the year.

On the other side of world, numerous endemic land birds have evolved on the scattered Pacific islands of Polynesia, Micronesia, and Melanesia. The geography of this vast region is variously defined, but while political affinities are complex – Hawaii, for instance, is part of the USA – the avifauna has in common both its evolutionary isolation and its extreme vulnerability. The Pacific Islands have more threatened bird species per unit of land than any other region in the world.

Bird conservation across these disparate realms throws up a host of challenges. BirdLife International has identified seabirds and endemic island species as the two most threatened of all bird groups – the first being especially vulnerable to modern fishing techniques, and the second to predation by invasive species. The recognition of IBAs in these realms is ongoing, and includes plans to map marine IBAs that extend from coastlines into the open ocean.

Vomiting voyager

The Northern Fulmar (*Fulmarus glacialis*) is the most widespread of the Northern hemisphere "tubenoses" (Procellariiformes), and ranges vast distances across the north Atlantic and Arctic Oceans. It has even been recorded over the North Pole. This species will defend itself at the nest by vomiting up its oily stomach contents, which can foul the feathers of a predator – even in some cases causing it to drown.

Small bird, big numbers

The Little Auk (*Alle alle*) is the smallest and most numerous of the auk species. More than 2.5 million breed on Northumberland Island, one of 55 IBAs identified in Greenland, several of which boast similar seabird numbers.

Arctic Ocean

Northumberland Island

GREENLAND

Atlantic Ocean

Tropical wanderer

The Red-tailed Tropicbird (*Phaethon rubricauda*) breeds on islands across the Pacific and Indian oceans. Colonies are generally sited on coral atolls, where pairs make their nests under low shrubs or in limestone cavities. This species feeds singly, and disperses as far as Japan outside the breeding season.

▲ IMPORTANT BIRD AREAS

IBA
IMPORTANT BIRD AREA

Identified by BirdLife International in Greenland *March 2010*

wholly or partially protected IBA

IBA with no or unknown protection

Back from the brink

The Hawaiian Goose, or Nene (*Branta sandvicensis*), is the world's rarest goose. Found only in the Hawaiian island group, its population was reduced by hunting and invasive predators from around 25,000 to just 30 in 1951. It has since bred well in captivity, been reintroduced to three islands, and the wild population now stands at around 1,000 geese.

Pacific Ocean

Hawaii

Nauru

Small but special

The Pacific Island of Nauru, which measures just 18 square km (7 sq miles) has recorded the fewest bird species of any sovereign state on Earth, with between 24 and 27 – depending upon which taxonomy is followed. Two are threatened and one, the Nauru Reed Warbler (*Acrocephalus rehsei*), occurs nowhere else.

Copyright © Myriad Editions

Part Three

A Crested Caracara (*Caracara cheriway*), a member of the Falconiformes, pursues
a Great Egret (*Ardea alba*), a member of the Ciconiiformes, for its catch.

BIRDS IN ORDER

The great filing cabinet of avian taxonomy contains some 10,000 species. Scientists have divided these into a number of orders, according to their evolutionary affinities, each of which in turn comprises one or more families. The identity of most orders is the subject of ongoing research and debate, as advances in molecular science overturn traditional taxonomic wisdom, severing some ties while establishing many new ones.

Ratites & Tinamous

By the end of the Cretaceous Period, some 65 million years ago, birds were already evolving within two distinct lineages, known by some as "super-orders": the Palaeognathae and the Neognathae. The former, which is the more primitive, today comprises only two orders. The latter comprises all the rest and thus accounts for some 99.4 percent of modern species.

The Palaeognathae derive their name from the ancient Greek for "old jaws". This refers to the complex structure of their bony palate, which is more reptilian than in other birds, and indeed paleognaths are the most primitive of living birds. The group falls into two orders. The Struthioniformes, or ratites, are a disparate collection of large, flightless birds – further divided by some authorities into four distinct orders. The Tinamiformes comprise the very different and somewhat partridge-like tinamous, which are confined to South and Central America. In all paleognaths it is the male that incubates the eggs, only receiving some female assistance in the case of the ostrich.

▼ Size of orders

Number of species in order
Percentage of total bird species

Tinamiformes
47 species
0.47%

Struthioniformes
10 species
0.1%

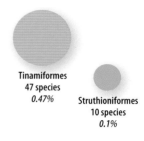

Emu (*Dromaius novaehollandiae*)

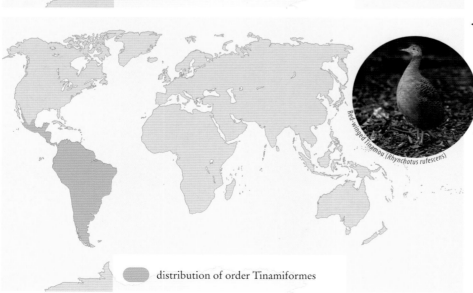

distribution of order Struthioniformes

distribution of family Dromaiidae (emus)

distribution of order Tinamiformes

Red-winged tinamou (*Rhynchotus rufescens*)

◄ Struthioniformes: ostrich, kiwis, allies

Struthioniformes are also known as ratites, from the Latin for "raft". This refers to the birds' lack of a keeled sternum for anchoring the wing muscles, and so points to their defining characteristic: flightlessness. Associated features include reduced wings and feathers that lack stiffened vanes. Modern ratites are divided into five families, considered by some authorities to be full orders. The largest ratite – indeed the largest living bird – is the Ostrich (Struthionidae) of Africa, which may top 2 metres (6 ft 7 in) in height. Next, are the emus and cassowaries (Casuariidae) of Australasia, followed by the rheas of South America (Rheidae). With the exception of the jungle-dwelling cassowaries, these birds inhabit open country, where strong legs enable them to get around at speed. Much smaller are the five species of kiwi (Apterygidae) from New Zealand. These chicken-sized, nocturnal birds use an acute sense of smell to sniff out food beneath the soil.

◄ Tinamiformes: tinamous

The tinamous look superficially like partridges. In fact, these plump, ground-dwelling birds are closely related to the ratites and are among the most ancient of birds, with a fossil record that goes back at least 10 million years. The single family (Tinamidae) is confined to South America and comprises at least 47 species across nine genera, ranging in size from 20 to 53 cm (8 in to 1 ft 8 in). Unlike ratites, tinamous have a keeled breastbone and can fly short distances on their short, rounded wings. Nonetheless, they spend most of their time on the ground, where strong legs help them get around and find food – including seeds, fruits and insects – and cryptic camouflage plumage helps conceal them from predators. Tinamous occur in all habitats, from tropical rainforest to grassland and alpine tundra. Though seldom seen, they often betray their presence with loud, whistled calls.

The basics of bird taxonomy

The taxonomy of birds – the way in which they are classified within the animal kingdom – has evolved over time. Recent decades have seen a shift away from a traditional system based largely on anatomical similarities towards one based on evolutionary affinities traced via genetics. Nonetheless, the basic hierarchy of taxonomic rankings pioneered by Swedish scientist Carolus Linnaeus (1707–78) has changed little and still provides a useful navigation tool around the world of birds.

At the broadest level, modern birds are the only extant members of the class Aves, to which they all belong. Aves is one of seven classes within the subphylum Vertebrata (animals with internal skeletons), the others being mammals, reptiles, amphibians, and three groups of fishes. These are all part of the phylum Chordata, within the kingdom Animalia.

Classification within Aves varies by authority. Anything from 23 to 29 orders of bird are recognized. Collectively, these comprise (again, depending on authority) 172 families, 2,057 genera and 9,845 species. The chart below gives an example of the taxonomic status of just one bird species.

Out of order?

Bird taxonomy remains highly contentious. Many scientists disagree about the orders into which birds are divided, and the relationships between them, as fresh studies of anatomy, DNA and the fossil record continue to challenge accepted wisdom. The integrity of species is also under question, with many birds that were once thought of as different races of a single species having since been assigned full species status; a process known by birdwatchers as "splitting".

For consistency and ease of reference, this chapter loosely follows the taxonomic model adopted by the British Trust for Ornithology, which in turn is based largely on Perrins (2003), following Sibley and Monroe (1990).

▼ Taxonomic status of Malachite Kingfisher

Class
Aves (birds)

Order
Coraciiformes
— The class Aves falls into a number of orders: 28 are recognized in this chapter.

Family
Alcedinidae
kingfishers
— Each order falls into a number of families. Among 10 other families in the order Coraciiformes are the Meropidae (bee-eaters) and Coraciidae (rollers).

Genus
Alcedo
river kingfishers
— Each family falls into a number of genera. There are two other genera in Alcedinidae: *Ceyx* (dwarf kingfishers) and *Ispidina* (pygmy kingfishers)

Species
Alcedo cristata
Malachite Kingfisher
— The Malachite Kingfisher is one of 17 similar species in the genus *Alcedo*. Others include the Common Kingfisher (*Alcedo atthis*).

The naming of species

The unique two-word scientific name assigned to each bird is known as a binomial. The first word denotes its genus, the second its species. In the above example *cristata*, which means "crowned", refers to the distinctive crest of the Malachite Kingfisher. Scientific names constitute a universal language, avoiding the confusion of common names, which may vary between countries.

Some species have two or more different geographical forms, which are not distinct enough to be treated as separate species. These are known as subspecies, or races, and are assigned a three-part name, or trinomial. For example, the Common Buzzard, *Buteo buteo*, has up to eight recognized subspecies across the Old World, including the East Asian race *Buteo buteo vulpinus* and the Canary Islands race *Buteo buteo insularum*.

Copyright © Myriad Editions

Game Birds to Grebes

The Galliformes (game birds) and Anseriformes (waterfowl) are the most primitive orders in the super-order Neognathae, or "new jaws", which accounts for more than 99 percent of modern birds. As such, they generally follow ratites and tinamous in bird classification systems. Both orders have played a pivotal role in human history, as they contain many species – including ducks, chickens, and pheasants – that have been exploited since prehistoric times for food and other resources.

The divers (Gaviiformes) and grebes (Podicipediformes) were once thought to be among the most primitive of birds, due largely to their superficial resemblance to the extinct Cretaceous order Hesperornithiformes. In fact, they have different ancestries, and their similarities to one another – being specialized diving birds with legs set far back on their bodies – are due simply to convergent evolution. Each order contains just one family and a handful of species, all of which are tied to aquatic habitats.

▼ **Size of orders**
Number of species in order
Percentage of total bird species

Galliformes
285 species
2.9%

Anseriformes
165 species
1.7%

Podicipediformes
22 species
0.2%

Gaviiformes
5 species
0.05%

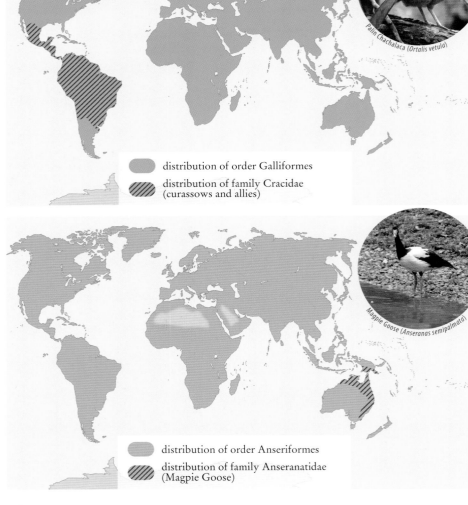

Plain Chachalaca (Ortalis vetula)

distribution of order Galliformes

distribution of family Cracidae (curassows and allies)

Magpie Goose (Anseranas semipalmata)

distribution of order Anseriformes

distribution of family Anseranatidae (Magpie Goose)

◀ **Galliformes: game birds**
Galliformes are plump-bodied, ground-dwelling birds with short thick bills and stout legs, which feed on a variety of plant and animal material, and tend to run from danger. They fly on their short, blunt wings only when pressed. The order includes chickens, pheasants, guinea fowl, and other species prized by people for food, either as domesticated fowl or wild game. Males of many species sport striking colours and/or plumes. Some perform spectacular courtship displays and may fight using spurs on their legs. Galliformes are prolific breeders, with large clutches. They occur widely, with most species largely sedentary. The six families comprise some 285 species, from the sparrow-sized Asian Blue Quail (*Coturnix chinensis*) to the hefty Wild Turkey (*Meleagris gallopavo*). The biggest family is the Phasianidae, which includes the quails, partridges, and pheasants. Others include the South American Cracidae, whose members – curassows, chachalacas, and guans – are more arboreal.

◀ **Anseriformes: waterfowl**
Anseriformes are found in aquatic habitats and occur on all continents except Antarctica. Most belong to the Anatidae family, which comprises over 140 species of ducks, swans, and geese. Anatids are well adapted to an aquatic existence, with webbed feet and heavily waterproofed plumage. Some species dive, some feed from the surface, and a few – notably geese – graze on land. The distinct flattened "duckbill" is adapted to filter food from the water. Flight is powerful and direct, and many northern species migrate large distances. Sexual dimorphism is pronounced in most ducks, with males generally the more colourful. A few species have been domesticated, notably the Mallard (*Anas platyrhynchos*), and many are hunted for food and sport. The two other families in this order are the Anseranatidae, which contains only the Magpie Goose (*Anseranas semipalmata*) of Australasia, and the Anhimidae, which comprises three species of screamer – largely terrestrial birds found only in South America.

Gaviiformes: divers/loons ▶

Divers, known as loons in North America, are medium-sized to large waterbirds found in North America and northern Eurasia. They have a distinctive dagger-shaped bill, held tilted upwards like a cormorant's, and a tail-less profile like a grebe's. The single family, Gaviidae, comprises just five species. All sport a breeding plumage of intricate markings, but moult in winter to plain dark above and white below. Divers swim strongly both on and below the surface, using webbed feet to propel themselves after fish and other aquatic prey. Like grebes, their feet are set too far back on the body for efficient walking, and they only visit land regularly when nesting. Courtship involves exuberant displays and far-carrying wailing calls. Nests are built close to the water on freshwater lakes. As in grebes, young chicks may ride on their parents' back. Flight is powerful and direct, on narrow wings. All species winter at sea.

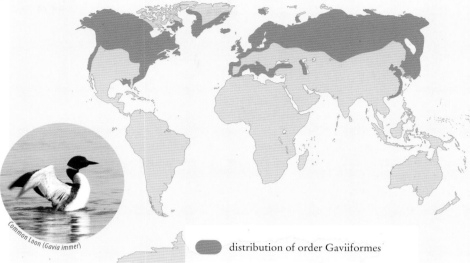

Common Loon (*Gavia immer*)

distribution of order Gaviiformes

Podicipediformes: grebes ▶

Grebes are small to medium-sized waterbirds found in aquatic habitats on every continent but Antarctica. Superficially duck-like, they are distinguished by their pointed bill and tail-less profile. Grebes are excellent swimmers and divers: unusually dense plumage provides excellent waterproofing, while lobed toes propel them underwater in pursuit of fish and smaller aquatic prey. They move awkwardly on land, however, with legs set far back on the body. Most species seldom fly (two South American species are completely flightless), although some migrate considerable distances. In breeding plumage, many sport ornate head plumes and perform elaborate courtship displays. The single family, Podicepedidae, comprises 19 species in six genera, ranging from the Least Grebe (*Tachybaptus dominicus*) at 23.5 cm (9 in), to the Great Grebe (*Podiceps major*) at 71 cm (28 in). Another three species have become extinct since 1977. Grebes build floating nests of plant material on fresh water. Many species winter at sea.

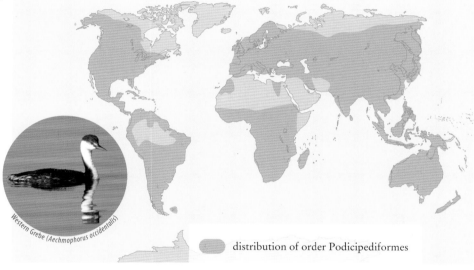

Western Grebe (*Aechmophorus occidentalis*)

distribution of order Podicipediformes

▼ Feeding techniques in Anatidae

Members of the Anatidae family (order: Anseriformes) have evolved a variety of feeding techniques and adaptations, offering a range of niches to different species in a shared environment, and thus circumventing competition.

Goosander (*Mergus merganser*)
Dives below surface to catch fish, using wings for propulsion and catching prey in its thin serrated bill.

Mute Swan (*Cygnus olor*)
Uses long neck to reach aquatic vegetation, snails, and other food items on the bottom.

Northern Shoveler (*Anas clypeata*)
Feeds on surface, using spatulate bill with sieve-like lamellae around the edge to extract tiny organisms from the water.

Pink-footed Goose (*Anser brachyryhnchus*)
Feeds on land, using short strong bill to pluck grass and other plant matter.

Copyright © Myriad Editions

Seabirds & Shorebirds

The five orders described on this spread embrace a variety of birds that make their living on or beside water. Some, including albatrosses, frigatebirds and penguins, are exclusively pelagic – adapted to survive far from land for months on end. Others, including many shorebirds, make their living on the water margins, using specialized bills or feeding techniques to glean food from beaches, mudflats and shorelines.

Many of nature's greatest travellers belong among these orders, from terns and shearwaters, which circumnavigate the globe on their seasonal wanderings, to godwits and turnstones, which migrate from the Arctic to the southern hemisphere. Most are also highly gregarious – either, like gannets, nesting in large colonies in inaccessible locations or, like knot, gathering in huge flocks outside the breeding season. As ever, there are the exceptions: coursers (Glareolidae), which are closely related to gulls, thrive in deserts far from any water, and seedsnipes (Thinocoridae), which are confined to South America, have adapted to an herbivorous diet.

▼ Size of orders
Number of species in order
Percentage of total bird species

Charadriiformes
342 species
3.5%

Procellariiformes
125 species
1.3%

Pelecaniformes
62 species
0.6%

Sphenisciformes
20 species
0.2%

Phaethontiformes
3 species
0.03%

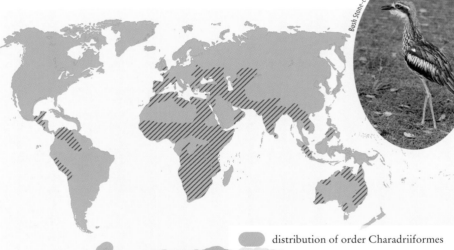

Bush Stone-curlew *(Burhinus grallarius)*

distribution of order Charadriiformes

distribution of family Burhinidae (thick-knees)

◀ Charadriiformes: gulls, waders, allies

This diverse order is traditionally held to include some 350 species in up to 20 families worldwide, notably the shorebirds and gulls. Most feed on invertebrates or other small animals, and are associated with water, both coastal and inland. The shorebirds – or waders, in the UK – include the Scolopacidae (snipe and sandpipers), Charadriidae (plovers and lapwings) and Recurvirostridae (avocets and stilts), all with long legs, and bills adapted for gleaning food from the substrate. The gulls (Laridae) are generally larger birds that take a wider variety of food and are closely related to terns (Sternidae), which plunge for fish, and skuas (Alcae), which scavenge and pirate food from other birds. Auks (Alcidae), including puffins and murres, nest on sea-cliffs and catch fish underwater. Smaller families include the Jacanidae (jacanas), adapted for walking on floating vegetation, and Burhinidae (thick-knees), that are largely nocturnal.

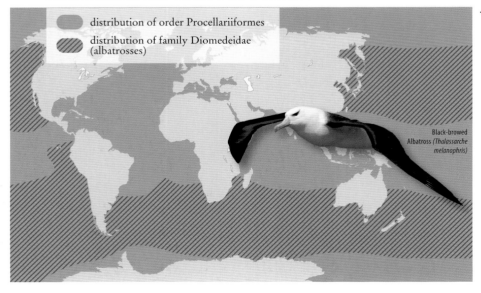

distribution of order Procellariiformes

distribution of family Diomedeidae (albatrosses)

Black-browed Albatross *(Thalassarche melanophris)*

◀ Procellariiformes: albatrosses, petrels

The Procellariiformes are seabirds. They comprise some 125 species in four families, and range in size from the huge Wandering Albatross (*Diomedea exulans*), with its record-breaking 3.6-m (12-ft) wingspan, to the Least Storm-petrel (*Halocyptena microsoma*), which weighs just 20 g (0.71 oz). All are exclusively pelagic, nesting on predator-free islands and ranging widely across the world's oceans. Specialized adaptations include nostrils enclosed in tubes, allowing them to smell prey from afar, and long, narrow wings for gliding with minimal effort. Fish, squid, and other food is either caught underwater or scavenged at the surface. All nest colonially, with smaller species avoiding predators by using burrows and returning to the colony only at night. Procellariiformes are long-lived, with a slow breeding cycle. They are also among the most endangered bird taxa, with many species threatened by such hazards as invasive predators, marine pollution, and long-line fishing.

Pelecaniformes: pelicans, ▶ cormorants, allies

The four families traditionally grouped in this order comprise a variety of medium-sized to large birds found worldwide in both fresh and marine waters – although recent DNA research links some families with the Ciconiiformes. Adaptations include totipalmate feet (all four toes webbed), a bare throat patch, and reduced nostrils. All species feed on fish, squid, and similar aquatic life. Pelicans (Pelecanidae) are large birds, known for their capacious bill pouch that acts as a fish scoop. Cormorants (Phalacrocoracidae) dive underwater for fish and are easily recognizable from their habit of holding out their wings to dry. Gannets (Sulidae) are exclusively marine, and plunge for fish from the air. Frigatebirds (Fregatidae) cruise tropical oceans on long wings, scavenging from the surface without alighting. All nest in large colonies.

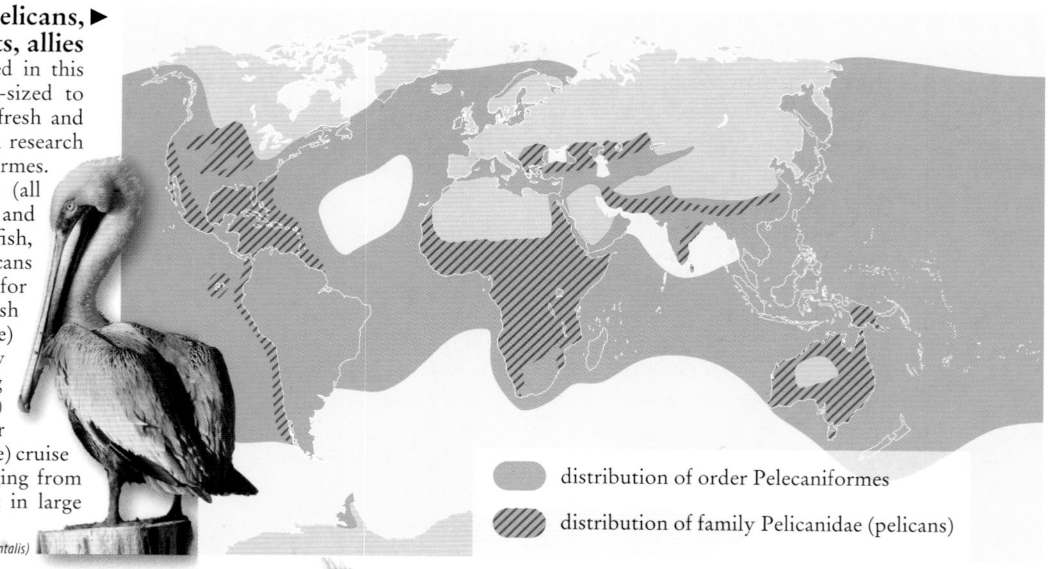

Brown Pelican (*Pelecanus occidentalis*)

distribution of order Pelecaniformes

distribution of family Pelicanidae (pelicans)

Phaethontiformes: tropicbirds ▶

The tropicbirds were once grouped among the Pelecaniformes but are now generally classified in an order of their own, with their relationship to other birds remaining unclear. They are medium-sized seabirds of tropical oceans that are adapted to a marine lifestyle similar to that of frigatebirds, cruising great distances over the open sea in search of fish. There are three species in a single family, Phaethontidae. All have predominantly white plumage and elongated central tail feathers, and can be distinguished from one another by fine black markings. Their small, feeble legs are set far back on the body, leaving them unable to move properly on land. Small, loose colonies are sited on oceanic islands, where breeding pairs perform fluttering display flights overhead.

Red-tailed Tropicbird (*Phaethon rubricauda*)

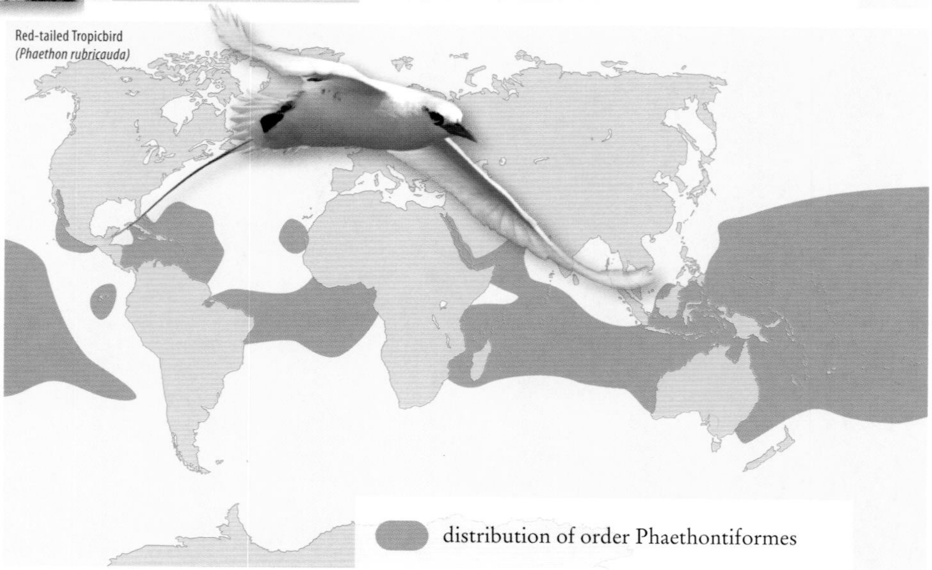

distribution of order Phaethontiformes

distribution of order Sphenisciformes

Sphenisciformes: penguins ▶

Penguins comprise a single family (Spheniscidae) of aquatic, flightless birds found exclusively in the southern hemisphere, including Antarctica. They are highly evolved for life in the water, with underwater vision, plumage adapted for insulation and buoyancy, and wings that have evolved into flippers. They swim underwater with great speed and agility in pursuit of krill, fish, and other sea life, and larger species can descend several hundred metres. The 17 to 20 species (according to authority) range in size from the 35 kg (75 lb) Emperor Penguin (*Aptenodytes forsteri*) to the 1kg (2.2 lb) Little Blue Penguin (*Eudyptula minor*), although some prehistoric species were as large as humans. Penguins breed in large colonies. On land they walk upright or slide on their bellies.

Rockhopper Penguin (*Eudyptes chrysocome*)

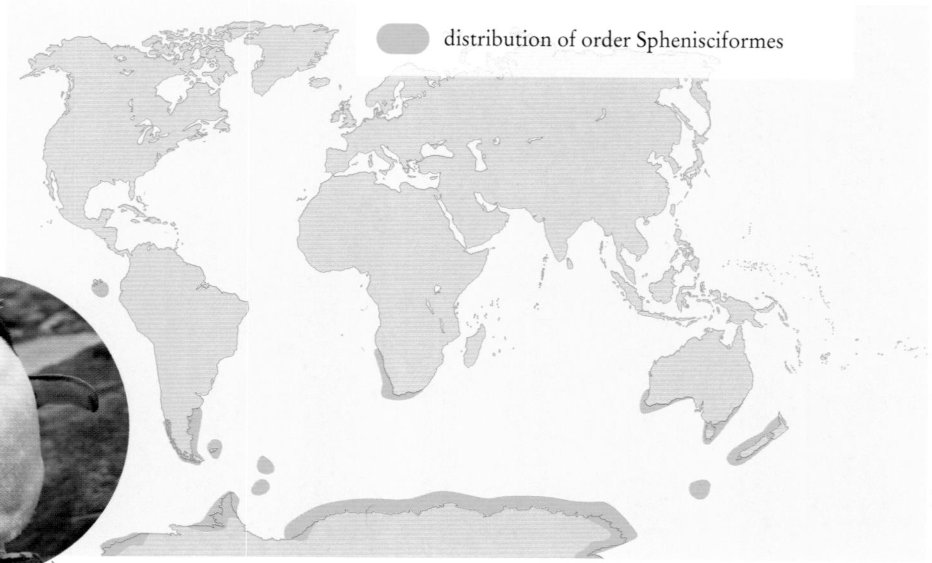

Copyright © Myriad Editions

51

— Kingfishers to Mousebirds —

The orders featured on this spread include many of the planet's most eye-catching bird families. Some, such as kingfishers and rollers, are known for their dazzling plumage. Others, such as toucans and hornbills, sport preposterously big bills. Though smaller species in some groups may superficially resemble songbirds, all have a number of key anatomical differences from the Passeriformes, and none can sing.

These orders also share many features of their breeding behaviour, with the majority of families and species nesting in holes, and many performing flamboyant courtship displays. The exception to this rule are the Coliiformes of Sub-Saharan Africa, which are neither colourful nor cavity nesters – they build a simple cup-shaped nest in foliage – and have an evolutionary history that sets them apart from other near-passerines.

▼ Size of orders
Number of species in order
Percentage of total bird species

Coraciiformes
403 species
4.1%

Piciformes
403 species
4.1%

Trogoniformes
37 species
0.37%

Coliiformes
6 species
0.06%

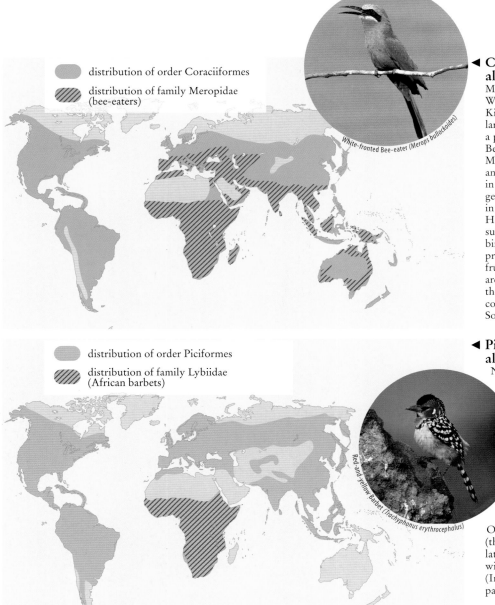

distribution of order Coraciiformes

distribution of family Meropidae (bee-eaters)

White-fronted Bee-eater (*Merops bullockoides*)

distribution of order Piciformes

distribution of family Lybiidae (African barbets)

Red-and-yellow Barbet (*Trachyphonus erythrocephalus*)

◄ Coraciiformes: kingfishers, rollers, allies

Most families in this order are confined to the Old World, especially tropical and subtropical regions. Kingfishers (Alcedinidae) are striking birds with large heads and powerful bills. They hunt from a perch: some for fish, others for terrestrial prey. Bee-eaters (Meropidae) catch insects in agile flight. Most are highly colourful, with slender bodies and often elongated central tail feathers, and nest in large sandbank colonies. Rollers (Coraciidae) get their name from the aerial courtship acrobatics in which they flaunt their bright blue plumage. Hornbills (Bucerotidae), found in tropical and subtropical Africa and Asia, are generally larger birds with hefty bills that, in some species, carry a prominent casque. They prey on everything from fruit to small animals. New World coraciiformes are – except for a few kingfishers – confined to the tiny todies (Todidae), of the Caribbean, and colourful motmots (Momotidae), of Central and South America.

◄ Piciformes: woodpeckers, toucans, allies

Nearly all birds in this order have zygodactyl feet – two toes forward and two back – which offer more stability when climbing tree trunks. Most are insectivores and, apart from jacamars (Galbulidae), do not grow down feathers. The best-known and largest family is the woodpeckers (Picidae), which also includes the piculets and wrynecks. Its members are found worldwide, except Madagascar, Australasia, and the polar regions, with most frequenting forest or woodland – though a few have adapted to treeless habitats. Other families include the fruit-eating barbets (three families) and toucans (Ramphastidae), the latter confined to the Neotropics and equipped with a huge but lightweight bill. The honeyguides (Indicatoridae), of Africa and Asia, are brood parasites and uniquely able to digest beeswax.

Trogoniformes: trogons ▶

Trogons make up a single family, the Trogonidae, which numbers seven genera, including the spectacular quetzals (*Pharomachrus* spp.) of South and Central America. Their weak feet are unique among animals in having a heterodactyl toe arrangement: first and second toes facing backwards; third and fourth toes forwards. They are colourful but retiring birds that inhabit tropical forests worldwide – with the greatest diversity in the Neotropics – and use their short, broad bill to feed on insects and fruit, generally gleaned from the branches in a brief fluttering flight. Trogons are typically located by their soft, insistent call, given from just below the canopy. All species have soft, richly coloured plumage – often featuring greens and reds – and are strongly sexually dimorphic, with females much duller than males.

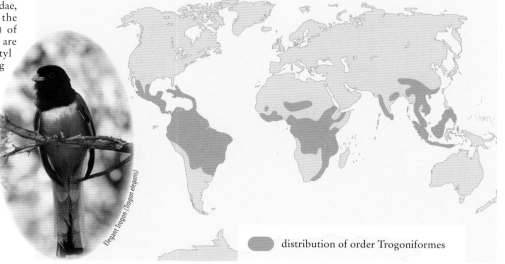

Elegant Trogon (Trogon elegans)

distribution of order Trogoniformes

Coliiformes: mousebirds ▶

Mousebirds comprise a single family (Coliidae) of just six species, which has no clear links with other modern birds and is all that remains today of a much more diverse prehistoric line. Entirely confined to Sub-Saharan Africa, they are the only bird order endemic to that continent. These smallish, slender birds have long tails and soft, greyish-brown plumage. They feed on buds, fruit and berries, clambering acrobatically among the foliage and often scurrying around at low-level like rodents, hence their common name. Other characteristic features include a small crest and short, stubby bill. Small flocks frequent lightly wooded country, moving from one feeding area to another in direct flight, and often sunbathing on top of bushes to dry out after rain.

Speckled Mousebird
(*Colius striatus*)

distribution of the order Coliiformes

▼ Digging deep

The Coraciiformes, Piciformes and Trogoniformes all nest predominantly in holes. Many species, including most woodpeckers and trogons, use tree holes. Others, including most bee-eaters and many kingfishers, use a hole in a sand or earth bank. Most are "primary cavity-nesters", which means that they use their bill to chisel out their own hole, rather than taking over an existing one. Few make a nest, though some may line the hole with a little plant material. Eggs are generally white, for better visibility in the darkness.

Perhaps the most peculiar nesting arrangement is that of the Bucerotinae hornbills. The female seals herself into the egg chamber by blocking up the entrance hole, using a mixture of mud, droppings and fruit pulp, leaving only a tiny slit through which the male can feed her. She remains there for the entire incubation, until the chicks have grown too large for her to remain inside the chamber with them, and undergoes a complete moult in the process.

Southern Yellow-billed Hornbill
(*Tockus leucomelas*) flying with
food to tree hole.

59

Passerines: Perching Birds

The Passeriformes is by far the largest order of birds, comprising close to 6,000 species. Known loosely as "perching birds", its members differ from other orders in various fine anatomical details, and are themselves divided into suborders. In simple terms, however, and with a few exceptions, passerines can be described as small birds that sing.

The word passerine derives from the Latin passer, for sparrow, and indeed a sparrow is a typical passerine. It has an anisodactyl arrangement of toes: three facing forward, two facing back, and all meeting the foot at the same level. It can also sing – though admittedly some sparrow species are more tuneful than others – by virtue of the specialized syrinx muscles around its trachea.

Passerines are thought to have evolved some 55 to 60 million years ago in Gondwana. The first great speciation took place in Australasia and New Guinea, later expanding westwards into Eurasia and Africa with an explosion of new lineages. Today, anything from 80 to well over 100 different families are recognized, with the taxonomy of many groups a matter of ongoing research. Species range in size from the hefty Common Raven (*Corvus corax*), at 1.5 kg (3 lb 5 oz) and 70 cm (2 ft 3 in), to the diminutive Short-tailed Pygmy Tyrant (*Myiornis ecaudatus*), at just 4.2 g (0.14 oz) and 6.5 cm (2 ½ in). The majority, however, are thrush-sized or smaller, with the average passerine being smaller than the average bird in any other order.

Authorities divide passerines into two or three sub-orders according to their evolutionary histories. Much the largest is the Passeri, which comprises some 5,000 species, known as oscine passerines. These include most of the familiar families, from sparrows (Passeridae), finches (Fringillidae), and thrushes (Turdidae), to swallows (Hirundidae), starlings (Sturnidae), and Old World warblers (Sylviidae). Oscine derives from oscen, Latin for songbird, and this group has a highly developed syrinx muscle, responsible for the complex sounds of such celebrated songsters as larks, nightingales, and lyrebirds – though some noises, such as those of crows (Corvidae), may not appeal to the human ear.

The Tyranni is a smaller sub-order that comprises about 1,000 species, known as suboscines. These are distinguished from oscines by the structure of the syrinx, and DNA research has confirmed the different evolutionary origins of the two groups. Most suboscines are found in the Tyrannides, a South American group that includes such families as the tyrant-flycatchers (Tyrannidae), cotingas (Cotingidae), manakins (Pipridae), and ovenbirds (Furnariidae). A separate Old World group, the Eurylaimides, including the broadbills (Eurylaimidae) and pittas (Pittidae), is found mainly in tropical regions around the Indian Ocean.

One family of passerines remains in taxonomic limbo. The New Zealand wrens (Acanthisittidae) comprise just two species, endemic to New Zealand. Though outwardly similar to Old World wrens (Troglodytidae), studies have revealed that they represent an ancient lineage that pre-dates the speciation of later passerines. Traditionally placed among the suboscines, some authorities now believe these diminutive birds warrant their own sub-order: the Acanthisitti.

▼ Size of order
Number of species in order
Percentage of total bird species

**Passeriformes
5,899 species
60%**

The South Island Wren (*Xenicus gilviventris*) is one of just two extant species in the sub-order Acanthisitti, both confined to New Zealand. Four other species became extinct as a result of human colonization; two of them within the last century.

◄ **World distribution of Passeriformes**

Passeri (oscine passerines)

Tyranni (suboscine passerines)

Acanthisitti (New Zealand wrens)

Cardinal virtues

The Northern or Common Cardinal (*Cardinalis cardinalis*) belongs to the cardinal family (Cardinalidae) of passerines. Like the various tanagers, grosbeaks and other members of this diverse group, it has a thick, strong bill adapted to feeding on seeds and fruit. Males, from whose vivid red plumage the family is named, are much more colourful than females.

Insect-eating voyager

The Common Redstart (*Phoenicurus phoenicurus*) was once thought to be a member of the thrush family (Turdidae), but is now known to belong to the Old World flycatchers (Muscicapidae). Its narrow bill is adapted to eating insects, and like many insect-eaters that breed in northern Europe and Asia, this species migrates to Sub-Saharan Africa in winter, where it is assured of a constant food supply.

Multi-purpose passerine

The Common Magpie (*Pica pica*) belongs to the crow family (Corvidae), which includes many of the larger passerines. Like many crows, it is a generalist, with a robust bill adapted to feeding on anything from small animals to eggs, carrion, insects, and grain. Crows are among the most intelligent of birds, and this species is the only non-mammal ever to have passed a mirror self-recognition test.

Passerine predator

The Bokmakierie (*Telophorus zeylonus*) belongs to the bushshrike family (Malaconotidae) of African passerines, notable for their bright colours and the synchronized calls with which pairs duet. This family is closely related to the true shrikes (Laniidae). Like them, it has a partly carnivorous diet, using a hook-tipped bill to capture small lizards, birds, and frogs, as well as large insects.

Broad of bill

A pair of Black-and-red Broadbills (*Cymbirhynchus macrorhynchos*) perch on a rainforest branch in Sabah, Malaysian Borneo. Broadbills (Eurylaimidae) are one of just three Old World families in the suborder Tyranni, or suboscine passerines. Most are insect-eaters, and use their broad, flat bills to snatch their prey in flight – either from the air or from among the forest foliage.

Oven ready

The mud nest of the Rufous Hornero (*Furnarius rufus*) resembles an old wood-fired clay oven. This distinctive structure explains the common name "ovenbird", often used for the Furnariidae family of suboscine passerines to which this species belongs. In fact, most other members of this South American group build their nests from sticks. The Rufous Hornero is the national bird of Argentina.

Champion songster

The impressive tail plumes flaunted by the male Superb Lyrebird (*Menura novaehollandiae*) in its courtship display make this Australian species, at 1 metre (3 ft 3 in) in length, the longest of the Passeriformes (and second in weight only to the ravens). Lyrebirds also boast the greatest vocal virtuosity of any bird. Their repertoires include not only the songs of numerous other species but also many non-avian sounds, from human voices and musical instruments to camera shutters and even chainsaws.

Copyright © Myriad Editions

Part Four

NORTHERN GANNETS (*Morus bassanus*).

HOW BIRDS LIVE

So thoroughly have birds adapted to the planet's many habitats that it seems there are few things, collectively, they cannot do. Many species are as adept at getting around on land or water as others are in the air. The avian toolkit of bills equips them for virtually any diet, from sieving plankton to tearing flesh. And they have risen to the challenge of breeding, with a suite of behavioural skills, from nest building to song, that is unmatched elsewhere in the animal world. What's more, birds can ensure conditions always suit them, simply by migrating with the seasons from one part of the world to another.

Taking to the Air

Birds are not the only animals that can fly. But they have risen to the challenges of flight with a suite of adaptations unrivalled among other groups. Flying has, in turn, allowed them lifestyles that are unimaginable for earth-bound creatures – whether simply travelling faster to capture food and dodge predators, or journeying around the globe to make the most of the seasons.

The mechanics of flight are straightforward enough. A flying bird must overcome gravity with an upward force, known as lift, and counter drag using a forward force, known as thrust. It does this by beating its wings. Once aloft, the bird must keep flapping, unless it can glide or soar. The aerofoil shape of its wings continues to generate lift, with the faster flow of air over the curved upper surface reducing the air pressure above the wing and creating a relatively higher pressure underneath it. Manoeuvring is then a matter of making adjustments, such as tilting one wing or beating the other faster in order to make a turn.

When landing, birds first flap more slowly to allow gravity to take effect, then spread and lower their tail as a brake, and drop their landing gear – their feet – into position. In small birds, this process happens too fast for the human eye. With larger birds, however, landing can be visibly difficult, and in tricky conditions, such as on a windy cliff-top, they may need several attempts.

Flight technique depends on wing shape. Birds with short, rounded wings can accelerate quickly and manoeuvre skilfully, but can't keep flapping for long. Those with longer, narrower wings can sustain higher speeds for greater distances. This allows species that are otherwise relatively similar to behave in quite different ways: the short broad wings of a Sparrowhawk (*Accipiter nisus*), for instance, enable it to twist and turn after prey through dense woodland, while the longer, pointed wings of a Peregrine Falcon (*Falco peregrinus*) give it the sustained speed needed to overhaul prey over distance.

Many large birds save energy by soaring or gliding. Those with long, broad wings, such as vultures, can use air currents to stay aloft for hours and manoeuvre at low speeds without stalling. To gain height they hitch a ride on thermals – the columns of warm air that spiral up from the sun-heated ground. Seabirds such as albatrosses (Diomedeidae) have long, narrow wings that create minimal drag, and allow them to exploit the updrafts generated on the windward slopes of waves. Thus they can glide low over the ocean in almost windless conditions, without flapping.

Birds' powers of flight may remain miraculous to the human eye and imagination. Ultimately, however, flying is simply a matter of natural selection harnessing the laws of physics in order to exploit a new habitat: the air. In the process it has given birds access to more of our planet than any other class of vertebrate has.

Winged record breakers

Greatest wingspan: Wandering Albatross (*Diomedea exulans*), at 3.63 m (11ft 11in)

Greatest wingspan of extinct bird: a prehistoric condor in the genus Teratornis, at more than 7 metres (23 ft)

Greatest wingspan of any land bird: Andean Condor (*Vultur gryphus*) and Marabou Stork (*Leptoptilos crumeniferus*), both at 3.2 m (10 ft)

Heaviest flying bird: Great Bustard (*Otis tarda*), at up to 21 kg (46.3 lb)

Fastest recorded bird: Peregrine Falcon (*Falco peregrinus*) at 188 km/h (117 mph), when diving

Fastest recorded bird in flapping flight: White-throated Needletail (*Hirundapus caudacutus*), at 170 km/h (106 mph)

Fastest recorded bird in level flight: Red-breasted Merganser (*Mergus serrator*), at 161 km/h (100 mph)

Slowest recorded flying bird: American Woodcock (*Scolopax minor*), at 8 km/h (5 mph)

Most aerial bird: Sooty Tern (*Onychoprion fuscatus*) may fly for over seven years without landing

Most aerial land bird: Common Swift (*Apus apus*) may fly for three years without landing

Fastest recorded wingbeats: Hummingbirds, at 90 beats per second or more, in the smaller species

Slowest recorded wingbeats: Large vultures, at just one beat per second

Magnificent Frigatebird (*Fregata magnificens*)

▼ Wing loading

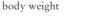
● body weight   ● flight feathers

The ratio of a bird's weight to its wing area – known as "wing loading" – determines how it flies. Birds with a low wing loading can remain airborne and continue manoeuvring even at low speeds. Birds with a high wing loading must flap much quicker and fly faster, and have a much wider turning circle.

Wing loading is calculated by dividing a bird's mass by the total surface area of its wings. The lower this figure, the less energy a bird need expend in order to fly. Smaller species can get away with a relatively lower wing loading: there is an upper limit in size, beyond which a bird would need to store so much energy to stay airborne that it would be too heavy to take off. Frigatebirds, for example, have the lowest wing loading of any bird, and expend much less energy in staying airborne than do heavy, fast-flapping divers.

Magnificent Frigatebird
wing loading 0.15

**Great Northern Diver
(Common Loon)**
wing loading 2.00

Copyright © Myriad Editions

Flying on the spot

A Ruby-throated Hummingbird (*Archilochus colutris*) feeding on a bottlebrush flower. Hummingbirds are the only true hoverers among birds, being able to remain stationary in perfectly still air. They beat their wings exceptionally fast – over 100 times per second in some species – hence the insect-like buzz that explains their name.

Hot air

Thermals allow storks, raptors, and other large migrating birds to make journeys that would otherwise demand too much energy. At peak migration times huge numbers of such birds wheel above favoured sea-crossing points, waiting to gain enough height before gliding down to the other side. These White Storks (*Ciconia ciconia*) are gathering over the Straits of Gibraltar on their annual spring journey north from Africa to Europe.

Always airborne

Swifts, such as the Common Swift (*Apus apus*), are almost exclusively aerial, feeding, mating and even sleeping on the wing, and landing only in order to breed. Their tiny feet are little more than simple grappling hooks, enabling them to cling to the vertical surfaces on which they nest, but not to walk. A newly fledged swift will not reach breeding maturity for three years, and may spend all that time continuously on the wing before it first touches down.

Power dive

The Peregrine Falcon (*Falco peregrinus*) catches other birds in a high-speed aerial dive known as a "stoop". Having spotted its prey from on high, the falcon accelerates into a long dive, folds back its wings and drops like a missile on its target. The kill is generally made with talons balled into fists, and the prey is often killed outright on impact.

Mile-high club

Most birds seldom fly higher than 150 metres. There is usually little point expending the energy to rise any higher. Vultures, however, use height to gain a vantage point from which to scan for food – and to observe other vultures doing the same. A Ruppell's Vulture (*Gyps rueppellii*) recorded over West Africa at a height of 11.3 km (7 miles) holds the high-altitude record for any bird. No mammal could last long at this height, but birds' efficient respiration gets them the oxygen they need, while their feathers insulate them against the cold.

78–79 Birds on the Move; 80–81 Flyways ▶▶

By Land & Water

Birds may have given over their front limbs to flight, as wings. But most species spend substantially more time out of the air than in it, and so still need their hind legs for getting around, perching, and many other everyday tasks. As birds have adapted to exploit almost every environmental niche on the planet, so these lower limbs have evolved a rich diversity of form and function.

There are various ways in which birds travel on foot. Most passerines tend to hop, moving both feet simultaneously, with tree-dwellers using their wings to help power their jumps from perch to perch. Others walk, moving one foot at a time. Many terrestrial birds have an impressive turn of speed, and will run from danger rather than take flight. The flightless Ostrich (*Struthio camelus*), whose huge 1.2-metre (4-ft) legs have just two toes each, can top 75 km/h (45 mph) at full stretch – faster than most birds can fly.

Wading birds, such as the aptly named stilts (*Himantopus spp*), have the longest legs. Game birds, which scratch and dig for food, have exceptionally strong legs – as do many raptors, whose legs must both withstand the impact of a killing strike, and carry away their prey through the air. Other birds, such as swifts and hummingbirds, have legs so short they cannot walk at all. The legs of some swimming birds, such as grebes, are placed at the rear, like propellers, and are effectively useless on land.

A bird's claws are made of keratin, like our hair, and grow continuously to counteract being worn down by use. In some birds, such as raptors, they have developed into lethal talons for stabbing and gripping. In others, such as game birds, they are more spade-like, for digging.

Birds also have many means of getting around on water. Most swimming birds have webbed feet, which work as paddles, although not all use them in the same way. Divers (loons) use both feet together, while ducks make alternating strokes with each leg. And when it comes to venturing below the surface, some birds – notably penguins and their northern counterparts, auks – use their wings as flippers, effectively flying underwater.

Feet are not only for locomotion and perching. For eagles they are weapons, used both to dispatch and butcher prey. For parrots they are hands, used to grip and manipulate food while the bill gets to work. Feet also help a bird to preen, especially around the head, where the bill can't reach. They can act as brakes when lowered in flight, or as a rudder when lowered in water. For the male Blue-footed Booby (*Sula nebouxii*) they are sexual signals, waved during courtship displays, while for the male Emperor Penguin (*Aptenodytes forsteri*) they are an incubating platform for his single egg above the Antarctic ice.

Blue-footed Booby engaged in courtship display.

▼ Feet: form and function

A bird's toes reflect its lifestyle. Most perching birds have an arrangement, called anisodactyl, with three forward-facing toes that form a broad foot for walking, and a backward-facing hind toe to wrap around a perch. (A muscle reflex that causes birds' claws to tighten when their legs relax prevents them from falling off.) The hind toe on non-perching birds, including waders, game birds and those with webbed feet, is generally reduced and raised out of the way, or even completely absent. That of a bird of prey, however, is particularly strong in order to grip and subdue struggling prey. Most woodpeckers have an arrangement called zygodactyl, with two toes facing forward and two back – in order to brace the bird against a vertical tree trunk, while owls can move their third toe either way to offer a choice of grip.

Heron (walking on mud)   **Sparrow** (perching)   **Duck** (walking)   **Eagle** (grasping prey)   **Woodpecker** (climbing)

▼ Plumbing the depths

Diving seabirds can reach some impressive depths

European Shag
20 m

Northern Gannet
40 m

Sooty Shearwater
60 m

Common Guillemot
100 m+

Record dive
by Emperor Penguin:
**564 metres
21 minutes 48 seconds**

Emperor Penguin
500 m+

Going down

Nuthatches, such as this White-breasted Nuthatch (*Sitta carolinensis*), climb tree trunks to winkle out food items from beneath the bark. They do not have the zygodactyl feet of woodpeckers, which also find food in this way. But they have evolved a method of walking – placing one foot directly in front of the other – that makes them the only birds able to descend tree trunks headfirst.

Hooked

The Osprey (*Pandion haliaetus*) can adjust the configuration of its toes, moving one behind in order to provide back-up when dealing with a struggling fish. In addition to its long, fishhook claws, this raptor's toes are coated with sharp spines that offer a better grip on its slippery catch.

Legging it

The fastest runner among flying birds is the aptly named Greater Roadrunner (*Geococcyx californianus*), which can race along at 40 km/h (25 mph). A close relative of the cuckoos, it captures small reptiles and other prey in lightning dashes across the desert terrain, and only takes flight as a last resort.

Getting a grip

Parrots such as this Blue-and-yellow Macaw (*Ara ararauna*) use their dextrous toes like fingers to manipulate food and bring it to their bills for feeding.

Lily-trotting

Members of the jacana family, such as this African Jacana (*Actophilornis africanus*), have proportionally the longest toes of any bird. By spreading the bird's weight, the toes allow it to walk across floating vegetation – hence its nickname "lilytrotter" – and thus get at the aquatic invertebrates that gather underneath.

Hanging about

Rainbow Lorikeets (*Trichoglossus haematodus*), use their strong grip to clamber acrobatically along branches, often hanging upside down in the process.

Copyright © Myriad Editions

Finding Food

Nowhere is the diversity of the bird world more apparent than in the variety of ways birds go about finding a meal. Almost anything is on the menu for one species or another – from seeds and berries to fruit, nectar, fish, flesh, insects, shellfish, carrion, and even dung.

One reason for this versatility is the bill, or beak. This unique appendage has adapted to exploit almost every ecological niche on the planet. One glance at a bird's bill gives an immediate indication of its diet. Insect-eaters have a short, fine bill for snapping up their miniscule food; seed-eaters have a short, thick bill for crushing theirs. Other categories include meat-eaters, with a hooked bill for butchering carcasses, fish-catchers, with a dagger-shaped bill for seizing their prey, and waterfowl, with a broad flat bill for filtering food underwater.

Technique is also important, and flight plays a vital role in feeding for many birds. Hummingbirds hover in front of a flower while extracting its nectar, vultures soar on thermals to scan for carrion, and gannets plunge dive to capture fish in the sea. But flight is not the only route to food: herons use long legs and infinite patience to capture fish in the shallows, while a parrot's bill serves as an extra limb when clambering around the canopy in search of fruit.

This proliferation of tools and techniques has produced some extraordinary specializations. Skimmers, for instance, have a uniquely long lower mandible that slices through the water as they fly low over the surface, and flips fish down their throat, in a lightning-fast reflex action.

By contrast, there are generalists, such as crows, whose versatile bill and keen intelligence enable them to exploit a variety of feeding opportunities. New Caledonian Crows (*Corvus moneduloides*) are known to fashion their own tools from leaves and twigs in order to obtain various foodstuffs, while Hooded Crows (*Corvus corone cornix*) have been observed using bread crumbs for baiting fish, and Common Ravens (*Corvus corax*) calling larger predators such as wolves to come and open up a carcass.

Other birds also employ a little help. Cattle Egrets (*Bubulcus ibis*) forage around the feet of large grazing mammals, snapping up any disturbed insects, while oxpeckers feed on the animals' backs, scissoring out parasites from their hairy hides. A few birds, such as skuas, have even turned pirate, snatching other birds' food on the wing in a smash-and-grab raid.

In short, from the steaming rainforest to the frozen tundra, there is scarcely a corner of the planet where birds have not evolved a canny means of grabbing a bite.

Built for flight

The bill, or beak, is thought to have evolved largely as an adaptation to flight. It weighs proportionally less than the jawbones and teeth of a mammal, which means that the bird carries less weight when airborne.

▼ What birds eat
Percentage of bird families by primary food source for the majority of species

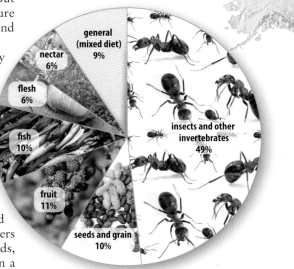

- general (mixed diet) 9%
- nectar 6%
- flesh 6%
- fish 10%
- fruit 11%
- seeds and grain 10%
- insects and other invertebrates 49%

The bill of the Sword-billed Hummingbird makes up 56% of the bird's total length.

▼ Fitting the bill

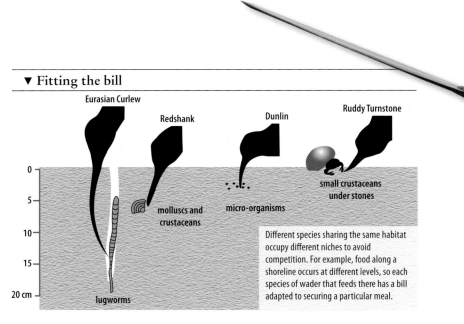

Eurasian Curlew

Redshank

Dunlin

Ruddy Turnstone

small crustaceans under stones

molluscs and crustaceans

micro-organisms

lugworms

0
5
10
15
20 cm

Different species sharing the same habitat occupy different niches to avoid competition. For example, food along a shoreline occurs at different levels, so each species of wader that feeds there has a bill adapted to securing a particular meal.

Hide and seek

Clark's Nutcracker (*Nucifraga columbiana*) is one of several members of the crow family known to practise "scatter-hoarding". It buries surplus food in the ground – as many as 2,500 caches over an area of up to 20 sq km (7.5 sq miles). Its impressive spatial memory enables it to relocate most caches, even months later and when buried under snow. Those that remain undiscovered may germinate and grow into new trees, thereby perpetuating the bird's habitat.

Bone breaker

The Bearded Vulture (*Gypaetus barbatus*) is, like most vultures, a scavenger. Unlike others, however, 90% of its diet is bone marrow, which it gets at by dropping bones from a great height to smash them on the rocks below. It may also use the same technique with live tortoises.

Shady deal

The Black Heron (*Egretta ardesiaca*) employs a unique fishing strategy called "canopying". Having found a promising spot in the shallows, it stretches out its wings to enclose its slim body in an umbrella-like canopy. The shadow this casts on the water offers a tempting refuge to unsuspecting fish, allowing the heron to snatch its prey as they swim within range.

Expert extractor

The two mandibles of the Common Crossbill (*Loxia curvirostra*) cross at the tip, enabling it to feed on pinecones. The bird opens the cone by inserting its bill between the scales and twisting the lower mandible, enabling it to extract the hidden seed with its tongue.

Size matters

The impressive bill of the Toco Toucan (*Ramphastos toco*) is the largest in relation to body size of any species. This massive appendage enables the bird to save energy while feeding, as it can perch in one spot and pluck fruit from surrounding branches. The bill is also thought to play an important role in temperature regulation.

Ocean wanderer

Albatrosses, such as the Black-browed albatross (*Thalassarche melanophris*), feed on squid, fish, and other food, taken mostly from the ocean surface. Highly efficient gliding on long narrow wings allows them to cover vast distances with minimal effort, while a strong sense of smell – highly unusual in birds – enables them to locate food from several kilometres away.

Copyright © Myriad Editions

Sense & Sensitivity

Birds' senses are finely tuned, as you might expect from animals for whom acute perception and split-second judgement are prerequisites for survival. But not all senses are equally developed: different groups have evolved different adaptations according to the particular demands of their environment.

Most birds have excellent eyesight. Indeed, their eyes are relatively larger and more developed than those of most mammals. Birds of prey, for instance, may have five times as many light-receptor cells per square millimetre in their retinas than do humans. This means strong night vision, too, which is important not only for nocturnal species but also for the many birds that migrate after dark.

Birds also boast excellent colour vision. Their retinas have five types of colour-sensitive cone cell, compared with just three in humans, which allows them to see a richer colour spectrum than we do, including ultraviolet. The eyes of some seabirds even have a polarizing layer that enables them to filter out reflected light from the water's surface and thus see prey beneath it.

Hearing is no less important than sight for most birds, and their ability to perceive and differentiate between sounds is essential, given the role of vocal communication – whether alarm call or courtship song – in their survival. Birds do not have the external ears of mammals, but openings on the sides of their head – most obvious in naked nestlings – lead to the inner ear, where sound vibrations are detected. The apparent "ears" of some owls are merely feathers used to enhance camouflage or display.

Relatively little is understood about birds' sense of smell. A poorly developed olfactory apparatus in the brain has long suggested that it plays little part in their lives, but recent evidence indicates smell may help many birds in finding food, mates, and directions. In certain specialized groups, a sense of smell is undoubtedly vital: New World vultures use enhanced olfactory powers to help locate carrion at some distance over land, while albatrosses and other tube-nosed seabirds do the same at sea.

Taste appears to be less developed in birds than in most mammals, with taste buds not found on the tongue – which is a hard, bony tool – but in the soft tissues inside the mouth. Food passes quickly through a bird's mouth so it has little time to evaluate what it picks up, though it generally receives enough information to identify the taste.

Birds' tongues do, however, have a sense of touch – which is of surprising importance to many species. The bills of many wading birds, for instance, are also packed with sensitive nerve endings. These enable them to find food entirely by tactile means as they probe blindly into the mud and seize any small animals they feel moving around below.

Bird-brained?

Birds can display impressive mental agility. Take memory: a Clark's Nutcracker (*Nucifraga columbiana*) may retrieve over 90% of the 30,000 pine kernels it buried separately several months earlier. Or communication: a captive African Grey Parrot (*Psittacus erithacus*) proved to have a functional vocabulary of over 100 words and an ability to count. Birds can also use tools: witness the Woodpecker Finch (*Camarhynchus pallidus*) winkling out grubs using a cactus spine (see below).

And then there are social skills. A Western Scrub-Jay (*Aphelocoma californica*) will conceal its cache of food from a nosy companion, demonstrating the ability to empathize with another – once thought unique to higher primates. Many other species of jay, including the Blue Jay (*Cyanocitta cristata*) shown left, also cache their food.

But do these tricks constitute intelligence as we understand it – a set of cognitive learning skills – or merely instinct? Certainly, some birds behave in a way that suggests the former: Carrion Crows (*Corvus corone*) in Japan, for instance, have learned to place walnuts in front of cars waiting at traffic lights. When the lights turn green, the cars drive on, cracking open the nuts, and the crows fly down to collect their meal. Species with larger brains, notably crows and parrots, do appear to be more intelligent than relatively small-brained ones such as ostrich or quails. Our idea of "intelligence", however, may not be the best yardstick by which to judge the many impressive mental adaptations of birds.

African Grey Parrot

▼ Field of view

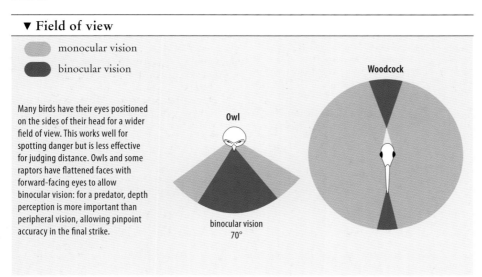

- monocular vision
- binocular vision

Many birds have their eyes positioned on the sides of their head for a wider field of view. This works well for spotting danger but is less effective for judging distance. Owls and some raptors have flattened faces with forward-facing eyes to allow binocular vision: for a predator, depth perception is more important than peripheral vision, allowing pinpoint accuracy in the final strike.

Owl

binocular vision 70°

Woodcock

Ultraviolet trails

The ability of a hovering Common Kestrel (*Falco tinnunculus*) to spot a tiny vole scurrying through the long grass far below may seem miraculous to the human observer. In fact, the falcon's task is made easier by its capacity to perceive ultraviolet light. This highlights the trails of urine that mark the rodents' regular runways, and reveals exactly where the next one will pop up.

The ears have it

Large eyes may be the most prominent feature of most owls, but hearing is just as important in catching prey. Owls have their ears placed asymmetrically on the sides of their head. This allows them to determine the exact source of a sound by calculating its position in the vertical as well as the horizontal plane. A Barn Owl (*Tyto alba*) can reputedly catch a vole in complete darkness using hearing alone.

Sound effects

The Oilbird (*Steatornis caripensis*) of Trinidad and northern South America roosts in caves by day and feeds in forests by night. Not only does it have the most light-sensitive eyes of any birds, but it can also navigate through the darkness by echo-location, sending out a stream of high-pitched calls and – like bats – responding to their echoes as the sounds bounce back from the surrounding surfaces.

Touchy-feely

The Painted Stork (*Mycteria leucocephala*) of southern Asia is one of a number of wading birds that rely upon a sense of touch to find their food. It feeds in silty water, where visibility is poor, and thrusts its long, open bill into the mud. Any small organisms that come into contact with the sensitive tip are immediately snapped up.

Sniffing it out

A Stewart Island Brown Kiwi (*Apteryx australis lawryi*) probes among leaf-litter in search of earthworms. New Zealand's kiwis are unique among birds in having their nostrils positioned at the tip of the bill, making them one of the few bird groups that rely on smell for feeding. Their eyesight is correspondingly poorer than that of most birds.

Copyright © Myriad Editions

Showing Off

Birds are at their most conspicuous during the breeding season, when each species sets out to advertise its charms using song, dance, costume, or a combination of all three. There is nothing frivolous about such performances. The next generation, after all, depends upon their success.

First, birds must secure a safe place in which to breed. This is generally the job of the males, and for many species their principal strategy is song. The vocal virtuosity of birds ranges from the simple two-note chime of a Chiffchaff (*Phylloscopus collybita*) to the complex improvised melodies of a Nightingale (*Luscinia megarhynchos*). Larks are among a number of birds that perform a choreographed "song flight" in order to broadcast their voice more widely. But the message – "keep out, this is my patch" – is always the same.

True singers are found only among the Passeriformes. But other birds, such as doves, may use a simple "advertising call", while some employ non-vocal techniques, of which one striking example is the drumming of a woodpecker on a hollow branch.

Song also serves to attract a mate. As well as revealing the singer's identity, it carries information about the singer's health, age, and experience that influences a female's selection. Studies have shown that, in any given species, the males that sing the loudest, the most often, or the most inventively tend to enjoy the most breeding success.

Once a male has caught the attention of a female he will usually flaunt his breeding prowess in a courtship display. Each species has its own routine: a drake Common Goldeneye (*Bucephala clangula*) will bob its puffed-up head, while a European Roller (*Coracias garrulous*) will flash its electric-blue wings. Many have evolved special feathers for this purpose, from the Elizabethan collar of a Ruff (*Philomachus pugnax*) to the fabulous fan of an Indian Peafowl (*Pavo cristatus*). Posture and movement maximize the impact, and there are few sights in nature more spectacular than the upside-down displays of New Guinea's birds-of-paradise, golden plumes cascading over their bowing, trembling bodies.

Some birds pair for life, others just for the season, and many only momentarily. Those that stay together to raise their young will periodically strengthen their bond with further courtship routines, which vary from the dances of cranes to the bill fencing of gannets. Male birds of some species reinforce their credentials as providers by bringing gifts of food or nest material to their partners.

It is the demands of courtship and display that account for the striking sexual dimorphism of so many bird species, males generally being much more colourful than females. But all this extravagance comes at a cost: male birds are more conspicuous to predators – and often more exhausted – when decked out in their breeding finery. Thus, most moult into a more subdued costume outside the breeding season, discretion then being the better part of valour.

Colour-coded

Birds may also display colours and markings for purposes other than courtship. A striking pattern revealed on take-off, such as the white rump of a Bullfinch (*Pyrrhula pyrrhula*), sounds the alarm and helps birds keep track of one another. The Sunbittern (*Eurypyga helias*) flashes false eye markings on its wings, known as ocelli, to alarm a predator, while some small owls have similar markings on the back of their head. Many colourful birds, including kingfishers, are unpalatable, and their bold colouration is thought to be a warning to would-be predators.

Fewer than 1 percent of birds are polyandrous, meaning that the female takes the lead in courtship and may mate with several males, while the males perform all subsequent parental duties. In such birds, this Red-necked Phalarope (*Phalaropus lobatus*) being an example, females are generally larger and brighter than males.

▼ Personal space

Relative size of territory of six European birds

Tawny Owl
c.260,000 m² (310,000 sq yd)

Robin
10,000 m²
(12,000 sq yd)

Yellowhammer
600 m² (717 sq yd)

Guillemot
0.05 m² (0.5 sq ft)

The size and shape of a bird's breeding territory depends upon the species, the habitat and the competition. Some species of eagles defend an area of several hundred kilometres. Conversely, many seabirds cram together into dense breeding colonies – each defending a territory that is just the immediate vicinity of the nest.

Golden Eagle
up to 250 km² (96 sq miles)

Ensemble piece

In a number of bird species, males gather to display before assembled females in a carefully chosen arena. Greater Sage Grouse (*Centrocercus urophasianus*) choose a clearing among dense stands of sage brush to perform their "strutting display". This group performance, known as a lek, enables females to choose the most promising suitor. After mating, the female brings up the young alone.

Fishy gift

A male Common Kingfisher (*Alcedo atthis*) offers a fish to his mate. This behaviour, known as courtship feeding, strengthens a pair bond. The female, in turn, may beg and flutter her wing like a fledgling as she receives the gift.

Musical colours

This male Bluethroat (*Luscinia svecica*) displays the markings from which the species is named, while singing from a prominent song post. The blue throat is moulted after the breeding season.

Fan base

The Indian Peafowl (*Pavo cristatus*), commonly known as a peacock, performs perhaps the best known of all courtship displays. The elongated plumes that make up his spectacular fan are in fact modified upper tail coverts; the tail itself is short and brown.

Building with blue

A male Satin Bowerbird (*Ptilonorhynchus violaceus*) constructs a "bower" of sticks, which he decorates with feathers, flowers and even litter, showing a marked preference for the colour blue. This serves as a stage set on which he sings and performs in order to attract a female. Mating only takes place once he lures her inside.

Waving the bill

A pair of Waved Albatrosses (*Phoebastria irrorata*) on the Galapagos Islands fence and click their bills in a ritualized courtship display. This performance also involves bowing and calling. It helps strengthen the pair bond, which may last for life.

Copyright © Myriad Editions

From Egg to Adult

The breeding strategies of birds include many of the animal kingdom's most ingenious adaptations. From nest design to egg shape, natural selection has found a solution to every environmental challenge, ensuring that each species offers its next generation the best possible start in life.

Nests vary from a plover's simple scrape in the ground to a weaver's elaborate apartment. All manner of materials are used, from sticks and stones to mud, moss, and saliva. Building may last anything from a few days to several weeks – and while some birds start afresh every season, others make one nest last a lifetime. The labour can be highly skilled: tailorbirds (*Orthotomus spp*) stitch leaves together with plant fibres using their bill as a needle. Although most birds choose a hidden or inaccessible location, some – notably most seabirds – prefer the social whirl of a colony, where they can exploit a common food source and benefit from safety in numbers.

A bird's egg protects the developing embryo inside while allowing the exchange of vital gases through the permeable shell. Clutch size varies from just a single egg in many seabirds to 15 or more in some game birds. Most parents incubate their eggs by simply sitting on them until they hatch, using moulted areas of bare skin called brood patches to transfer their body heat directly. When ready, the chick uses a sharp projection on its bill, called an "egg tooth", to break out. This falls away after hatching.

Birds pursue one of two main strategies in rearing their young. Many, including most songbirds, brood their young in the nest. Their chicks – known as "altricial" – hatch helpless and naked, and depend upon their parents for food, warmth and protection. With others, such as ducks and game birds, the young hatch in a more advanced state. They leave the nest early and can feed themselves immediately. Such chicks are called "precocial".

Either way, most parents continue to offer some form of care after their young have fledged, driving away predators or – in the case of grebes – even offering a ride on their backs. Many birds of prey will actively encourage their offspring's early attempts at hunting. And it is not only parents that do the work: in certain colony-dwelling species, including Shelduck (*Tadorna tadorna*), the young gather in crèches under the care of unrelated birds known as "aunts".

As a rule, the fewer young a species has, the more time and energy it spends on raising them, and the greater their chances. The survival odds of a single albatross chick, which may take nine months to fledge, are much higher than those of a baby Blue Tit (*Cyanistes caeruleus*), one of a clutch of ten – most of which will never see adulthood. The slow breeders also mature later and live longer than other birds.

Perhaps the most hands-off approach to parenthood comes from the Common Cuckoo (*Cuculus canorus*) and other so-called brood parasites. These "nest-cheats" simply deposit their eggs in the nest of another bird and leave their host to do the work. No Common Cuckoo has ever knowingly met its parents.

▼ A WORLD OF BREEDING STRATEGIES

Material needs
Gathering nesting material is a full-time job as birds prepare their nests for the start of the breeding season. Choice of material depends upon nest design. A Tufted Puffin (*Fratercula cirrhata*) collects vegetation and feathers to line its burrow.

The hole story
Holes – in tree trunks, sandbanks and other secure locations – offer prime nest sites. Some birds, such as the Burrowing Owl (*Athene cunicularia*), may take over the old burrow of a prairie dog or armadillo on the grasslands in North and South America.

Extreme nests

Largest tree nest: that of a Bald Eagle (*Haliaeetus leucocephalus*) pair in Florida was 6 m (20 ft) deep by 3 m (10 ft) wide, and weighed close to three tonnes

Largest nest: Australia's Orange-footed Scrubfowl (*Megapodius reinwardt*) builds a breeding mound and buries its eggs inside. One was recorded at 3 m (10 ft) tall, with a footprint of 18 x 5 m (59 x 16 ft)

Smallest nest: the Bee Hummingbird (*Mellisuga helenae*) builds a tiny cup measuring just 2 cm (3/4 in) in diameter and depth

Longest nest burrow: those of the Rhinoceros Auklet (*Cerorhinca monocerata*) of the Northern Pacific are up to 8 m (26 ft) long

Largest nesting colonies: those of the Red-billed Quelea (*Quelea quelea*), a small African finch, may cover more than 80 hectares (200 acres) of thorn bush, and house over 1 million birds

Most northerly nesting bird: the Ivory Gull (*Pagophila eburnea*) breeds at the edge of the pack-ice in the Arctic Circle

▼ Hatching calendar
Clutch size and incubation time in five European birds

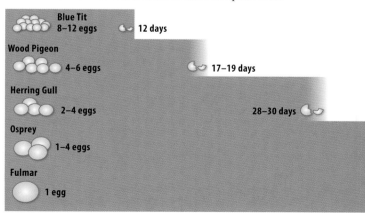

Blue Tit 8–12 eggs — 12 days

Wood Pigeon 4–6 eggs — 17–19 days

Herring Gull 2–4 eggs — 28–30 days

Osprey 1–4 eggs

Fulmar 1 egg

Copyright © Myriad Editions

Lining up

Some parents go to extraordinary lengths to provide for their offspring. A pair of Great Tits (*Parus major*) may bring in 1,000 caterpillars a day while their young are in the nest – and will continue to feed them for a week or more after they have fledged.

Kept in suspense

The Olive-backed Sunbird (*Cinnyris jugularis*) suspends its nests from a thin branch and camouflages it using moss, lichen and spider's webs. The clutch of one or two eggs hatches after about ten days, and both male and female take turns in feeding the young.

Practice makes perfect

Nest-building skills improve with experience. Young male weavers, such as this Southern Masked Weaver (*Ploceus velatus*), generally produce a series of shoddy trial nests before they manage to create one good enough to attract a female.

Bare minimum

Many ground-nesting birds simply scrape a shallow depression in the sand or soil with their feet. The eggs and youngsters depend upon the warm body of a parent for insulation. When no parent is at hand, camouflage helps them escape the notice of predators – as with this clutch of Killdeer eggs (*Charadrius vociferus*).

Dad duties

The male Emperor Penguin (*Aptenodytes forsteri*) uses his feet to support first an egg and then a chick while his mate is away for three months, fishing. A roll of skin on his belly provides warmth and additional protection.

Chamber of secrets

The Malleefowl (*Leipoa ocellata*) does not brood its eggs. Instead, the pair builds an incubation chamber by scraping a long hollow in the ground and filling it with layers of rotting vegetation and sand. Both adults tend the mound, adding or removing sand to ensure the temperature inside remains at an optimum 30°C (86°F). But by the time the hatchlings emerge, 50 to 100 days later, their parents are long gone.

40–45 days

60 days

Living Together

No bird is an island. Even the most solitary species must interact regularly with other birds. Some breed communally. Others gather together as circumstances dictate – at roosts, on migration, or when feeding. A few even enjoy a special relationship with another species altogether.

Flocks offer protection. Although gathering in one place may make birds more visible to predators, the odds of each individual being targeted fall sharply once it joins a crowd. Flocks also mean more eyes to look out for danger. Single birds must be more vigilant than those in a flock, thus constantly interrupting valuable feeding time by looking around.

Many birds flock outside the breeding season, when territorial ties weaken and collective foraging makes food easier to find. Mixed feeding flocks, in which several species forage together, are a feature of many woodland and forest habitats. Such flocks typically have "core" species, such as chickadees in North America and antbirds in South America, whose conspicuous plumage or behaviour serves to attract others. Different species may also gather to exploit a temporary food bonanza, such as a mass termite emergence on the African savanna or shoaling sardines at sea.

Communication is vital in any such gathering. "Contact calls" help birds stay in touch when foraging or travelling, while "alarm calls" warn of approaching predators. Calls are quick messages – as opposed to song, which is a ritualized performance – and can be understood across species. The Greater Racket-tailed Drongo (*Dicrurus paradiseus*) of southern Asia will even attract other birds to a mixed feeding flock by mimicking their calls, thus boosting its own chances of foraging success.

Many species flock to roost, including some, such as wagtails, that are largely solitary at other times. Communal roosts can act as information centres: birds monitor the condition of their neighbours and, if they appear well fed, will follow them to their feeding sites the next morning. Roost sites are generally either concealed or inaccessible. Gulls and geese may simply roost on the open water.

Some birds gather to breed but disperse widely at other times. Breeding colonies typically have a major food source nearby, such as the sea, but limited suitable habitat. Thus, the 95 percent of seabird species that are colonial breeders crowd onto breeding cliffs or other terrain in huge numbers. The cramped conditions offer certain advantages: members may gang up to drive away predators, and can follow one another to feeding grounds. But there is also a cost: parasites and disease are more easily transmitted between birds, and the colony as a whole is vulnerable to environmental disaster, such as oil spills.

Safety in numbers

Large flocks of geese, such as these migrating Snow Geese (*Chen caerulescens*), comprise an aggregation of many family parties. When in flight they keep up a constant honking to stay in touch. When on the ground they continually rotate position, allowing those at the centre to feed or rest while those towards the edge remain vigilant.

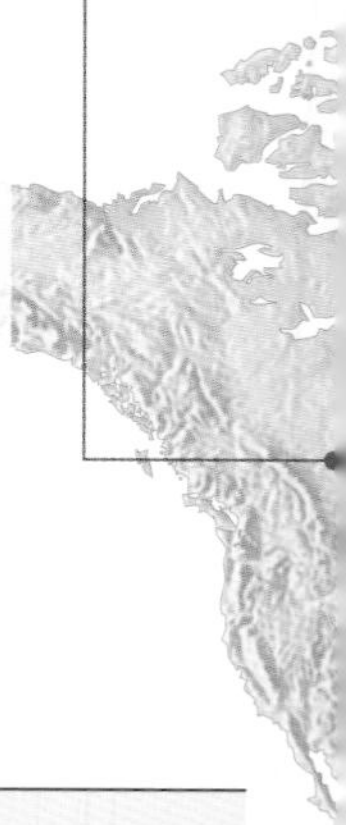

Commensalism

This is a relationship in which one species benefits from the activities of another. In Australia, for example, Yellow Robins (*Eopsaltria spp*) follow foraging Brush Turkeys (*Alectura lathami*) to snap up any insects they disturb. In the Arctic, geese often site their nests close to that of a Snowy Owl (*Bubo scandiacus*), whose aggression deters nest-raiding Arctic foxes. Commensalism may even involve non-avian partners: enterprising Pale Chanting Goshawks (*Melierax canorus*) in the Kalahari will follow a foraging honey badger and pounce on any rodents it flushes from burrows.

▼ Gannet colonies in southern Africa

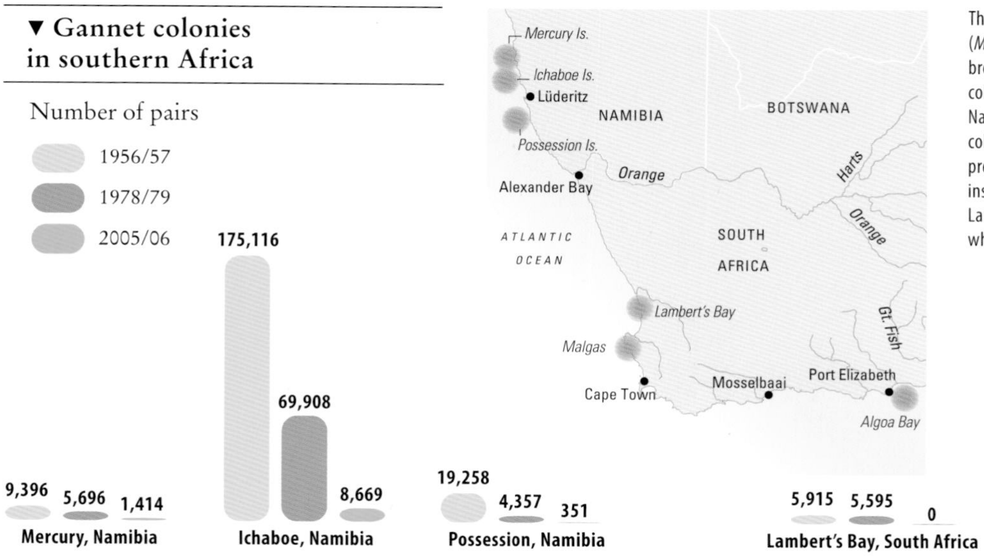

Number of pairs

- 1956/57
- 1978/79
- 2005/06

The worldwide population of the Cape Gannet (*Morus capensis*) comprises about 150,000 breeding pairs. These are restricted to just six colonies: three in South Africa and three in Namibia. Numbers fluctuate over time as each colony is affected by local factors. Increased predation by Cape fur seals in 2006, for instance, caused complete abandonment at Lambert's Bay. This leaves the species as a whole highly vulnerable.

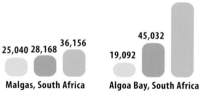

Mercury, Namibia: 9,396 — 5,696 — 1,414

Ichaboe, Namibia: 175,116 — 69,908 — 8,669

Possession, Namibia: 19,258 — 4,357 — 351

Lambert's Bay, South Africa: 5,915 — 5,595 — 0

Malgas, South Africa: 25,040 — 28,168 — 36,156

Algoa Bay, South Africa: 19,092 — 45,032 — 98,419

Map labels: Mercury Is., Ichaboe Is., Lüderitz, NAMIBIA, BOTSWANA, Possession Is., Orange, Harts, Alexander Bay, ATLANTIC OCEAN, SOUTH AFRICA, Orange, Lambert's Bay, Malgas, Gt. Fish, Mosselbaai, Port Elizabeth, Cape Town, Algoa Bay

Starling flight

Large flocks of European starlings (*Sternus vulgaris*) perform synchronized aerobatic displays in cloud-like formations. Each member responds to the movements of others almost instantaneously, enabling the flock to behave like a single organism and baffle any would-be predators.

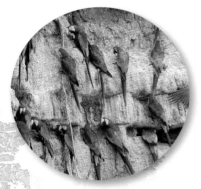

Mud, glorious mud

Red-and-green Macaws (*Ara chloropterus*) gather at a "clay-lick" in Manu National Park, Peru. Like many parrot species, they ingest soil and mud in order to supplement their fruit-rich diet with important minerals. Noisy flocks of several hundred birds, comprising several different species, congregate daily at favoured sites.

Our mutual friends?

Oxpeckers (*Buphagus spp*) feed on ticks and other skin parasites gleaned from the bodies of large mammals such as buffalo. This arrangement was long assumed to be of mutual benefit to bird and beast: the oxpeckers get a meal while their host gets a grooming service. But recent studies have shown that the birds feed mostly on blood, taking ticks only once already engorged, and also probing wounds, suggesting their services are more parasitic than beneficial.

The swarm

The Red-billed Quelea (*Quelea quelea*) is a small African finch that forms the largest flocks of any bird. Breeding colonies may number several hundred thousand pairs, while non-breeding flocks may number into the millions. Such swarms may take five hours to pass and can strip crops like locusts.

Follow the plough

Cattle Egrets (*Bubulcus ibis*) habitually follow cattle and grazing mammals in order to feed on invertebrates they disturb. In this Sri Lankan paddyfield they have developed a commensal relationship with the farmer, flocking around the tractor to snap up any goodies that emerge from the boggy ground.

Apartment block

Sociable Weavers (*Philetairus socius*), of Africa's arid Kalahari region, work together to build one huge communal nest. This haystack-like construction measures up to 8 m (26 ft) across by 2 m (6 ft) high, and may support more than 300 birds in up to 100 individual nesting compartments. Its dense thatch insulates the colony against both the desert's cold nights and baking hot days.

Copyright © Myriad Editions

Birds on the Move

For centuries the swallow's arrival has heralded summer for people all over Europe. But it wasn't until the 20th century that scientists discovered where the bird disappeared to in winter. Even now that we know the truth about migration, it still seems barely conceivable that such a fragile-looking creature can complete an annual 20,000-km (12,400-mile) round-trip to South Africa and back.

Of course, the Barn Swallow (*Hirundo rustica*) is not alone. Over half a billion birds migrate twice a year between Europe and sub-Saharan Africa. Similar numbers make similarly staggering journeys in the Americas, Asia, and Oceania, criss-crossing the equator between their breeding grounds in the northern hemisphere and their wintering quarters in the tropics. Indeed, more than 4,000 bird species are migrants.

Birds migrate because, quite simply, the risks of staying behind outweigh those of moving on. For the Barn Swallow, Europe's summer may offer abundant food and long daylight hours for feeding a family, but winter is a cold, dark death trap. Conversely, southern Africa offers warmth and food year round, but there is too much local competition when it comes to breeding.

Migration is thought to have evolved at the end of the last Ice Age, when species from the tropics began heading northwards to take advantage of new habitats exposed by the retreating ice, but had to return each winter. Today, most species of birds that breed in northern regions are migrants, whereas most species that breed in the tropics – where food and weather are more reliable – tend to stay put.

▼ Barn Swallow migration routes

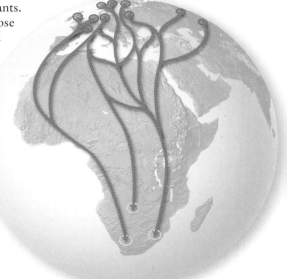

- 🔵 breeding grounds
- ⚪ wintering grounds

A Barn Swallow's annual migration round-trip may exceed 20,000 km (12,400 miles). The northbound leg takes about four weeks; the return journey (with no rush to breed), a week or so longer. Different populations follow different routes.

Around **40%** of bird species are migrants

Barn swallows gather on power lines prior to departure.

▼ Migration altitude

—— exceptional altitude

—— usual altitude

Most migrating birds usually fly at between 200–1,500 m (640–4,800 ft) above sea level. They fly lower when the wind is against them, as ridges, trees and buildings lessen its force. When the wind is behind them they fly higher, to benefit from its full force. Mountains compel birds to gain altitude. Bar-headed Geese (*Anser indicus*) in central Asia regularly cross the Himalayas.

9,000 m / 29,000 ft

Bar-headed Geese

6,700 m / 22,000 ft

4,900 m / 16,000 ft

eagles, hawks, vultures

3,000 m / 10,000 ft

ducks, geese

3,000 m / 10,000 ft

1,800 m / 6,000 ft

crows

1,200 m / 4,000 ft

swifts, swallows

600 m / 2,000 ft

Copyright © Myriad Editions

Not all migration is from north to south. Some species travel from east to west or, in the southern hemisphere, south to north. Highland birds may migrate downhill, seabirds track seasonal ocean currents, and desert species follow the rains. "Partial migrants", such as the European starling (*Sterna vulgaris*), may sit out the winter in some parts of their range, but migrate away from the areas where winter is harsher.

Most small birds travel hard and fast, fuelled by fat reserves, and flying largely by night when the air is calmer. Many larger species make slower progress, stopping periodically to feed and rest. Some birds migrate in flocks, while others scatter across a broad front, gathering at communal roosts en route.

Much of the science behind migration remains poorly understood. Shortening day length triggers departure, birds orientating themselves by instinct. Navigation then involves a combination of cues, most importantly the sun, but also the moon and stars, and landmarks such as valleys and coastlines. Meanwhile, various other specialized adaptations – including sensitivity to polarized light, infrasound and the Earth's magnetic field – allow birds a navigational accuracy far beyond the grasp of humans.

Whatever the science, birds perform some astounding feats. Take the Manx Shearwater (*Puffinus puffinus*) that was transported 4,000 km (2,500 miles) from its breeding site in Wales to be released on the US coast near Boston, and was back at its burrow just 15 days later. Or the Bar-tailed Godwits (*Limosa lapponica*) that flew 11,000 km (6,800 miles) non-stop from Alaska to New Zealand in just six days. For such global wanderers it is indeed a small world.

▼ BIRD RINGING

Number of records from birds originally ringed in Britain and Ireland
1909–2010

- more than 20,000
- 10,001 – 20,000
- 5,001 – 10,000
- 1,001 – 5,000
- 101 – 1,000
- 1 – 100

Feeding frenzy

Many small migrants have the capacity to turn food quickly into fat, forming a layer beneath the skin that is converted into energy as they fly. Smaller species can gain 3% to 4% of their body weight each day, and a Sedge Warbler (*Acrocephalus schoenobaenus*) almost doubles its weight, putting on 10 g in a three-week feeding frenzy prior to departure. This fuel allows it to undertake a single, non-stop 4,000 km flight to West Africa.

With this ring

We owe our knowledge of bird migration largely to the practice of ringing, or banding, individual birds. Small birds, such as this Black-throated Green Warbler (*Dendroica virens*) are usually caught in a "mist net" that has been strung across their flight path. The net is designed so that the birds are not harmed and can be removed safely. Larger, ground-feeding birds, such as geese, may be caught by a more substantial net, which is "fired" over the top of them.

Researchers fit a ring of an appropriate size onto a bird's leg. If the bird is subsequently recovered, a unique number on this ring reveals where and when it started its journey. Only a tiny proportion of ringed birds are recovered. Many are found dead, but live birds may also be recaptured. Either way, the recovery of any bird reveals vital clues about its migratory behaviour. Larger rings, coloured dyes and other more visible markers used on the biggest species can be identified from a distance, without the need to recapture the bird.

Some young birds may be ringed in the nest. Ringers handling large, aggressive species, such as this Ural Owl (*Strix uralensis*), wear protective clothing to guard against attack from the parents.

Information about bird movement is only slowly building up, since many ringed birds migrate to remote areas where there are no researchers to capture or observe them. But, over the decades, sufficient birds have been recovered to reveal consistent patterns of migratory behaviour.

The British Trust for Ornithology (BTO) has been ringing birds in the UK since 1909. The map of their records illustrates the wide range of bird migration from the British Isles, but also reflects the level of activity by researchers around the world. South Africa, for instance, has a more active ringing programme than most other African countries, and thus records a good recovery rate, while the migration routes of British birds wintering in central Africa remain very poorly known.

Flyways

The routes taken by migratory birds do not simply criss-cross the world arbitrarily. Each species takes its place among many others in one of several migratory highways that, like intercontinental conveyor belts, transport huge numbers of birds to their destination. These aerial routes are known as flyways.

Flyways reflect the prevailing weather conditions and topography of the areas that birds must overfly. Some follow coastlines, while others cross oceans or continental interiors. Most include key pit stops – often wetlands – where birds can top up on food, water and rest. Many follow river valleys and other landforms, often funneling through mountain passes, sea straits, and other natural bottlenecks, where migrants congregate in large numbers.

The three main global flyways, in the broadest sense, are the Americas, the Afro-Palearctic, and the Asian–Australasian, each of which comprises a number of more defined routes, many of which overlap. Some species may cross or change flyways, and different breeding populations within a species may take different directions. Some fly the full length of the flyway; others just travel along part of it.

Although very general, these flyways indicate similar patterns of behaviour exhibited by numerous species. All species that spend the summer months in Greenland tend to winter in Scandinavia, Europe, or the west coast of Africa, for example. The flyways are clearly enough defined to provide an important focus for bird conservation efforts. This is especially important, as the dependence of each species upon a particular flyway makes them very vulnerable to any disruption to their route.

Many disruptions are man-made, including such obstacles as lighthouses, power lines, and gas flares, all of which kill many migrating birds. Flyways have evolved over thousands of years, and evolution hasn't prepared birds for these modern hazards. In some regions of the world, such as West Africa and the Mediterranean, the birds must also run the gauntlet of hunters' traps and guns; over 50 million migrants die each year on the tiny island of Malta alone.

Most serious, however, is the loss or destruction of habitat along flyways. The drainage of wetlands, especially, can have disastrous consequences. Broader climatic factors also play a part. The desertification of the Sahel, due to overgrazing and climate change, is extending the desert crossing for many species on the African-Eurasian flyway. This is thought to explain why some, such as the Sand Martin (*Riparia riparia*), no longer visit Europe in the same numbers they did 50 years ago.

Wrong flyway
Birds do get lost, despite their navigation skills. Inexperience, bad weather or a faulty internal compass can all lead individuals astray. Those that turn up far from their usual routes are known as vagrants. This may involve a complete change of flyway: the Pallas's Leaf Warbler (*Phylloscopus proregulus*), for instance, breeds in Siberia and China and migrates south down the East Asian flyway to winter in tropical Asia, but every year a few reach the UK, having travelled west by mistake. Such individuals are generally too weak to survive for long and few will ever find their way back home.

▼ MAIN GLOBAL FLYWAYS

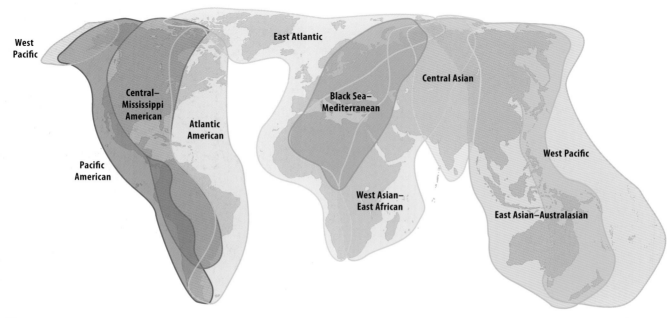

West Pacific

East Atlantic

Central Asian

Central–Mississippi American

Black Sea–Mediterranean

Atlantic American

Pacific American

West Pacific

West Asian–East African

East Asian–Australasian

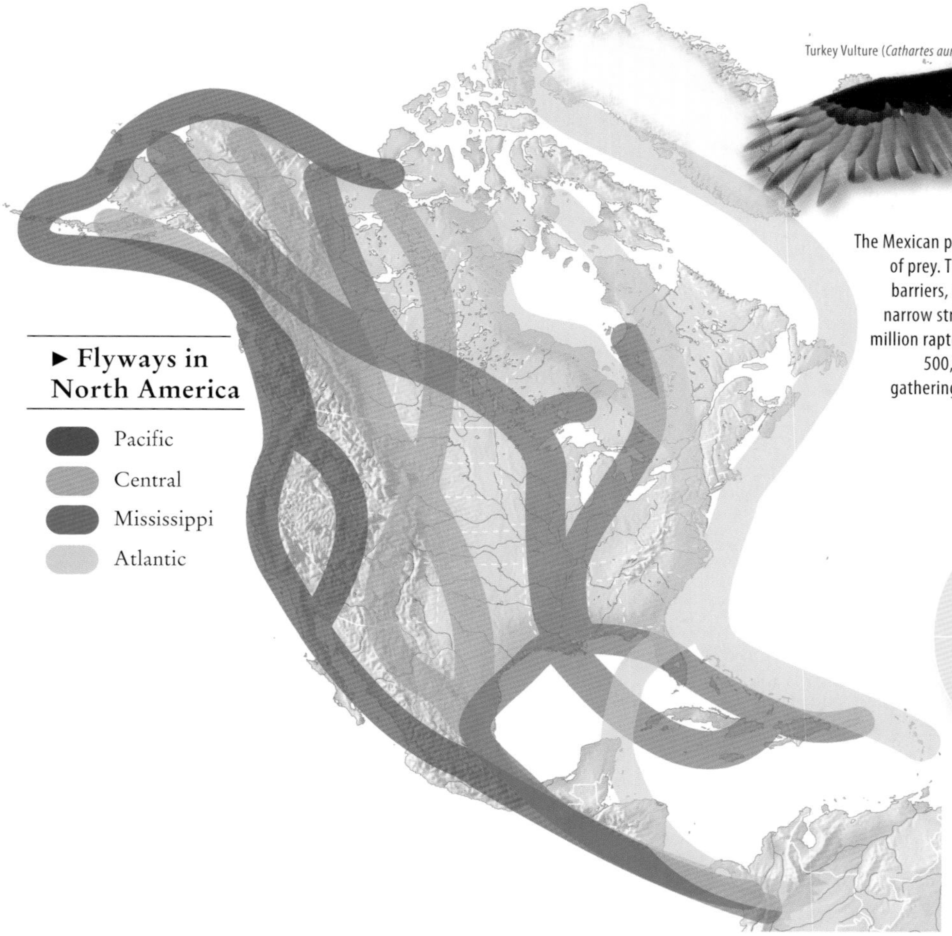

Turkey Vulture (*Cathartes aura*)

▼ Veracruz migration

The Mexican port of Veracruz witnesses the world's largest annual migration of birds of prey. This phenomenon, known as the "river of raptors", is due to two natural barriers, the Gulf of Mexico and the Sierre Madre, which funnel the birds over a narrow strip of land as they head south from North to Tropical America. Nearly 5 million raptors and vultures, from over 25 species, are counted each autumn, with 500,000 having been recorded on a single day. The birds circle overhead in gatherings thousands strong, known as kettles, as they await thermals to carry them onward.

▶ Flyways in North America

- Pacific
- Central
- Mississippi
- Atlantic

Mississippi Kite
270,500

Swainson's Hawk
865,800

Broad-winged Hawk
1,841,500

Turkey Vulture
1,603,400

Total: 4.6 million

Proportion of main species that passed through *Autumn 2007*

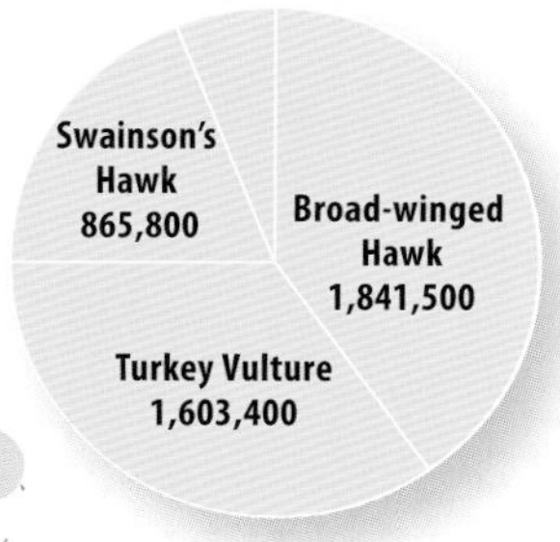

Other species recorded include American Kestrel Sharp-shinned Hawk Osprey Cooper's Hawk Peregrine Falcon, and unidentified hawks of the *Buteo* genus.

▼ Migrant meals

◦ breeding sites of Eleanora's falcon

routes of migrating birds

Shorebird service station

The Banc d'Arguin national park on the coast of Mauritania in West Africa is the world's largest pit-stop for migrating shorebirds. An estimated 2,250,000 waders winter there, more than 30% of the estimated total population using the East Atlantic Flyway. Peak counts include 920,000 Dunlin (*Calidris alpina*) (shown here). This huge area protects 40% of the Mauritanian coastline, and comprises a rich habitat mosaic of seagrass beds, intertidal flats, channels, and creeks. It was designated a World Heritage Site in 1989 but remains threatened by offshore fishing.

Many predators feed on migrating birds. Eleonora's falcon (*Falco eleonorae*), however, is unusual in that its entire lifestyle is specifically adapted to this food source. This fast-flying hunter of small songbirds nests on rocky cliffs in the Mediterranean. Its chicks fledge in August, much later than most birds, thus enabling the parents to take advantage of the autumn songbird migration in order to feed their growing chicks. Once fledged, the falcons themselves migrate south to Madagascar.

Copyright © Myriad Editions

Different Journeys

The popular idea of a migrant's journey is the swallow's long-distance, cross-continental epic, travelling thousands of miles south from its breeding quarters in autumn and returning north by the same route in spring. But there are many variations on this theme: some shorter, others even longer and many much more complex.

Some long-distance migrants take the shortest route possible, even if this means braving perilous stretches of desert or sea. A Ruby-throated Hummingbird (*Archilochus colubris*) migrating south from North America, for instance, will fly directly across the Gulf of Mexico in order to reach its Central American wintering quarters as quickly as possible. Eurasian species, such as the Willow Warbler (*Phylloscopus trochilus*), will cross the Sahara in much the same way. These tiny birds may virtually double their body weight prior to departure as they take on the fuel they need to reach their destination.

Large birds do not have the same capacity to sustain long, flapping flight, and so must take more circuitous routes in order to negotiate natural barriers. Thus, most storks and raptors migrating between Europe and North Africa traverse the Mediterranean at Gibraltar or the Bosphorus, hundreds of thousands of birds funneling through these narrow straits at peak times.

Not all birds arrive and depart by the same route. Some follow an elliptical or "loop" migration, returning by a different route from their outward journey in order to exploit seasonal food supplies or prevailing weather conditions. Sand Martins (*Riparia riparia*), for instance, fly to Africa over the western Mediterranean, passing to the west of the Alps, but return in a loop via the eastern Mediterranean, passing to the east of the Alps.

Many of the longest and most complex migration routes are those of pelagic seabirds. Their journeys seldom follow a simple north–south or east–west axis, but instead loop from breeding ground to feeding ground in order to exploit the most productive ocean currents at peak times. Sooty Shearwaters (*Puffinus griseus*) that breed in New Zealand embark on an annual oceanic odyssey that takes them around much of the Pacific in a giant figure-of-eight.

Not all journeys follow regular, predetermined routes. Some species migrate only when food stocks run out, heading out en masse in mid-winter in search of more supplies, and sometimes continuing to move on as conditions dictate. And not all journeys are long, either. Many birds from highland regions simply head downhill during winter to find easier conditions at lower altitudes. The Mountain Quail (*Oreortyx pictus*) of North America even makes this journey on foot. But however far a bird migrates, and whatever the twists and turns of its route, all species are essentially doing it for the same reason: to find a place where survival is easier. And, in that sense, it's always worth the effort.

Coming down

Some birds migrate by altitude rather then latitude. The Wallcreeper (*Tichodroma muraria*) is a small alpine bird of Europe and Asia that breeds on rocky mountain slopes at altitudes of up to 3,000 m (10,000 ft). In winter, when its food supply is largely buried beneath snow, it descends to the foothills, sometimes taking up temporary quarters in villages and quarries.

▼ **Satellite assistance**

The return route of Harri the Osprey
2002–03

→ southbound   → northbound

In recent years, scientists have refined their understanding of birds' migration routes using satellite telemetry. By fitting small transmitters to large birds, such as raptors and waterfowl, they have tracked the progress of individual birds, discovering how fast they travel and where they stop en route. An Osprey, named Harri by researchers, was tagged at its nest in Finland in 2002, and tracked all the way to South Africa and back.

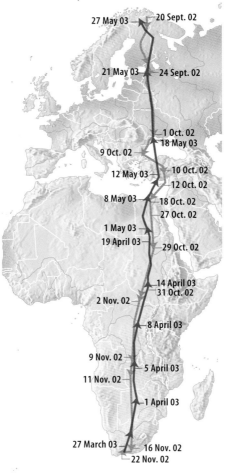

▼ **Looping the loop**

Examples of Sooty Shearwater Pacific migrations
2006

→ bird 1   → bird 2

The satellite tracking of Sooty Shearwaters (*Puffinus griseus*) has revealed that these small seabirds make the longest known annual migration of any species. Nineteen birds tracked from their breeding grounds in New Zealand were found to traverse the entire Pacific Basin in a giant figure-of-eight, most covering around 65,000 km (39,000 miles) in the process. Each made prolonged stopovers in the north before returning via a corridor in the central Pacific. Their routes took advantage of the richest feeding grounds in both hemispheres, from the Antarctic waters in the south to the productive coastal currents off California, Alaska, and Japan in the north.

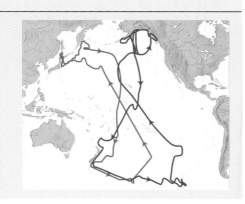

◀◀ *78–79 Birds on the Move; 80–81 Flyways*

The variety and length of migration routes

← **Arctic Tern** (*Sterna paridisaea*): the only bird known to migrate between the Arctic and Antarctica, completing a 30,000–40,000 km (18,000–25,000 mile) round trip

← **European Bee-eater** (*Merops apiaster*): separate populations migrate to west and southern Africa from western and eastern Europe respectively

← **Manx Shearwater** (*Puffinus puffinus*): completes a loop between breeding grounds on coasts in the northeast Atlantic, and wintering quarters in the southwest

← **Amur Falcon** (*Falco amurensis*): Crosses the Indian Ocean en route to South Africa; returns via an overland route

← **Bar-tailed Godwit** (*Limosa lapponica*): its southbound migration from Alaska to New Zealand is the longest known non-stop flight of any bird; it returns via the Yellow Sea in eastern Asia

← **American Golden Plover** (*Pluvialis dominica*): migrates south over the Atlantic to South America; returns north overland to the Arctic

◄ Irruptions
Areas where Common Redpolls were recorded in winter garden survey

///// 1999   ⬤ 2000

Species from northern regions may turn up in winter quarters far beyond their usual range if they exhaust their food supplies. This is known as an irruption. In North America the Common Redpoll (*Carduelis flammea*) periodically irrupts into areas where there is still a plentiful supply of its principal food – birch and alder catkins – as happened in the winter of 2000.

Change of feathers

The Common Shelduck (*Tadorna tadorna*) migrates in order to moult. Most adult birds in the UK depart immediately after breeding for the Heligoland Bight off the coast of Germany, joining a gathering of up to 100,000 birds from all over northwest Europe. Once they have re-grown their flight feathers in October, they start returning to their breeding grounds.

Copyright © Myriad Editions

Part Five

Domestic Chicken *(Gallus domesticus).*

BIRDS AND PEOPLE

Humankind has long had a somewhat ambivalent attitude towards birds. On the one hand, birds have provided us with vital resources, from food, fertilizer and feathers to the less tangible – but no less valuable – gifts of companionship and inspiration. On the other, we have persecuted them wherever they get in our way, and exploited many species to the point of extinction. Certain domesticated species, such as the chicken, have been pivotal to human history and culture. Today, the ever-growing popularity of birdwatching has opened a new window on our relationship with birds – and one that is potentially of great benefit to both us and them.

Birds on the Menu

An estimated 7 percent of the world's 10,000 species of bird have been an important source of food throughout human history. Some, through breeding and domestication, are consumed in their billions every year. Others, sadly, have not survived our appetites.

Tastes vary with culture. Songbirds such as larks and thrushes figured prominently in ancient Roman cuisine – a taste that has endured in the Mediterranean region to this day. The most widely consumed species, however, have been from among the wildfowl (Anseriformes) and game birds (Galliformes). The latter, which include species such as partridge, grouse, and guineafowl, have powerful leg and pectoral muscles that make for good eating.

One wild game bird species looms large in human culture and history. The Red Junglefowl (*Gallus gallus*) of southern Asia, first domesticated more than 10,000 years ago, is the ancestor of the farmyard chicken. Today, chickens are reared by the tens of billions worldwide to provide meat and eggs. In the UK alone, more than 29 million chicken eggs are consumed daily.

Other species of global economic importance include the domestic duck, descended from the Mallard (*Anas platyrhynchos*), of which more than two-thirds are consumed in China, and the turkey, descended from the Wild Turkey (*Meleagris gallopavo*) of North America, which still accounts for more than half global production.

Red Junglefowl (*Gallus gallus*)

▼ From jungle to battery farm

Ever since the Red Junglefowl was first domesticated, both chickens and their eggs have become an increasingly important staple food worldwide, with over 50 billion chickens reared annually. In many developing countries, most birds are free to roam. In many industrialized countries, however, high demand has led to intensive farming techniques – battery farming – in which chickens are housed in very confined spaces, up to 90,000 in one shed. This produces very high yields, with battery chickens laying over 300 eggs a year. In 2006, some 74 percent of poultry meat and 68 percent of eggs were intensively produced.

Such methods have received much criticism on the grounds of both animal welfare and public health. Chickens may suffer damage to skin and eyes from ammonia generated by droppings, and develop brittle bones that leave them unable to support their own weight. To guard against cannibalism, their beaks are removed. Battery cages are due to be phased out in the European Union by 2012. In the USA, however, they remain the dominant mode of production.

▼ Egg consumption

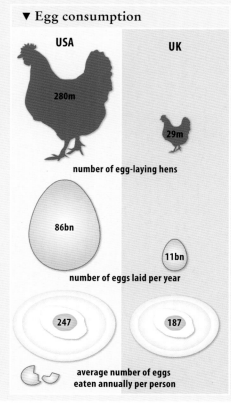

USA

280m

UK

29m

number of egg-laying hens

86bn

11bn

number of eggs laid per year

247

187

average number of eggs
eaten annually per person

▼ Turkeys and ducks
Number in each continent
2006

- Asia
- Central America & Caribbean
- Europe
- Middle East & North Africa
- North America
- Oceania
- South America
- Sub-Saharan Africa

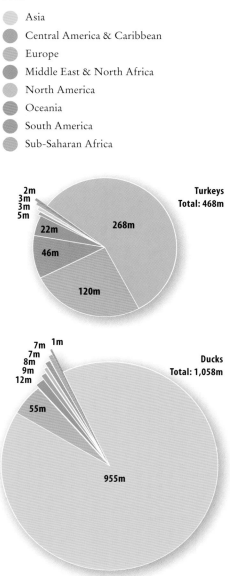

**Turkeys
Total: 468m**

2m
3m
3m
5m
22m
46m
268m
120m

**Ducks
Total: 1,058m**

7m 1m
7m
8m
9m
12m
55m
955m

A duck farmer herds his flock on the backwaters of Kerala, Southern India. The majority of the world's domestic ducks are farmed in east and south Asia – notably in China, where they are a prominent component in traditional cuisine. The turkey market, on the other hand, is dominated by North America.

Historically, some communities sustained themselves almost entirely upon wild birds – especially those on remote islands, without other livestock or crops. Many Melanesian islanders still collect the buried eggs of megapodes. But the hunting of wild birds in industrialized countries is these days more for sport than the pot, and is restricted by law to certain species. Though these birds are no longer important as a food source, they play a significant role in the economy: in the USA, the sale of "duck stamps" (licences to hunt wildfowl) raised over $25 million in 2000.

Certain game bird species have been reared and introduced widely for hunting purposes. The Common Pheasant (*Phasianus colchicus*), a bird indigenous to Asia, is now bred in huge numbers for sports hunting worldwide, from Europe and North America to Chile, New Zealand, and St. Helena. This species now occupies a greater part of the total UK bird biomass than any other.

While the common pheasant has prospered from human appetites, at least in terms of numbers, other species have fared less well. The Passenger Pigeon (*Ectopistes migratorius*), which once swept across North America in the largest known flocks of any bird, was slaughtered on a massive scale in the 19th century – primarily as a cheap food for slaves and the poor. By 1914 the species was extinct.

Seabird storage

The sea-cliffs of the remote island of St. Kilda house some of Europe's largest seabird colonies, and its original inhabitants – who probably never numbered more than 180 – depended upon them for food and other resources.

▼ UK pheasants in figures

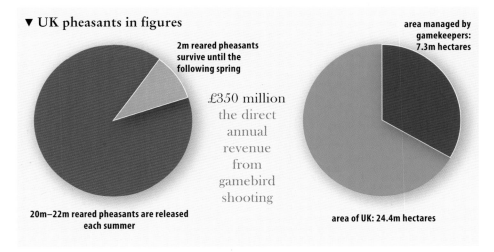

2m reared pheasants survive until the following spring

20m–22m reared pheasants are released each summer

£350 million the direct annual revenue from gamebird shooting

area managed by gamekeepers: 7.3m hectares

area of UK: 24.4m hectares

Traditional traps

A San bushman in Botswana's Kalahari sets a trap for a bustard. Such small-scale harvesting of wild birds has been practised by hunter-gatherer peoples from ancient times, and has a negligible impact on bird populations.

▼ Hunting in the USA

Target practice

The Common Pheasant, originally from Asia, has been widely introduced around the world for sport hunting. First brought to Britain by the Romans, it was rediscovered as a game bird in the 1830s and has since been reared extensively by gamekeepers. In 1857, it was introduced to North America – also for shooting – and has since spread across much of the USA, Canada, and Mexico. Other countries where pheasants are now found include Chile, St. Helena, and New Zealand.

End of the line

Martha, the last known Passenger Pigeon, died in September 1914 in Cincinnati Zoo, Ohio. This species once formed migratory flocks containing more than a billion birds. In the second half of the 19th century it was slaughtered in prodigious numbers: 50,000 birds were killed each day at just one nest site at Petosky, Michigan in 1878, with the hunt continuing for nearly five months.

Turkey shoot

A hunter poses with a Wild Turkey (*Meleagris gallopavo*). Unlike their domesticated descendants, wild turkeys can fly strongly and roost in trees. Native American people hunted them from ancient times. The related California Turkey (*Meleagris californica*), also hunted by early settlers, is now extinct.

Copyright © Myriad Editions

Putting Birds to Use

It is not only as food that birds have made a significant contribution to humanity. For centuries people have used them for everything from bedding to fertilizer – and arguably the most universal service that they have provided has been companionship.

In some traditional cultures, birds have proved a multifaceted resource. The Alutiiq people of Alaska's Kodiak Islands, for instance, harvested seabirds for their flesh, feathers, hides, bones, bills, and talons. Cormorant skins were stitched into durable outer garments – around 50 being required for one parka – while puffin bones were used as tools, and their bills as ceremonial rattles. The original St Kilda islanders fashioned shoes from entire gannets.

Feathers are an especially valuable commodity. The down of wildfowl such as eider and geese is much prized as an insulating material for bedding and winter clothing. The flight feathers of larger birds have provided everything from quill pens to "fletching" (stabilizers) for arrows. And as waste from poultry farming, feathers have yielded various industrial applications, including biodegradable polymers.

Plumage has also long figured prominently in the pageantry and fashions of many cultures. The feather trade in the West peaked in the late 19th century, when birds such as grebes and egrets were slaughtered by the million to provide decorative headwear. Between 1870 and 1920 alone, an estimated 20,000 tons of plumage was imported to the UK for this purpose. Opposition to the feather trade led to the formation of the Royal Society for the Protection of Birds (RSPB), and was a catalyst for the conservation movement.

Guano – seabird excrement – is an excellent fertilizer, due to its high levels of nitrogen and phosphorus. The word originates from the *Quichua* language of the Incas, and this product has been harvested in Peru for centuries, where deep accumulations on offshore islands, deposited primarily by the Guanay Cormorant (*Phalacrocorax bougainvillii*), were once mined on an industrial scale. Artificial fertilizers have today largely replaced guano.

Living birds have also provided numerous services, from the homing pigeons that carried wartime messages in Europe to the cormorants trained for fishing in China. Birds of prey have been especially valued for their hunting prowess, the art of falconry being thousands of years old in many parts of the world.

The use to which the largest number of bird species have been put, however, is as pets. Birds' colours and voices have always made them popular companions. Certain groups, notably parrots and pheasants, have proved especially popular – and many are now reared in captivity, where selective strains have been developed. Unfortunately the international market in cage-birds, as with raptors for falconry, has placed great pressure on wild populations of many sought-after species, driving some to the brink of extinction.

Pigeon post

Pigeons have been used to carry messages tied to their legs at various times. When Paris was besieged in 1870–71, during the Franco-Prussian War, messages were first posted in  specially printed envelopes (see below) to the headquarters at Tours, where they were converted into microfilm. Each message was then dispatched, attached to between 20 and 35 pigeons to ensure its delivery, indicating the level of risk to the bird.

Pigeons were also used to send messages during World War I, one of  which, Cher Ami, is credited with saving the lives of 194 US soldiers, and was awarded the French Croix de Guerre for heroic service. During World War II, 32 pigeons receiving the Dickin Medal, presented to honour the use of animals during wartime.

Pigeons have been pressed into service in peace time as well. A commercial pigeon post was established in New Zealand between Great Barrier Island and the mainland in 1897, and was operated until 1908 by two rival companies, who even issued stamps.

Research has subsequently revealed that traces of magnetite in the brains of pigeons allows them to navigate using the Earth's magnetic field, hence their prodigious homing abilities.

▼ How birds are used

Number of bird species for which a use has been recorded

3,649 — as pets

1,398 — for food

394 — hunted

▼ Multipurpose fowl

Ostriches have been farmed in South Africa for more than 100 years. Since the 1970s, however, this industry has spread to many other regions, including Europe and the USA. Ostriches are highly adaptable birds and potentially very profitable to farm, requiring relatively little maintenance and providing many products.

Around 43% of bird species are used by humans – some for more than one purpose

An average adult may yield the following:

- **eggs:** up to 50 a year for food or ornamental decorations
- **lean, protein-rich meat:** up to 30 kg (66 lb)
- **feathers:** up to 1.8 kg (4 lb), prized in the fashion and millinery trades
- **hide:** up to 1.3 sq m (14 sq ft), tanned into highly durable leather for clothing, bags, shoes
- **oil:** used in various natural cosmetic and health products

Avian anglers

A Chinese fisherman uses his trained cormorants to catch fish. A ring around the bird's lower neck means it can swallow only smaller fish, and brings larger fish back to the boat. This traditional technique was once also practised in Japan and parts of eastern Europe, but has today largely been supplanted by modern technology.

Fashion feathers

The hat worn in this 17th-century engraving of a painting by Peter Paul Rubens is crowned with ostrich plumes, indicating that the feathers of this African bird have been traded in Europe for many centuries. Ostrich feathers lack stiffened quills, the bird being flightless, and so are ideal for decorative purposes.

Precious plumes

A Snowy Egret (*Egretta thula*) displays its breeding plumes. This small species of heron was in great demand for the US feather trade during the late 19th century, when an estimated 193,000 egrets were killed to provide one year's supply of plumes for a single auction house. Today, the bird is the symbol of the National Audubon Society, which successfully campaigned to outlaw the trade in plumes.

Desert falcon

A Lanner Falcon (*Falco biarmicus*) perches on a falconer's glove in Dubai. Falconry remains popular in the Middle East, where approximately 3,000 falcons are employed for this use each year. The earliest evidence of the art comes from Mesopotamia, around the reign of the Assyrian king Sargon II (722–705 BC). Falconry was probably introduced to Europe around AD 400.

Caged colours

The Budgerigar (*Melopsittacus undulatus*) is a parrot species from arid parts of Australia, whose small size, low cost and playful nature have made it a popular pet around the world. Its natural colour in the wild is green and yellow, with black scalloped markings. Other colour varieties, such as blues, whites and yellows, are the product of captive breeding.

Muck raking

Andean villagers collect guano on Independencia Island, Peru. Competition for control of this important resource, produced by Guanay Cormorants, led to the War of the Pacific (1879 to 1883) between the Peru–Bolivia Alliance and Chile.

Copyright © Myriad Editions

94–95 Conflicts with Birds; 108–09 Birds Wanted ▶▶

Birds in Culture

The importance of birds to humankind has not been purely utilitarian. From time immemorial people have drawn inspiration from birds' beauty, song, and power of flight. These properties are celebrated to this day in culture, religion, and politics across the globe.

Some of the earliest representations of birds are found among the artefacts of Ancient Egypt, where many species enjoyed religious status. The Sacred Ibis (*Threskiornis aethiopicus*), regarded as the incarnation of the god Thoth, was mummified by the thousand to accompany burials in the Necropolis of Hermopolis. Vultures, symbolic of motherhood, were associated with the goddess Nekhbet.

Many traditional cultures have accorded symbolic value to feathers of certain birds. Eagle feathers, associated with power and divinity, were earned as tokens of honour among native North American tribes. To the Maya and Aztec Indians of Central America, the Resplendent Quetzal (*Pharomacrus mocinno*) was emblematic of the deity Quetzalcoatl, and its feathers used in ceremony and as tribute. Its legendary status survives in various forms today, including as the currency of Guatemala.

The cultural significance of some birds' feathers sometimes took a heavy toll on the birds themselves. A ceremonial cloak made for Kamehameha, the first king of Hawaii, consists of half a million yellow feathers from an estimated 80,000 Hawaiian Mamos (*Drepanis pacifica*), a bird that is now extinct. In traditional societies where feathers still remain important – as with the plumes of birds-of-paradise among tribal groups of Papua New Guinea – a more sustainable quota is now harvested.

Birds have always featured prominently in art, from the symbolism of the European Goldfinches (*Carduelis carduelis*) that adorn Renaissance religious paintings, to the scientific cataloguing of ornithologists such as Victorian John Gould. Birds are also a favourite motif in Japanese prints and ceramics, generally linked with the seasons and interpreted as reflections of human emotions and qualities.

In literature, too, birds are celebrated in works ranging from John Keat's "Ode to a Nightingale" to Paul Gallico's *The Snow Goose*, often used to embody themes of freedom and escape. Some 64 different species appear in the works of Shakespeare.

Modern cultures may no longer harvest birds for ritual purposes, but they continue to exploit their symbolic value. Thus, contemporary American politicians are characterized as "hawks" or "doves", according to their approach on military matters. Many species have been elevated to iconic status as "national birds", from the diminutive Dipper (*Cinclus cinclus*) of Norway to the massive Andean Condor (*Vultur gryphus*), shared by Bolivia, Chile, Colombia, and Ecuador. Images of these species appear everywhere, from coats-of-arms to postage stamps.

In the modern world, these emblematic values have great commercial clout. Images of birds sell everything from books (Penguin publishers) to beer (the Guinness toucan). And the multi-million pound UK market for Christmas cards would be sunk without the humble European Robin (*Erithacus rubecula*).

Tribal headdress made with feathers from Birds-of-Paradise, parrots, and lorikeets, Papua New Guinea.

£6.5m
Amount paid for a copy of John James Audubon's *Birds of America* in London, 2010

▼ **Shakespeare's top 20 birds**

Number of times the bird is mentioned in collected plays of William Shakespeare

"I know a hawk from a handsaw"
Hamlet, Act II, scene 2
"Handsaw" – a corruption of "hernshaw", the old name for a Grey Heron

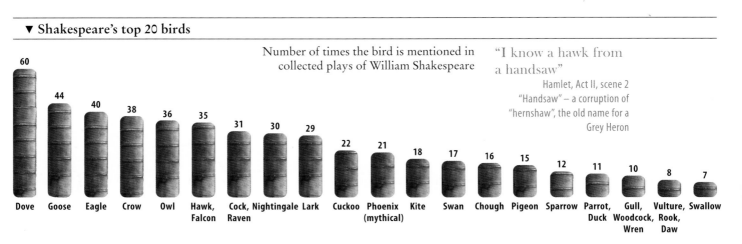

60	44	40	38	36	35	31	30	29	22	21	18	17	16	15	12	11	10	8	7
Dove	Goose	Eagle	Crow	Owl	Hawk, Falcon	Cock, Raven	Nightingale	Lark	Cuckoo	Phoenix (mythical)	Kite	Swan	Chough	Pigeon	Sparrow	Parrot, Duck	Gull, Woodcock, Wren	Vulture, Rook, Daw	Swallow

Eagle power

The Bald Eagle (*Haliaeetus leucocephalus*) has loomed large in the culture and folklore of North America for thousands of years. Its feathers once adorned headdresses worn by Native American peoples, including the Sioux, Crow, Blackfeet, and Cheyenne. Today, it is the national bird of the USA, and emblematic of national pride and military might.

Robin redbreast

The European Robin (*Erithacus rubecula*)appears in countless different forms on Christmas cards and other festive seasonal products. A British folk tale explains the bird's red breast as having originated from the wounds of Christ on the cross. Its association with Christmas, however, is more likely to have arisen from the fact that postmen in Victorian Britain wore red uniforms and were nicknamed "Robin".

Bird of doom

Not all birds have positive cultural associations. Ravens are associated with death and ill fortune in the folklore of many northern regions, perhaps originating in their habit of scavenging from corpses on the battlefield. This superstition is most famously expressed in Edgar Allen Poe's narrative poem "The Raven", published in 1845, in which the narrator refers to the bird as a "thing of evil".

Falcon in Egypt

Falcons, here depicted in a hieroglyph, are among more than 70 species of bird that have been identified in the artwork and artefacts of Ancient Egypt. The falcon was the sacred animal of the god Horus and symbolic of divine kingship.

Artistic gold

According to the distinguished ornithologist Herbert Friedmann, the European Goldfinch (*Carduelis carduelis*) is depicted in at least 486 devotional pictures from the Renaissance, representing the work of 254 artists, 214 of them Italian. The bird is invariably shown in the hands of the Infant Jesus, and symbolizes variously the soul, resurrection, sacrifice, and death. It also appears as an augur relating to the healing of the sick, and thus redemption. Among the most famous artists to have made use of this theme are Leonardo da Vinci, Raphael and Tiepolo.

Stamp of identity

A Crested Partridge (*Rollulus rouloul*) depicted on a Malaysian postage stamp. Stamps illustrating a country's indigenous birdlife have long been an important expression of national heritage. The first three were issued by Japan in 1875. The following year, Colombia issued a stamp with an Andean Condor, and Guatemala followed in 1879 with a Resplendent Quetzal, both these species being the national bird of their respective country.

African royalty

The scarlet primary feathers of the Purple-crested Turaco (*Tauraco porphyreolophus*), known locally as *Ligwalagwala*, are worn to denote royalty in the kingdom of Swaziland. This tiny country is Africa's last absolute monarchy, and the feathers play a prominent role in cultural festivals and pageantry.

Copyright © Myriad Editions

Learning from Birds

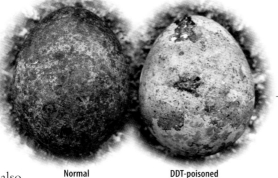

We know a lot about birds. They are the most easily observed, and so the best studied, of all animal groups. In turn, birds have taught us a great deal, from technological innovation to a deeper understanding of our environment – and how to look after it.

People have always watched and learned from birds. The earliest flying machines attempted to replicate a bird's flight action, and much of modern aeronautical engineering – including the aerofoil cross-section of an aircraft's wing – builds upon basic avian adaptations. Other technology derived from birds ranges from shock-absorption systems inspired by woodpecker skulls to camouflage patterning on ships' hulls based on the wing markings of seabirds.

As the most conspicuous and ubiquitous of all animal groups, birds have also opened for us a window onto the wider natural world. It was observations of the arrival and departure of summer migrants such as the Barn Swallow (*Hirundo rustica*), for instance, that first revealed animal migration to science. And in honing our capacity to monitor this behaviour, from simple metal rings to mini-satellite transmitters, so our technology has developed.

In modern times, our understanding of birds' behaviour has cast them – just like the original canary in a coalmine – in the role of environmental indicators. Studies of the puzzling decline of raptors across Europe and America during the 1960s, for example, alerted science to how pesticides were damaging food webs and thus ultimately posing a threat to human health.

Most recently, seabirds have proved to be key indicators of climate change. Significant breeding failures among, for example, Antarctic penguins, have alerted scientists to changes in the abundance and distribution of their food. This has revealed how global warming is disrupting marine ecosystems, with profound implications for our own species. It forms part of the chain of evidence that has prompted global action against this threat.

Bird populations are also an important indicator of biodiversity, suggesting patterns of species richness and endemism among other animal groups. The decline of birds in a particular region is often an early indication of wider environmental threats, and thus sounds the alarm bell to conservationists. Recent evidence suggests that the protection of important sites for birds – notably through the BirdLife International Important Bird Area network – tends also to safeguard most other terrestrial biodiversity.

Meanwhile, the gathering of information from and about birds shows no sign of abating. The year 2003 alone saw some 1,411 articles with the word "bird" in the title or abstract published in mainstream academic journals, while in 2004, the largest natural history book distributor was marketing three-and-a-half times more books about birds than about mammals. As people continue to learn more about birds – and more from them – so conservation becomes ever better informed and more effective.

Normal peregrine egg · **DDT-poisoned egg**

Poison alert

By the 1950s the once widespread Peregrine Falcon (*Falco peregrinus*) had become extremely rare in North America and northern Europe due to an insecticide called DDT that farmers were spraying on crops. DDT worked its way up the food chain, from grain to seed-eating birds such as pigeons, and on to raptors such as Peregrines. The chemical residue inhibited the falcons' capacity to produce calcium, thus weakening their eggshells, which cracked or overheated before hatching. By the 1970s, DDT was banned across much of the world and Peregrines have since recovered well. This episode helped inspire Rachel Carson's *Silent Spring*, published in 1962, which proved inspirational to the modern conservation movement.

▼ Eastern US peregrines

Number of breeding pairs east of Mississippi

1930	350–400 *(estimate)*
1964	extinct in wild
1997	174
2008	600

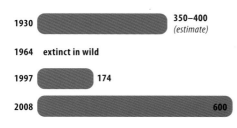

The delicate feather patterns of the Barnacle Goose resemble the waving tentacles of barnacles, which led people to believe that the birds hatched from the shells of these crustaceans.

▼ Getting it wrong

Science sometimes takes a while to find the right answer. Before the advent of bird ringing first revealed the truth about bird migration, many outlandish ideas had been advanced to explain why birds came and went with the seasons. Aristotle suggested that over winter some species metamorphosed into others: the Common Redstart (*Phoenicurus phoenicurus*), for instance, becoming a Robin (*Erithacus rubecula*). For centuries, British scientists believed that swallows hibernated at the bottom of ponds – a theory perhaps explained by the discovery of dead swallows in the mud below the reedbeds where they had been roosting. Even more bizarrely, the Barnacle Goose (*Branta leucopsis*), which visits Britain in winter, was believed to hatch from barnacles, and it was not until 1891 that a European scientist visited Greenland and saw the birds on their summer breeding grounds. In North America, the Cree Indians thought that small birds, such as wood warblers, migrated on the backs of larger ones, such as cranes. But perhaps the truth – that all these birds make biannual inter-continental journeys of many thousands of miles – would have seemed no less astonishing.

Male pride

Studies of sexual behaviour in birds, especially the lengths that males will go to in their efforts to impress a potential mate, have generated insights into human social problems. Studies of the male Arabian Babbler (*Turdoides squamiceps*), for instance, reveal that this small brown desert bird uses displays of altruism to demonstrate greater access to resources and thus advertise its status. Scientists believe such studies may yet prove informative as western civilization addresses the problems of overconsumption.

All fished out

In the northeastern Atlantic, climate change and overfishing have severely depleted the population of the Lesser Sandeel (*Ammodytes marinus*), a small fish that is a key prey species for many seabirds, including the Black-legged Kittiwake (*Rissa tridactyla*). At the same time, the warming ocean conditions have hastened the proliferation of Snake Pipefish (*Entelurus aequoreus*), which are less nutritious and can choke seabird chicks. The resulting population crashes in kittiwake colonies have alerted the authorities to the wider environmental and economic consequences of overfishing.

Cushioning the blow

Woodpeckers, such as this Black Woodpecker (*Dryocopus martius*), have a layer of spongy tissue between the bill and skull that shields their brain from the violent shockwaves generated when hammering a tree with their bill. Studies of this shock-absorption system have inspired research into biomimetic shock isolation systems to protect micro-machined electronic devices (MEDs) for high-g military applications.

Joining in

The Bateleur Eagle (*Terathopius ecaudatus*) is in decline as a breeding species across much of southern Africa. Breeding statistics for this and every other southern African bird appeared in 1997 in The Atlas of Southern African Birds, published by BirdLife South Africa. This project, the largest biodiversity project ever conducted in Africa, collated 7.3 million records collected by 5,000 observers, many of them volunteers. Bird populations are relatively easy to monitor compared to those of other taxa, which means that people from outside the scientific community can contribute directly to important scientific research.

Copyright © Myriad Editions

Conflicts with Birds

irds and people do not always rub along well together. Where wild birds threaten human interests – whether commercial, agricultural, or health-related – they have often come into conflict with humankind. Losses on both sides can be considerable.

Perhaps the greatest declaration of hostilities was Mao Zedong's injunction to "kill a sparrow" in 1958, part of the "four pests" campaign that was central to China's Great Leap Forward. Sparrows were targeted because they ate grain seeds, with peasants across China instructed to destroy nests and scare birds to exhaustion by banging pots and pans. Mao called off the campaign in 1960 when his scientists advised that sparrows ate more insects than seeds, but by then it was too late: with no sparrows to keep them in check, locust populations exploded – leading to the Great Famine, in which around 30 million people died of starvation.

Some birds do cause serious agricultural damage. Various species of crow, pigeon, parrot, and goose are among those responsible for significant commercial losses among cereal and fruit farmers. Most devastating is the Red-Billed Quelea (*Quelea quelea*), which was considered a direct cause of food insecurity in southern and eastern Africa in 2009.

Conflict at a more local level arises when avian predators are perceived to compete with people for the same prey species, notably game birds. In the UK, for example, gamekeepers systematically eradicated raptors during the late 19th and early 20th centuries. By 1918, five species, including the White-tailed Eagle (*Haliaeetus albicilla*), had been exterminated, and another three reduced to critical levels. Fishing birds, from Ospreys (*Pandion haliaetus*) on trout farms to cormorants on angling lakes, have suffered similar persecution.

Problems also occur where birds live in human environments: sparrows entering bakeries, supermarkets, and livestock-feed stores spread disease and compromise hygiene; swifts, swallows, and other roof-nesting birds block gutters and introduce parasites; gulls in seaside towns tear open refuse bags; and huge urban starling roosts damage trees and make pathways hazardous. Deterrents range from anti-roost netting to spikes on ledges, and birds may be legally destroyed under licence where they are deemed to pose a threat to pubic health.

Diseases occasionally passed from birds to humans include avian tuberculosis, salmonellosis and psittacosis – the last contracted from the droppings of parrots and other cagebirds. In recent years, however, all these have been eclipsed by the H5N1 strain of the influenza virus, popularly known as bird – or avian – flu.

Collision course

Mid-air collisions between birds and aircraft, known as "bird-strikes", are on the increase in the USA. Birds may strike the aircraft's cockpit, or be sucked into its jet engine intakes, and can cause serious damage. In 2007, such events caused 3,094 precautionary landings and 1,442 aborted takeoffs. This increase has been attributed to rising populations of wildfowl and other large birds, as well as quieter modern jet engines. Since 1960, more than 25 large aircraft around the world have crashed as a result of bird strikes.

Number of US bird strikes

7,439

1,738

1990   2007

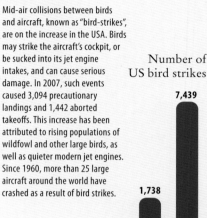

Whooper Swans (*Cygnus cygnus*) were among more than 6,300 migratory wildfowl found dead around Qinghai Lake in Northwest China between April and June 2005. Many tested positive for the H5N1 virus, which they are thought to have contracted from captive wildfowl or an unidentified poultry source.

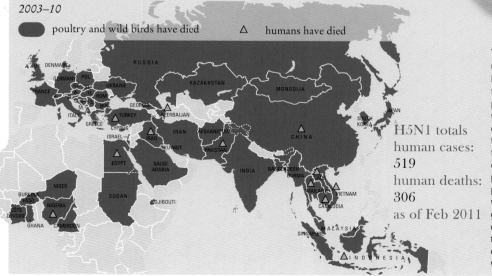

▼ Impact of H5N1

2003–10

⬤ poultry and wild birds have died   △ humans have died

H5N1 totals
human cases:
519
human deaths:
306
as of Feb 2011

The spread of bird flu

Outbreaks of H5N1 bird flu in South-East Asia during the late 1990s grew to pandemic proportions by 2008, claiming the lives of billions of birds, and causing huge losses to poultry farmers. The disease spread across much of the world, largely through the movement – often illegal – of domestic poultry. The mass die-offs of wildfowl revealed that wild birds also carry the disease, and suggested that they may pass it along their migration routes. The virus does not easily pass from bird to human, or from person to person, so human cases have been few, although 60% have proved fatal. The danger lies in possible mutation of the virus, which, scientists warn, could cause a catastrophic global human pandemic. Vaccines are currently being developed in many countries. Meanwhile, scientists stress that improved biosecurity in poultry farming is key to combating the threat, and that proposed schemes to cull wild birds are misguided and ineffective.

◀◀ *86–87 Birds on the Menu; 88–89 Putting Birds to Use*

Fighting back

Very few species of bird will attack humans directly, but some – including skuas, owls, and this Arctic Tern (*Sterna paradisaea*) on the Farne Islands, UK – will defend their nest sites vigorously against all-comers. Birds known to have caused human fatalities include the Ostrich (*Struthio camelus*) and Southern Cassowary (*Casuarius casuarius*), both much larger birds and equipped with a deadly kick. Such incidents are extremely rare and generally involve birds in captivity.

Feed the birdie

Feral pigeons being fed in St Mark's Square, Venice. The risk of disease transmission via direct contact between humans and birds is generally low. Only 176 such cases were documented between 1941 and 2003. Nonetheless, these birds, which have adapted successfully to many urban environments, cause other problems: their droppings can make pathways unsafe and, over time, cause acid corrosion to limestone buildings or monuments, while their nest materials can block gutters and down-pipes.

Bird scarer

A scarecrow planted in a Balinese paddy field aims to deter birds from eating rice seed. Balinese farmers traditionally use materials such as coconut palm leaves to replicate a human form, with some scarecrows also serving a cultural role as a protection against supernatural spirits. Research worldwide has shown that birds quickly become habituated to scarecrows. Today, those in the West seldom take a human form, and their impact is generally reinforced by sound, such as the loud report of an automatic propane gun.

$50m
Annual losses caused by quelea across Africa

Crops lost to Quelea
On 19,000-ha farm in Botswana
2009

845 tonnes

387 tonnes

sorghum   millet

The swarm

Red-billed Quelea gather across Africa in flocks of millions, their breeding triggered by seasonal food and rainfall. Each bird eats around 10g of seeds a day, so a 2-million-strong flock may consume 20 tonnes of cereal crop in that time. Breeding colonies are eradicated by aerial spraying with the organophosphate pesticide fenthion or, in Kenya and South Africa, by fire-bombing. Such operations can cause great damage to wider biodiversity.

Copyright © Myriad Editions

Birds for Pleasure

The last century has seen people take their interest in birds into a new dimension, simply by watching them. The dramatic recent growth of the birdwatching industry, with such related activities as feeding garden birds, has had a major impact on economies and conservation worldwide.

The founding in America of the National Audubon Society in 1886, and in the UK of the Royal Society for the Protection of Birds in 1889, reflected a new popular interest. It was no longer only hunters or scientists in pursuit of wild birds. The advent of field guides and affordable optics made this leisure pursuit increasingly accessible. And in recent years, fuelled by the internet, interest has grown exponentially.

Today, the majority of the world's birdwatchers are from either the UK or USA. The RSPB estimates that at least 30 million UK residents feed birds in their gardens, including around 2.9 million who are "active" birdwatchers. The US Fish and Wildlife Service estimated in 2006 that around 48 million Americans were birders, 20 million of whom pursued their hobby "away from home". Other countries where bird watching is popular range from Sweden to South Africa.

The most dedicated birdwatchers spend substantial time and money in pursuit of their hobby. For many it has become a competitive sport, with individuals racing around, trying to see as many species as possible within a particular time frame or area; top "world listers" have "ticked" more than 8,600 of the world's 10,000 species. Others may devote their energies simply to the birds in their garden.

Recent years have seen a proliferation of birdwatching organizations, including local clubs, national societies, and special interest groups such as the Disabled Birders Association. Numerous festivals and events feed this enthusiasm: the British Birdwatching Fair, held at Rutland Water for three days every August, attracts more than 20,000 visitors; the US Christmas bird count draws more than 50,000 participants nationwide. Bird watching celebrities, such as British television presenter Bill Oddie, and North American authors Jonathan Franzen and Margaret Atwood, have helped raise the pastime's public profile.

This all generates impressive revenue. Americans spent an estimated $45 billion watching wildlife in 2006, with birds accounting for much of this. The UK industry is valued at around £200 million per annum. And such estimates of total economic value do not include possible savings in healthcare costs from the significant "quality-of-life" benefits that birdwatching undoubtedly also brings.

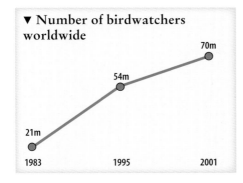

▼ **Number of birdwatchers worldwide**

70m
54m
21m

1983   1995   2001

The biggest twitch

In 2008, British birdwatchers Alan and Ruth Davies set a new world record for the greatest number of different bird species seen in one calendar year. They notched up 4,341 species, visiting 26 countries in the process. The story is told in their book *The Biggest Twitch*.

▼ BIRDWATCHING IN THE UK

The UK has more birdwatchers than any other European country, with numerous organizations, societies, publications, and websites dedicated to this pastime.
- The Royal Society for the Protection of Birds (RSPB) is the world's largest bird conservation organization, with over 1 million members.
- Over 40,000 volunteer birdwatchers collect data for the British Trust for Ornithology (BTO).
- More than half the adults in the UK feed birds in their garden.
- There are at least 110 local bird clubs and societies in the UK.

Pulling power

The appeal of charismatic species such as the Osprey (*Pandion haliaetus*) is a valuable tool in conservation. The RSPB found in 2001 that an estimated 290,000 people visit UK sites with nesting Ospreys each year, notably at their famous Loch Garten reserve in Scotland, where the species first returned to breed in 1954 after 38 years' absence from the UK. These visitors contribute an estimated expenditure of £3.5 million per year and create around 90 jobs.

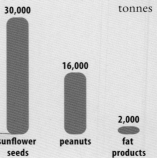

£200m
Amount spent in UK each year on food for wild birds

▼ **Feeding the birds in the UK**
British Trust for Ornithology estimate of bird food purchased
2006
tonnes

30,000 — sunflower seeds
16,000 — peanuts
2,000 — fat products

Percentage of people in each region
who say they participate
2006

19% Northeast   27% Midwest

21% West   33% South

54%
of birders
in the USA
are female

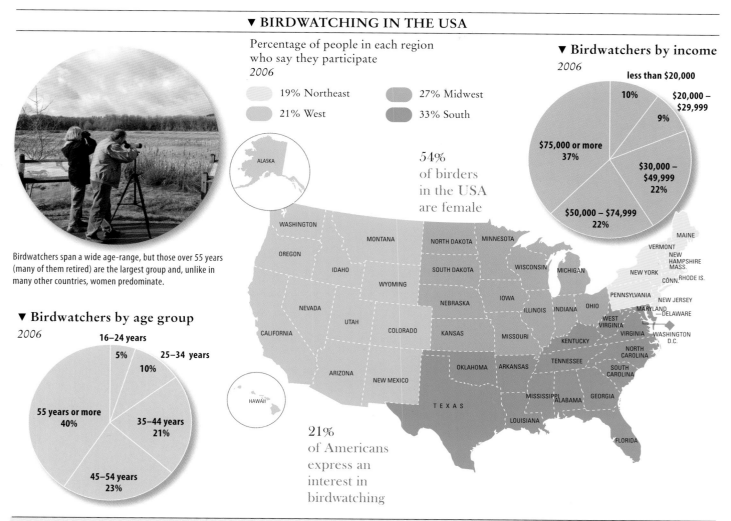

ALASKA

WASHINGTON
OREGON
MONTANA
NORTH DAKOTA
MINNESOTA
IDAHO
SOUTH DAKOTA
WISCONSIN
MICHIGAN
WYOMING
NEVADA
NEBRASKA
IOWA
ILLINOIS
INDIANA
OHIO
CALIFORNIA
UTAH
COLORADO
KANSAS
MISSOURI
WEST VIRGINIA
VIRGINIA
KENTUCKY
NORTH CAROLINA
ARIZONA
NEW MEXICO
OKLAHOMA
ARKANSAS
TENNESSEE
SOUTH CAROLINA
T E X A S
MISSISSIPPI
ALABAMA
GEORGIA
LOUISIANA
FLORIDA
HAWAII

MAINE
VERMONT
NEW HAMPSHIRE
MASS.
NEW YORK
CONN. RHODE IS.
PENNSYLVANIA
NEW JERSEY
MARYLAND
DELAWARE
WASHINGTON D.C.

▼ **Birdwatchers by income**
2006

less than $20,000

10%

9%

$20,000 – $29,999

$75,000 or more
37%

$30,000 – $49,999
22%

$50,000 – $74,999
22%

21%
of Americans
express an
interest in
birdwatching

Birdwatchers span a wide age-range, but those over 55 years
(many of them retired) are the largest group and, unlike in
many other countries, women predominate.

▼ **Birdwatchers by age group**
2006

16–24 years
5%

25–34 years
10%

55 years or more
40%

35–44 years
21%

45–54 years
23%

▼ **The value of birdwatching tourism**

While birdwatchers
themselves are concentrated
in the industrialized world,
today's birdwatching
industry has a global reach.
With more than 130
dedicated tour groups
offering birdwatching
holidays worldwide, it not
only brings considerable
revenue to many developing
countries, but also stimulates
local interest and expertise.
All this plays a vital part in
conservation.

Costa Rica
This small nation offers one of the most
successful global models of ecotourism,
generating an estimated $410 million from
birdwatching alone in 2001.

Macaws for celebration
The value of each red-and-green macaw (*Ara chloroptera*) visiting a clay-lick at Manu
National Park, Peru, one of the natural world's favourite photographic spectacles, has
been estimated as up to $4,700 a year in tourist receipts. That was in 1992, and bird
tourism to the region has increased considerably since then.

Rwanda boosts birding
A Ruwenzori Double-collared
Sunbird (*Cinnyris stuhlmanni*) is
one of Rwanda's 44 "Albertine
Rift endemics", the main draw
for bird tours to this tiny but
bird-rich African nation. In
December 2009, the
government outlined a new
strategy to boost bird tourism,
hoping to attract some
$11 million annually by 2012.

Local guidance
A local tour guide leads a Bird Quest
tour to the Caucasus mountains,
Georgia. Visiting bird groups
contribute revenue and
employment to local communities,
and inspire knowledge and
expertise among local people, some
of whom find employment as
guides.

Copyright © Myriad Editions

Part Six

A ROAD SIGN IN QUEENSLAND, AUSTRALIA, WARNS MOTORISTS TO BEWARE OF CASSOWARIES.

98

BIRDS UNDER THREAT

Birds have long suffered at human hands: waves of extinctions accompanied the early Polynesian settlers and subsequent European expansion around the globe. But while people have always hunted and persecuted birds – some species in vast numbers – the greatest threats today arise from our destructive influence on their habitats. Deforestation, pollution, unchecked development, and the proliferation of invasive alien species have left one in eight of the world's bird species under threat. And climate change is already reflected in changing bird populations around the world.

Extinction

It is apt that the emblem of extinction, the Dodo, is a bird. This outsized, flightless pigeon from Mauritius is one of more than 150 species from the class Aves to have disappeared from the planet in the last 500 years.

Sources differ on how many species of bird have been lost since 1500. BirdLife International classifies 138 as officially extinct. With a further four remaining only in captivity, however, and another 14 that are currently classified as Critically Endangered but have not been seen for years, the list rises to at least 153.

Extinction is inherent to life on earth: many more species have died out over the 100-million-year history of birds than exist today. What has changed in recent times is the rate of extinction. Under natural conditions this would be on average one species lost per century, but since 1500 it has risen to one every three years. The rate continues to accelerate, with some 18 species becoming extinct in the last 25 years. By the end of this century, scientists calculate that, on average, one species will be lost each year.

Extinctions during recent human history have followed clear patterns. Most significantly, 88 percent have been island species, despite the fact that more than 80 percent of the world's birds live on continents. This partly explains why orders of bird that have proliferated on islands, notably rails (Gruiformes), parrots (Psittaciformes), and pigeons (Columbiformes), have lost a disproportionate number of species. Many are highly specialized and so exceptionally vulnerable to external threats.

The common denominator behind recent extinctions has been the influence of humankind around the globe. The expansion by 1280 AD of the Polynesians across the Pacific, bringing their livestock and other alien species, took a devastating toll on many previously uninhabited islands, from Hawaii to New Zealand. Europeans took over where the Polynesians left off, ruthlessly exploiting the natural resources, including birds, and irreversibly altering the natural environment.

Scientists worry that current statistics underestimate the number of bird extinctions. More than half today's known species were not discovered until after 1850, so humans may well have driven many others extinct before they became known to science. Furthermore, many subspecies have also disappeared over the same period. Today's subspecies are the species of tomorrow, so their loss could prove equally damaging to potential biodiversity.

Predictions are alarming. At current rates, an estimated 1,200 of the world's 10,000 bird species – roughly one in eight – faces extinction unless measures are taken to halt their decline. And scientists anticipate a higher proportion of extinctions in continental interiors, where habitat loss is creating ecological "islands" just as vulnerable as their oceanic equivalents.

The good news, however, is that humankind does have the capacity to save birds from extinction. An estimated 25 additional species would have been lost during the past 30 years had it not been for human intervention.

▼ Extinct birds since 1500

Number in each order
Total: 212

Order	Number
Passeriformes songbirds	69
Gruiformes rails and allies	33
Columbiformes pigeons, doves, dodo	19
Psittaciformes parrots	18
Anseriformes ducks, geese, swans	12
Charadriiformes shorebirds, gulls, auks	9
Strigiformes owls	9
Ciciniiformes herons and allies	7
Procellariiformes petrels, albatrosses, allies	6
Struthioniformes ostrich, kiwis, allies	5
Galliformes game birds	5
Apodiformes swifts and hummingbirds	5
Podicipediformes grebes	3
Cuculiformes cuckoos	2
Falconiformes birds of prey	2
Caprimulgiformes nightjars and allies	2
Coraciiformes kingfishers and allies	2
Piciformes woodpeckers and allies	2
Pelecaniformes cormorants and allies	1
Sphenisciformes penguins	1

▼ Continents and islands

Number of bird species extinctions per 25 years
1500–2000

- islands
- continents

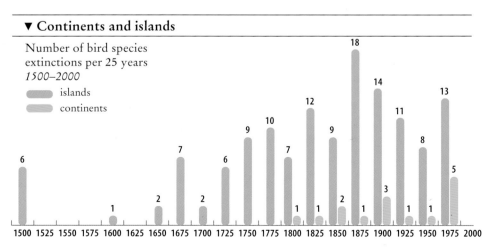

▼ Types of threat

Number of extinctions predominantly caused by each threat since 1500

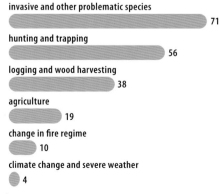

invasive and other problematic species — 71

hunting and trapping — 56

logging and wood harvesting — 38

agriculture — 19

change in fire regime — 10

climate change and severe weather — 4

The San Benedicto
Rock Wren
(*Salpinctes obsoletus exsul*)
became extinct around
9.00 am, August 1, 1952,
when its island habitat
was devastated by
a massive volcanic
eruption.

Seabird's demise

An artist's impression of Great Auks (*Alca impennis*). This flightless seabird, the largest of the family, nested on a number of rocky islands in the north Atlantic. The last known breeding colony was exterminated on Gunk Island between 1785 and 1841, killed for food and for use as fishing bait, and the last known birds killed at Edley Rock, Iceland in 1844.

Flightless and finished

Moas were large flightless birds endemic to New Zealand and commemorated here on a Cuban stamp. The largest species stood some 3.7 m (12 ft) tall with neck outstretched, and weighing up to 510 kg (1,124 lb). Until the arrival of the Maori sometime before 1300 9.5 AD, the Moas' only predator was the huge Haast's Eagle (*Harpagornis moorei*). By about 1400 AD almost all moas – along with Haast's Eagle, which had relied on them for food – are thought to have been driven to extinction by hunting and habitat clearance by humans, although rumours of isolated surviving individuals persisted until the late 19th century.

Hawaiian farewell

Roughly 30 percent of the species to have become extinct since 1500 were from Hawaii. The Hawaii O'o' (*Moho nobilis*) was one such bird. A member of the now-extinct family Mohoidae, its plumes provided native Hawaiians with robes and capes. The arrival of Europeans with muskets hastened its decline, and the last-known sighting was in 1934 on the slopes of Mauna Loa.

Uncomfirmed

It can be hard to ascertain whether or not a bird is extinct. The Ivory-billed Woodpecker (*Campephilus principalis*) is, or was, native to the swamp forests of the southeastern USA – along with a separate subspecies native to Cuba. Following its rapid decline during the early 20th century, due to habitat destruction and hunting, and with no confirmed sightings since the 1950s, the species is now listed by the IUCN as Critically Endangered and Possibly Extinct. Between 2004 and 2007, however, sightings were reported in Arkansas, Louisiana, and Florida, prompting intensive scientific investigation. Despite several high-profile reports, no conclusive evidence has yet been found.

Polly gone?

The last known wild Spix's Macaw (*Cyanopsitta spixii*) disappeared from its final stronghold in Brazil's Bahia Province at the end of 2000, leaving only captive birds remaining. Its decline was due to trapping for trade, the destruction of its caraiba forest habitat and the menace of introduced Africanized bees. The species cannot yet be presumed Extinct in the Wild, however, until all potential habitat has been thoroughly surveyed, so for now it is classified as Critically Endangered Possibly Extinct in the Wild. Meanwhile, the captive population, which officially totalled 71 individuals in 2010, but unofficially may number up to 120, forms part of an international breeding programme that aims to restore the bird to the wild.

Dead as ...

The Dodo (*Raphus cucullatus*) was a large flightless relative of the pigeon, endemic to Mauritius. Weighing around 40 kg (88 lb), it showed no fear of the first humans to arrive on the island. But by 1680, only 174 years after Europeans first learned of it, the Dodo was extinct, the victim of both uncontrolled hunting, and of the rats, dogs, and other invasive species introduced by early travellers. Today, it exists only as a few bones in museums and in various drawings and descriptions. Of the 28 native birds once found on Mauritius and the other Mascarene Islands, 27 were found nowhere else. Of these, 24 or 25 are now extinct.

Copyright © Myriad Editions

Birds under Threat

Roughly one in eight of the world's bird species is under threat. These birds are found all over the world, although some regions harbour a greater proportion than others. Meanwhile, many common birds are also in decline.

The majority of threatened species are concentrated in certain regions, notably the tropical Andes, the Atlantic Forests of Brazil, the eastern Himalayas, eastern Madagascar, and the archipelagos of South-East Asia. Around three-quarters occur in forest habitats, especially tropical lowland forest. The southern oceans and the islands of Oceania are among other biomes where a high percentage of the avifauna is threatened. Some bird families include a particularly high ratio of threatened species, including albatrosses, cranes, and parrots.

In national terms, Brazil and Indonesia have the most globally threatened species, but almost all countries and territories worldwide support at least one. Around 60 percent of threatened species (738 species) are confined to just one country or territory, but many cross borders, with some 170 threatened species recorded from five or more countries. Conservation for such species requires international cooperation.

Around 988 species of threatened birds have populations of fewer than 10,000 birds, and some species number fewer than 50. Most of these are declining in number. Most threatened species are also confined to small areas, with some 6 percent having a global range of less than 10 square km (4 sq miles) each. Threatened birds occur in all major habitat types, but three-quarters are found in forest. Most forest species are highly dependent on this habitat, and fare badly when it is disturbed.

It is not only threatened birds that are struggling. In North America, the populations of 20 common bird species declined by half from 1967 to 2007, while a 2005 study across 20 European countries found that 45 percent of common bird species had declined over the previous quarter of a century. Meanwhile, from water birds in Asia to Afro-Palearctic migrants, populations of once common birds in many other regions have fallen significantly in recent decades.

The decline of birds warns of a wider impoverishment in biodiversity that has profound implications for our own species. Without the complex web of living organisms working together, of which birds are an integral part, we would be left without the basic ingredients, such as oxygen, clean water, and fertile soil, which sustain life on Earth.

▶ THREATENED BIRDS

Number of species of birds classified as Critically Endangered, Endangered, or Vulnerable on a global basis *2010*

- 70 – 123
- 26 – 55
- 11 – 25
- 1 – 10
- none identified

The distribution of threatened birds among the countries of the world reflects a combination of factors, including the inherent species diversity, both past and recent. Brazil and Indonesia hold the most threatened bird species. Both have large tracts of lowland rainforest, the most species-rich habitat, and both have suffered massive and ongoing habitat loss.

▼ Threatened birds

BirdLife International assessment of status of bird species extant in wild *2010*

Total threatened species: 1,244 –12.6% of all birds

- Data Deficient 62
- Critically Endangered 190
- Endangered 372
- Vulnerable 678
- Least Concern 7,751
- Near Threatened 838
- Total number of species assessed: 9,891

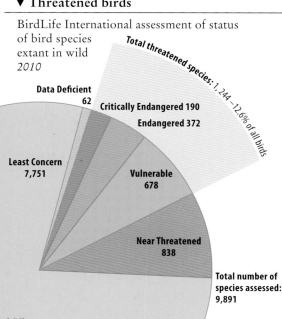

Parrot pressures

The twin dangers of habitat loss and collection for the cagebird trade have left parrots (Psittacidae) among the bird families with the highest proportion of endangered species. At one point, the 16 or so Yellow-eared Parrots (*Ognorhynchus icterotis*) pictured here at their Colombian roost would have represented one-fifth of the world population. Following intensive conservation action, their population had increased to 1,103 individuals by 2009.

CANADA

USA

BERMUDA

MEXICO

BAHAMAS
TURKS & CAICOS
CAYMAN IS. CUBA DOMINICAN REP. PUERTO RICO ANGUILLA
JAMAICA HAITI VIRGIN IS. (UK) ST BARTHÉLEMY
BELIZE VIRGIN IS. (US) ANTIGUA & BARBUDA
GUATEMALA HONDURAS ST KITTS & NEVIS GUADELOUPE
EL SALVADOR NICARAGUA MONTSERRAT DOMINICA
ARUBA GRENADA ST LUCIA MARTINIQUE
COSTA RICA N. ANTILLES BARBADOS
PANAMA VENEZUELA ST VINCENT & GRENADINES
TRINIDAD & TOBAGO
GUYANA
SURINAME
COLOMBIA FRENCH GUIANA

ECUADOR

PERU

BRAZIL

BOLIVIA

PARAGUAY

CHILE ARGENTINA

URUGUAY

Widespread but threatened

A Lesser Kestrel (*Falco naumanni*) at its rooftop nest site in Turkey. This small falcon exemplifies how a wide range is no guarantee of security. Although it occurs regularly in 96 countries in Europe, Asia, and Africa, it underwent a rapid decline over the last half of the 20th century. Breeding populations in Western Europe fell by about 46% each decade from 1950, while wintering populations in South Africa declined by about 25% over the same period. Consequently, the species was classified as Vulnerable, though there has since been some evidence of recovery.

Endangered ibis

In 1981, only seven Crested Ibis (*Nipponia nippon*) were known in the wild. Conservation efforts have since helped raise this population to an estimated 500, and the species has been downgraded from Critically Endangered to Endangered. Nonetheless, with an estimated breeding range of no more than 2,800 square km (1,080 sq miles), in one small region of Shaanxi province in central China, this bird remains the subject of serious conservation concern.

Scarce sandpiper

The Spoon-billed Sandpiper (*Eurynorhynchus pygmeus*), now listed as Critically Endangered, is one of 17 threatened species that have declined by over 80% over the course of three generations. Only 150 to 320 breeding pairs are thought to remain. The breeding range of this unusual wader is restricted to northeastern Russia, and its decline reflects habitat loss in its breeding, passage, and wintering grounds, as well as disturbance, hunting, and climate change.

85% of albatross species are threatened

Copyright © Myriad Editions

Losing Land

The biggest threat that birds face worldwide is the loss and degradation of their habitat. As agriculture and forestry have changed the face of the planet, leaving huge areas unable to support much of their native fauna and flora, many birds have been left with nowhere to go.

The impact of farming on natural habitats increases as the human population continues to grow. The past three centuries have seen the global extent of cropland and pasture expand nearly six-fold, from less than 6 percent of total land area in 1700 to around 32 percent today. In Europe and North America, unchecked agricultural development has already transformed many landscapes. That process is now underway in the tropics, where a dramatic increase in crops such as soybean, oil palm, coffee, and cocoa is partly fuelled by markets in the industrialized world.

In Europe, agricultural intensification and expansion threaten almost a third of IBAs. Many farmland birds have declined drastically in recent decades, particularly in European Union member states, where the Common Agricultural Policy (CAP) has encouraged intensive farming techniques that severely deplete biodiversity. A similar problem affects farmland and grassland species across North America.

Meanwhile, tropical forest continues to disappear. This habitat harbours the world's highest concentration of bird species, yet more than 1 million hectares are lost each year – cleared for crops, or felled for logging and paper production. The destruction has accelerated since the latter half of the 20th century, with the conversion of vast tracts of lowland forest in South America and South-East Asia to commercial oil palm and rubber plantations. Rising commercial demand fuels this process: Indonesia's production capacity for wood-pulp and paper has grown by 700 percent since the late 1980s, and has now reached an unsustainable level.

As deforestation continues, tropical forests that once stretched unbroken over vast areas are reduced to scattered islands in a sea of agriculture. These patches, whilst important local reservoirs of biodiversity, nonetheless invariably support fewer species than large areas, as they are corroded at the edges and often cannot support viable populations of species that require larger territories.

Biofuels were initially welcomed as a sustainable alternative to fossil fuels. However, the conversion of land for biofuel crops – such as oil palm in South-East Asia – is now accelerating the process of deforestation. In the European Union, the rush to grow biofuels in place of set-aside poses a further threat to declining farmland birds. Fertilizers used in cultivating biofuel crops also exacerbate water pollution and cause other environmental damage.

Such rampant human-generated habitat loss can reduce bird populations to the point where natural forces usually held in balance can become devastating. Fire is a natural part of many ecosystems, for example, but becomes highly destructive in human hands. Since Europeans first settled in Australia, fire has contributed to the extinction of at least five bird species, and today poses a threat to almost half of Australia's nationally threatened birds.

In South-East Asia
0.7%
of the remaining natural forest is lost to logging each year

▼ **Rainforest loss**
1990–2007

square kilometres lost

area lost as percentage of total forest in country

9%

Brazil
485,350

▼ **Major tropical crops**

Area under cultivation
1961–2009
hectares

● 1961
● 2009

98.8m

23.8m

3.6m

14.7m

3.9m

8.9m

soybeans   oil palm fruit   natural rubber

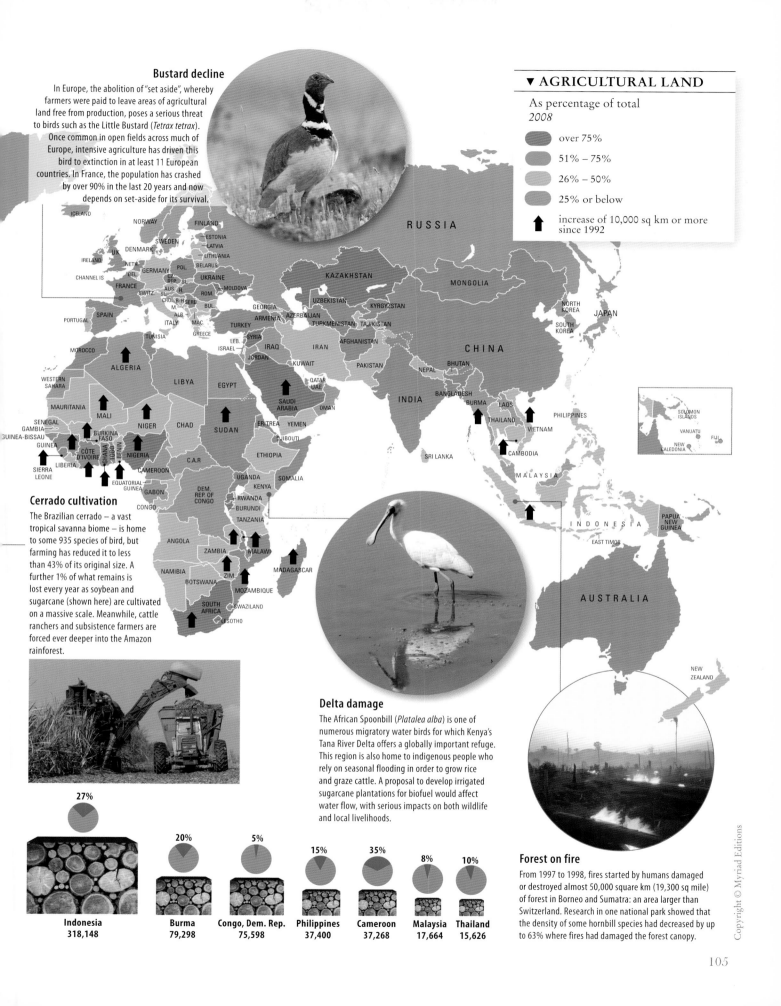

Bustard decline

In Europe, the abolition of "set aside", whereby farmers were paid to leave areas of agricultural land free from production, poses a serious threat to birds such as the Little Bustard (*Tetrax tetrax*). Once common in open fields across much of Europe, intensive agriculture has driven this bird to extinction in at least 11 European countries. In France, the population has crashed by over 90% in the last 20 years and now depends on set-aside for its survival.

Copyright © Myriad Editions

▼ AGRICULTURAL LAND

As percentage of total
2008

- over 75%
- 51% – 75%
- 26% – 50%
- 25% or below
- ⬆ increase of 10,000 sq km or more since 1992

Cerrado cultivation

The Brazilian cerrado – a vast tropical savanna biome – is home to some 935 species of bird, but farming has reduced it to less than 43% of its original size. A further 1% of what remains is lost every year as soybean and sugarcane (shown here) are cultivated on a massive scale. Meanwhile, cattle ranchers and subsistence farmers are forced ever deeper into the Amazon rainforest.

Delta damage

The African Spoonbill (*Platalea alba*) is one of numerous migratory water birds for which Kenya's Tana River Delta offers a globally important refuge. This region is also home to indigenous people who rely on seasonal flooding in order to grow rice and graze cattle. A proposal to develop irrigated sugarcane plantations for biofuel would affect water flow, with serious impacts on both wildlife and local livelihoods.

27%

Indonesia 318,148	**Burma** 79,298	**Congo, Dem. Rep.** 75,598	**Philippines** 37,400	**Cameroon** 37,268	**Malaysia** 17,664	**Thailand** 15,626

20% · 5% · 15% · 35% · 8% · 10%

Forest on fire

From 1997 to 1998, fires started by humans damaged or destroyed almost 50,000 square km (19,300 sq mile) of forest in Borneo and Sumatra: an area larger than Switzerland. Research in one national park showed that the density of some hornbill species had decreased by up to 63% where fires had damaged the forest canopy.

Infrastructure & Pollution

As humankind continues to modify the natural landscape to suit its own ends, so the trappings of development intrude ever more harmfully on the lives of birds. An expanding human infrastructure opens up habitats for further exploitation, while the environment becomes ever more cluttered with the waste our activities generate.

Scientists predict that by 2032 infrastructure development will have touched over 70 percent of the Earth's land surface. The consequences for birds are considerable: in Africa alone, development is damaging habitat in 21 percent of IBAs, and in Europe this figure rises to 37 percent.

Urbanization is a significant contributor, especially in Asia and the Pacific, which account for one-third of all species threatened by residential and commercial development. The transport networks that link developed area – roads, railways, shipping lanes, and flight paths – damage and break up habitats. They also spread invasive alien species, as well as being the direct cause of death for many birds.

Meanwhile, the growing global demand for energy, metals, and minerals increasingly targets regions that were previously untouched. Drilling for oil and gas damages natural habitats, while coal mining can lop off entire mountaintops, bringing wholesale destruction. Roads and settlements that service remote mines open up pristine habitats to further development. Some energy and mining companies work to minimize or offset their impact, but many do not – and government regulation is often ineffective.

The growing demand for water also causes problems, driving ever more ambitious hydro-engineering schemes. Dams, barrages, and canals damage river-basin ecosystems and their resident bird populations. In Africa, the Middle East, and Europe, dams and other hydrological structures are a threat to nearly 10 percent of the region's IBAs, most of them Ramsar sites.

Artificial structures, from farm fences to pylons, take a heavy toll on many birds, especially migrants. Some birds die in collisions; others may be electrocuted on poorly designed power lines. Italy has an average of 2.6 km of power lines criss-crossing every square kilometre of land, and recent censuses have found that birds from 95 different species have been killed when colliding with them. The proliferation of offshore wind farms around Europe and elsewhere is a further cause for concern.

Meanwhile, development generates pollution, from agricultural and industrial run-off that devastates wetland and coastal habitats, to oil spills at sea that can prove catastrophic to the marine ecosystem. Wide tracts of farmland, forest, and wetland are treated with synthetic pesticides, saturating the environment with persistent organic pollutants (POPs) that may affect both humans and wildlife. As well as poisoning birds directly, pollution can also reduce their fertility and degrade their food supplies. In the developing world, products banned or restricted elsewhere are increasingly popular among farmers, who often fail to appreciate their environmental impacts.

Solid junk also causes problems. Toxic lead shot can impair breeding success in scavenging raptors, waterfowl, and game birds, while floating plastic garbage can be mistaken for prey by albatrosses and petrels – often with fatal consequences.

▼ Disrupted wetlands

Sites of international importance threatened by dams, barrages, and embankments in Africa, Europe, and the Middle East
2004

34%
of species threatened by development are in Asia and the Pacific, where urbanization is most rampant.

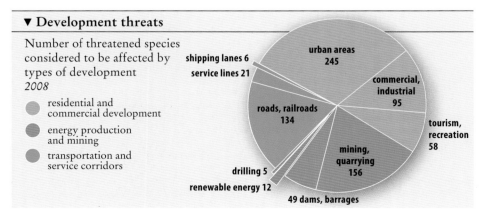

▼ Development threats

Number of threatened species considered to be affected by types of development
2008

- residential and commercial development
- energy production and mining
- transportation and service corridors

shipping lanes 6
service lines 21
urban areas 245
commercial, industrial 95
roads, railroads 134
tourism, recreation 58
mining, quarrying 156
drilling 5
renewable energy 12
49 dams, barrages

Full of lead

The globally threatened Spanish Imperial Eagle (*Aquila adalberti*) is one of at least 59 species worldwide known to have been poisoned by lead ingested from spent ammunition. The shot comes embedded in the bodies of Greylag Geese (*Anser anser*), the eagle's main winter prey, which is targeted by hunters during its migration between northern Europe and southern Spain. Up to 40% of all waterbirds in Europe and North Africa are calculated to ingest one or more lead pellets during a single hunting season. This small quantity can easily prove fatal – or leave a weakened bird more vulnerable to other threats.

Poisoned cranes

In 2002, some 145 Demoiselle Cranes (*Grus virgo*), together with several large raptor species, were among 340 dead or dying birds found scattered across a 3,500 square km (1,350 sq mile) area of Mongolian steppe. The area had been treated with the rodenticide bromadiolone following a population explosion of voles. The true number of casualties is thought to have been much higher.

Road kill

An Emu (*Dromaius novaehollandiae*) killed by a collision with a vehicle on an Australian highway. Road traffic is a significant cause of mortality for birds all over the world, whether flying or – like this species – flightless. Nocturnal birds are especially badly affected, as they can be disorientated by headlights or struck when pursuing prey illuminated in the beam.

Mine every mountain

The Cerulean Warbler (*Dendroica cerulea*) has declined by 82% since 1970. Its remaining core habitat overlaps with the Appalachian coalfields, where mountaintop mining poses an increasing threat to the species. By the end of 2012, an estimated 5,700 square km (2,200 sq miles) of forest will have been lost from the Appalachians, over half of this due to mountaintop mining. In 2004, the Cerulean Warbler was uplisted from Least Concern to Vulnerable.

Soda waters

Tanzania's Lake Natron is home to 2.5 million Lesser Flamingos (*Phoenicopterus minor*), some 75% of the world's breeding population. This IBA and Ramsar site is threatened by a planned soda extraction facility that, if it went ahead, would not only cause major habitat loss and damage through infrastructure and pollution, but would also alter the hydrology and chemical composition of the lake, rendering it unsuitable for the flamingos. The scheme has drawn widespread opposition and, as of November 2010, remains under review.

Strung up

A Barn Owl (*Tyto alba*) killed in collision with a wire fence in the Kalahari. Fences pose a serious hazard to many species of bird, particularly those that hunt just above ground level – such as certain owls and raptors – and large game birds, which tend to fly short distances fast and low.

▼ Vulture death drug

The anti-inflammatory drug diclofenac was first prescribed in India for cattle during the early 1990s, and has since permeated the food chain to devastating effect for vultures. From 1992 to 2007 three once-common species plummeted to Critically Endangered status: the Indian Vulture (*Gyps indicus*) and Slender-billed Vulture (*Gyps tenuirostris*) populations fell by almost 97 percent, while that of the White-rumped Vulture (*Gyps bengalensis*) dropped by a staggering 99.9 percent. These birds had provided a vital clean-up service on carcasses around human settlements. Their decline has brought a proliferation of feral dogs and a consequent steep rise in the incidence of rabies.

Declining numbers

Number of White-rumped Vultures recorded during surveys of specific locations in India 1992–2007

2007	2003	2002	2000
31	130	283	888

In a 1992 survey, over 21,200 vultures were recorded.

112–13 All at Sea ▶▶

Copyright © Myriad Editions

Birds Wanted: Dead or Alive

After habitat loss, direct exploitation poses the greatest threat to wild birds. Hunting for food and trapping for the cage-bird trade has taken a toll on more than 400 globally threatened species – one third of the total. The problem is worse in certain regions and for particular bird families.

At least 50 bird species have been hunted to extinction over the last 500 years. Today, few communities depend upon wild birds for food, but hunting remains enshrined in many cultures, and 1,398 extant species are recorded as having been exploited in this way. Some, such as the Swan Goose (*Anser cygnoides*), of China's lower Yangtze Basin, have declined significantly as a result.

In the Mediterranean region alone, an estimated 500 million birds are killed every year, the majority on migration between Europe and Africa. And legal protection is not always effective. Illegal hunting in southeast and central Europe, for instance, supplies a restaurant market in Italy estimated to be worth €10 million per year. Dead songbirds are smuggled over borders in huge numbers: in 2001, the Italian police seized a 12-tonne trailer-load of frozen songbirds comprising 120,700 specimens of 83 different species.

Birds are not killed only for food and sport. Raptors have long suffered persecution for their assumed predation on game birds. Today, all UK birds of prey enjoy full protection under the Wildlife and Countryside Act 1981, yet every year raptors continue to be shot, trapped or poisoned in significant numbers. Victims include national rarities such as the Golden Eagle (*Aquila chrysaetos*).

▼ Overexploited families

Number of species of threatened bird affected by overexploitation within larger families
2008

parrots
67

pigeons, doves
51

hawks, eagles
43

pheasants, quails, francolins
41

ducks, geese, swans
16

guans, curassows
16

buntings, sparrows
10

megapodes
9

hornbills
8

ibises, spoonbills
8

rails, crakes
8

▼ TAKING AIM

Harrying the harrier

The Hen Harrier (*Circus cyaneus*) is the most persecuted bird of prey in the UK relative to population size, largely because of its unpopularity on grouse moors. The last full survey, in 2004, indicated a total UK population of 749 pairs, but recorded significant decreases on grouse moors – especially in England. In 2008, just 10 pairs bred successfully in England, despite there being enough suitable habitat to support several hundred pairs. Most persecution takes place on private land and therefore often goes unrecorded.

Quail massacre

Some 38,000 Common Quail (*Coturnix coturnix*), more than the country's entire breeding population, were shot in Serbia over just two months in 2004 – up to 90% illegally, using automatic shotguns and tape lures. Quail populations have declined heavily in eastern and southeastern Europe, where such hunting persists. Elsewhere in Europe, populations are stable or increasing.

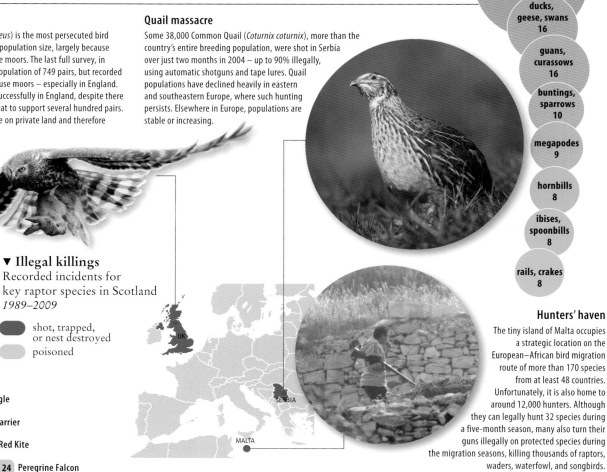

▼ Illegal killings

Recorded incidents for key raptor species in Scotland
1989–2009

11	Goshawk	shot, trapped, or nest destroyed
13	Sparrowhawk	poisoned
26	Kestrel	
17 24	Golden Eagle	
49 4	Hen Harrier	
5 64	Red Kite	
60 24	Peregrine Falcon	
137		344 Common Buzzard

Hunters' haven

The tiny island of Malta occupies a strategic location on the European–African bird migration route of more than 170 species from at least 48 countries. Unfortunately, it is also home to around 12,000 hunters. Although they can legally hunt 32 species during a five-month season, many also turn their guns illegally on protected species during the migration seasons, killing thousands of raptors, waders, waterfowl, and songbirds.

UK

SERBIA

MALTA

The bird trade

In terms of the number of species affected, the cage-bird trade represents an even bigger threat to birds than hunting, with at least 3,649 extant species recorded as having been exploited in this way. The largest markets are in Asia, notably China and Indonesia. Certain bird families are in particularly high demand. In Latin America thousands of wild parrots are illegally captured every year in a trade that puts at risk the populations of many species, some of them already globally threatened. Most are exported to foreign markets, with some fetching very high prices. A high proportion of birds die during capture and transit.

Egg collecting, popular in Europe during the 19th and 20th centuries, had a historical impact on the breeding success of many species. In the UK, this pastime became illegal in 1954, yet a handful of dedicated collectors – driven more by trophies than profits – continue to steal birds' eggs. Police who raided a house in Cleethorpes in November 2006 discovered a collection of 7,707 eggs, all collected by one individual and many of them from rare species.

Eggs are also stolen to hatch live birds, notably for the falconry trade. Of 17 raptors' nests raided by illegal collectors in the UK during 2008, 15 belonged to the Peregrine Falcon (*Falco peregrinus*), a species much prized by falconers. The stolen eggs are smuggled overseas in incubators, notably to the Middle East, where the chicks are reared for falconry.

Parrot prison

Trappers in Mexico capture up to 78,500 parrots every year. Most go to overseas markets, notably the USA, with the most sought-after species selling for $1,000 or more. This trade has significantly affected wild populations. The population of the Lilac-crowned Parrot (*Amazona finschi*), shown here, is estimated to have declined by 20% to 30% over the last decade.

Blue-fronted Amazons (*Amazona aestiva*) are among dozens of parrot species captured illegally throughout Latin America, from Mexico in the north to Argentina – where these birds were seized – in the south. On average, only a quarter of captured birds survive.

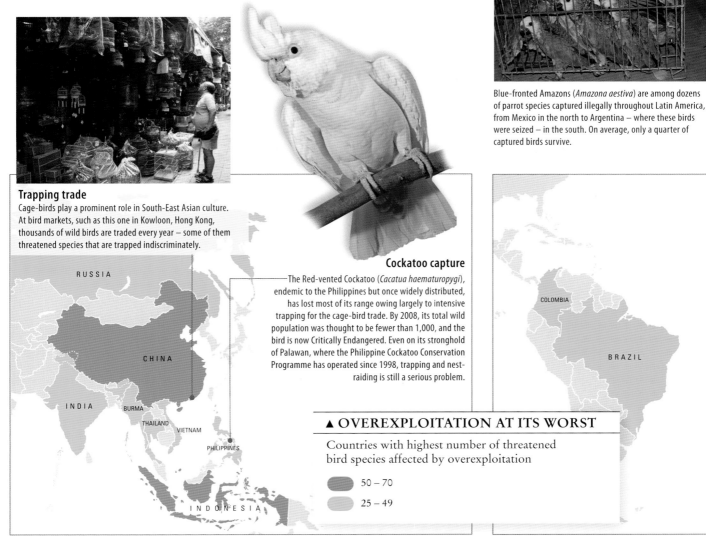

Trapping trade

Cage-birds play a prominent role in South-East Asian culture. At bird markets, such as this one in Kowloon, Hong Kong, thousands of wild birds are traded every year – some of them threatened species that are trapped indiscriminately.

Cockatoo capture

The Red-vented Cockatoo (*Cacatua haematuropygi*), endemic to the Philippines but once widely distributed, has lost most of its range owing largely to intensive trapping for the cage-bird trade. By 2008, its total wild population was thought to be fewer than 1,000, and the bird is now Critically Endangered. Even on its stronghold of Palawan, where the Philippine Cockatoo Conservation Programme has operated since 1998, trapping and nest-raiding is still a serious problem.

▲ OVEREXPLOITATION AT ITS WORST

Countries with highest number of threatened bird species affected by overexploitation

- 50 – 70
- 25 – 49

RUSSIA
CHINA
INDIA
BURMA
THAILAND
VIETNAM
PHILIPPINES
INDONESIA

COLOMBIA
BRAZIL

Copyright © Myriad Editions

Alien Invasion

Invasive alien species are thought to pose the greatest threat to biodiversity, after climate change and human population growth. Birds are especially vulnerable. At least 625 threatened species – more than half the total – are directly threatened by invasives.

Invasive alien species are non-native organisms that damage the ecology and threaten the native species of the areas they invade. It is generally humans who transport these aliens around the globe – either deliberately, as with pets and livestock, or accidentally, as when rats hitch a ride on boats. If they become established, these invaders invariably spell disaster for local fauna and flora. The problem is especially acute on islands, where many species that evolved in isolation are defenceless against the newcomers. New Zealand, for instance, has no indigenous terrestrial mammals and, in the absence of ground-level predators, many birds became flightless. The arrival of humans, with their cats, rats, and other voracious imports, has proved catastrophic for these species.

Cats and rats have, indeed, been the most destructive introduced predators. Others include stoats, foxes, mink, dogs, and pigs, some preying directly on birds, others raiding their nests or depleting their prey. Many species were introduced as biological controls: mongooses were exported to the Caribbean from India in the late 19th century to control rodents in cane fields, but have since devastated a whole spectrum of native fauna.

Being eaten is not the only danger. Invasive herbivores such as sheep and goats deprive birds of feeding and breeding grounds by over-grazing. And invasive plant species disrupt native plant communities and create ecological deserts for native fauna. Rhododendrons from the Himalayas may look attractive in European woodlands, for example, but they support virtually no native species.

Numerous bird species are themselves invasives, with three – the Common Myna (*Acridotheres tristis*), European Starling (*Sternus vulgaris*), and Red-vented Bulbul (*Pycnonotus cafer*) – all listed among the world's 100 most destructive alien species. Their impact ranges from direct predation, to competition for food and nest-sites. Some invasive birds even hybridize with native species, thus threatening their very identity.

Some of the most destructive invaders are the tiniest. Parasites and bacteria – often carried on the bodies of invasive animals – spread avian diseases. For forest birds on Hawaii, for example, the arrival of mosquitoes has brought devastating avian malaria. Avian flu, spread largely by the poultry trade, is now of particular concern, as much for generating public prejudice against wild birds as for its direct impact on their populations.

Today, many nations are vigorously battling the menace of invasive species. Measures range from aggressive eradication programmes to stringent customs legislation. Nonetheless, the proliferation of global travel and trade continues to exacerbate the problem, while habitat destruction and a warming climate allow new invasives to flourish in areas that were previously off-limits.

More than 50% of known bird extinctions since 1500 have been linked to invasive species

▼ The biggest killers

Number of bird extinctions caused by the most destructive invasive alien species since 1500

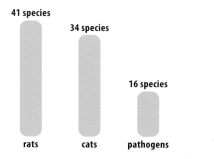

41 species — rats
34 species — cats
16 species — pathogens

A House Sparrow (*Passer domesticus*) peeks from its nest hole in a saguaro cactus, Arizona. The House Sparrow has been spread across the world by humans. In some cases its import was intentional, as when it was taken to Australia as company for the first European pioneers, but the species has also shown initiative in hitching rides on ships. Before 1850, the House Sparrow was unknown in the Americas; today there are at least 150 million in the USA alone, and it has had a severe impact on many native species. It out-competes other hole-nesters such as bluebirds, woodpeckers and tree swallows, and even destroys the eggs and chicks of rivals in order to secure space for new broods.

▼ Globe-trotting Sparrow

Number of bird extinctions caused by the most destructive invasive alien species since 1500

■ original range

■ invasive range

Going viral

The American Crow (*Corvus brachyrhyncho*) is one of the American birds hardest hit by the recently imported West Nile Virus (WNV). Indigenous to Africa, the Middle East, and southern Europe, this disease was accidentally introduced via New York in 1999, and has since swept over much of eastern USA, spreading south to Latin America and the Caribbean. Though carried largely by mosquitoes, WNV also passes directly between birds, with most American species highly vulnerable owing to their lack of previous exposure. Fatalities have been recorded in over 300 species, as well as among livestock and humans.

Killer kitty

A Great Tit (*Parus major*) falls victim to a domestic cat. Feral and domestic cats are ruthless predators, and take a heavy toll on wild bird populations in many parts of the world, often occurring in numbers far higher than any balanced ecosystem can sustain. The UK Mammal Society has calculated that cats in the UK catch up to 275 million prey items a year, of which 55 million are birds. Many more are likely to go unrecorded. The most frequent victims are House Sparrow (*Passer domesticus*), Blue Tit (*Cyanistes caeruleus*), Blackbird (*Turdus merula*) and European Starling (*Sternus vulgaris*).

Inbreeding interloper

The Ruddy Duck (*Oxyura jamaicensis*) (right) is an American native that established itself in the UK by escaping from wildfowl collections. It has since spread widely into Europe, where its willingness to interbreed with the closely related White-headed Duck (*Oxyura leucocephala*) (left) is a cause for conservation concern. The latter, a native Eurasian species, is now Endangered, and scientists fear that its hybridization with the Ruddy Duck threatens the genetic integrity of the small European population that remains – notably in Spain. Ruddy ducks are now culled in Spain, Portugal and France, and in 2005 a controversial programme got under way to eradicate the UK population of around 5,000.

Plummeting petrel

A Galápagos Petrel (*Pterodroma phaeopygi*) at its nesting burrow on the Galápagos Islands beside a baited trap set for invasive rats. This Critically Endangered species has declined rapidly since the early 1980s owing to threats posed by a number of invasive species, including predation by rats, cats, and dogs, and the destruction of its breeding habitat by goats and cattle. A 2008 survey estimated that fewer than 5,000 active nests remain.

Invasive species affect 7.5% of threatened birds on oceanic islands

Possum problems

The Brushtail Possum (*Trichosurus vulpecula*) was introduced to New Zealand from Australia in 1870 for food and the fur trade. This marsupial has since colonized most of the country, reaching a wild population of some 30 million, and is causing serious ecological damage to the habitat of native birds. By browsing on native trees, possums alter the forest structure and can eventually cause canopy collapse. They also eat bird eggs and chicks. A national campaign uses traps and poison to control possums. Studies have found that any losses this causes to native fauna are outweighed by their recovery once the competition for food and predation has been reduced.

Copyright © Myriad Editions

All at Sea

The marine environment is a rich one for birds, but also poses a range of threats that they will not encounter on land. Humankind's exploitation of the sea, both as resource and dumping ground, has seen ocean-going species decline faster than any other group of birds over the last two decades.

Commercial fisheries have proved disastrous for many species. Longline fishing, in which boats tow multiple hooks on long lines, is estimated to kill up to 300,000 seabirds annually, including 100,000 albatrosses. The birds are caught on the hooks, dragged underwater, and drowned as they scavenge behind the boats. Albatrosses and petrels also follow trawlers for the fish waste thrown overboard, often becoming entangled in the nets or struck by the cables. All 22 albatross species are now globally threatened or Near Threatened.

Gillnets – huge static nets set in the path of migrating fish – are equally lethal: at their height in the 1980s the driftnet fisheries of the North Pacific killed some 500,00 seabirds every year. These nets are now banned on the high seas, but continue to take a heavy toll on birds in territorial and coastal waters, especially species that fish underwater, such as divers, auks, and sea ducks.

At the same time, the fishing industry is exhausting the marine food supply. Having run down populations of larger fish, such as tuna and cod, fisheries are increasingly turning to smaller species, such as sandeels, anchovies, and krill, which are staple prey for many seabirds. This also destabilizes the entire marine foodweb.

An estimated 6.5 million tons of plastic is dumped annually by ships

▶ FISH PRODUCTION

Total commercial marine and freshwater fish catch
2008
metric tonnes

- 1 million or more
- 100,000 – 999,999
- 10,000 – 99,999
- fewer than 10,000
- no data

Percentage of fish stocks exploited at or beyond maximum sustainable yield
2008

- 71% – 80%
- 20% – 52%
- 10% or less

Deadly tangle

A Northern Gannet (*Morus bassanus*) killed by a discarded fishing net. Gannets may become entangled in nets when plunge-diving for food or collecting discarded netting to use as nest material. The consequences are often fatal.

Vanishing small fry

The sandeel is a key prey species for the Atlantic Puffin (*Fratercula arctica*) and other North Atlantic seabirds. Stocks have been decimated by over-fishing, which is thought to explain major breeding failures in several seabirds, including Atlantic Puffins, Arctic Terns (*Sterna paradisaea*), and Black-legged Kittiwakes (*Rissa tridactyla*).

The Benguela Current is one of the richest in the world, attracting high densities of seabirds and supporting productive fisheries. Namibia's demersal longline fishery is estimated to kill over 30,000 seabirds per year, while in 2005 to 2006 it was estimated that 18,000 seabirds were killed in the South African hake trawl fishery, most of which were globally threatened or Near Threatened species.

Meanwhile the sea is choking with pollution. Oil is especially damaging to birds, as it breaks down their waterproofing, leading to death through hypothermia. Birds also inhale and ingest toxic chemicals from oil when preening, while scavengers such as gulls are exposed to oil from the carcasses of contaminated fish and wildlife.

Big oil spills can be locally catastrophic: when the oil tanker *Exxon Valdez* spilled nearly 11 million gallons of crude oil into Prince William Sound, Alaska, in March 1989, between 375,000 and 435,000 birds are estimated to have died. Even more damaging, however, is the illegal dumping of oily waste from ships – done largely to save on cleaning costs back in port. This practice kills an estimated 300,000 seabirds off the south coast of Newfoundland alone – equal to another *Exxon Valdez* every year.

Anthropogenic debris – or junk – floating in the ocean affects over 44 percent of seabirds. Dumped by ships or washed down rivers, this lethal flotsam is carried vast distances on ocean currents. Some birds are trapped or entangled in it; many others mistake it for prey and swallow it – often with dire consequences. Toxic chemicals called polychlorinated biphenyls (PCBs) from floating plastics cause serious tissue damage when ingested by seabirds.

In the long term, climate change may yet prove the biggest threat of all to seabirds. Changes in the abundance and distribution of prey, attributed to global warming, are already having a detrimental impact on many species, from Antarctica to the north Atlantic.

Oil: the silent killer

Oil not only fouls seabirds' feathers but is also ingested when they attempt to preen, often with lethal toxic effects. Auks, such as this Common Guillemot (*Uria aalge*), are especially vulnerable to oil spills, as they swim on the surface and dive below in pursuit of small fish.

By clogging the barbs and barbules of its feathers, oil overcomes a bird's natural waterproofing. The wreck of the oil tanker *Prestige* off north-west Spain in November 2002 is thought to have contributed to the extinction of the rare Iberian breeding population of this species.

Cleaning and rehabilitating such birds is a skilled and laborious process. Over 35,000 dead birds were retrieved after the *Exxon Valdez* spill: fewer than one-tenth of the total estimated casualties. Once cleaned, the birds, such as the Common Goldeneye (*Bucephala clangula*) below, may need to be fed through a tube.

Hard to swallow

The carcass of a young Laysan Albatross (*Phoebastria immutabilis*) on Midway Atoll, Hawaii, reveals how much junk it swallowed. Toothbrushes, cigarette lighters, and bottle tops are among countless floating plastic objects the adult birds mistake for food, swallowing them and regurgitating them to their young.

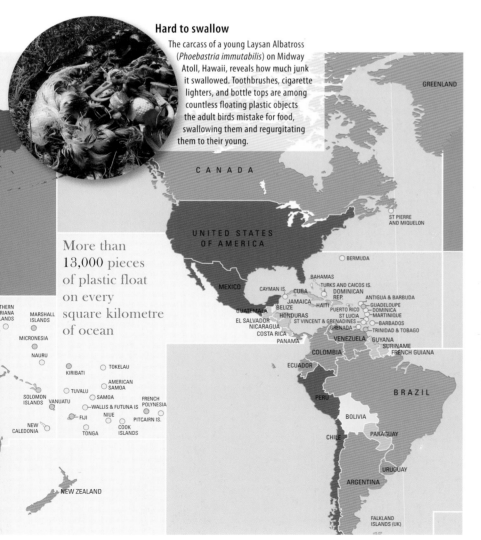

More than 13,000 pieces of plastic float on every square kilometre of ocean

GREENLAND

CANADA

ST PIERRE AND MIQUELON

UNITED STATES OF AMERICA

BERMUDA

MEXICO

BAHAMAS
TURKS AND CAICOS IS.
CAYMAN IS. CUBA
DOMINICAN REP.
JAMAICA HAITI PUERTO RICO
BELIZE
GUATEMALA HONDURAS
EL SALVADOR ST VINCENT & GRENADINES
NICARAGUA
COSTA RICA
PANAMA

ANTIGUA & BARBUDA
GUADELOUPE
DOMINICA
ST LUCIA
MARTINIQUE
BARBADOS
GRENADA
TRINIDAD & TOBAGO

VENEZUELA GUYANA
SURINAME
FRENCH GUIANA
COLOMBIA

ECUADOR

BRAZIL

PERU

BOLIVIA

PARAGUAY

CHILE

URUGUAY

ARGENTINA

NORTHERN MARIANA ISLANDS
MARSHALL ISLANDS
GUAM
MICRONESIA
NAURU
PAPUA NEW GUINEA
KIRIBATI TOKELAU
TUVALU
AMERICAN SAMOA
SOLOMON ISLANDS
VANUATU SAMOA
WALLIS & FUTUNA IS.
FRENCH POLYNESIA
FIJI NIUE PITCAIRN IS.
NEW CALEDONIA TONGA COOK ISLANDS

NEW ZEALAND

FALKLAND ISLANDS (UK)

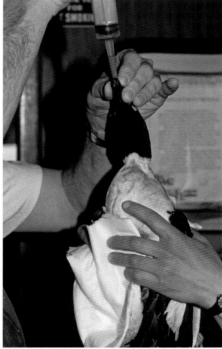

The Deepwater Horizon oil spill of 2010 was the largest accidental marine oil spill in the history of the petroleum industry. Oil flowed into the Gulf of Mexico for three months after an explosion of the undersea gusher on 20 April. By the time the well was capped on July 15, about 4.9 million barrels (206 million gallons) had leaked out, threatening 32 national wildlife refuges around the coasts of Louisiana, Mississippi, Alabama, and Florida.

Copyright © Myriad Editions

Warming Up

Our climate is changing. Global warming, largely caused by us, is having far-reaching effects on the Earth's ecosystems and the birds they support. Although some species may benefit in the short term, these temporary winners are far outnumbered by the many losers. Mass extinctions are likely, should warming continue at projected rates.

The evidence for global warming is now overwhelming: the global mean surface temperature increased by 0.4° to 0.8°C during the last century, and is projected to rise a further 1.4° to 5.8°C by the end of this one. The resulting changes – including rising sea levels, disrupted rainfall patterns, reduced snow cover, and extreme weather events – are already having a significant impact on the environment. Equally overwhelming is the evidence that most recent warming has been caused by greenhouse gas emissions resulting from human activity. Carbon dioxide concentrations have increased by 31 percent since 1750, due largely to deforestation and the burning of fossil fuels – a rate unprecedented during the last 10,000 years.

Global warming has already affected the distribution of at least 400 bird species. Studies in both the UK and North America show that numerous species have extended their range northward in recent decades, finding suitable conditions at previously inhospitable latitudes, while studies in Australia show a corresponding shift southwards. Other range shifts are altitudinal, with lowland species in the tropics advancing higher up mountains. Meanwhile, many species already adapted to high latitudes and altitudes are finding their habitat shrinking.

Warmer conditions exacerbate other threats. In Australia, for example, more frequent fires in eucalypt woodlands are facilitating the spread of the invasive African gamba grass (*Andropogon gayanus*), which promotes further fires and threatens habitat for many species. In Hawaii, introduced mosquitoes are spreading, and transmitting avian pox and malaria to endemic bird populations.

Climate change is also evident in birds' phenology – their response to the seasons. As spring creeps further up the calendar each year, many species are nesting earlier, and some migrants are arriving earlier. Not all can adapt at the same rate. Great Tits (*Parus major*) are struggling because the timing of their egg-laying has not kept pace with the changing phenology of plants and insects, which means their spring food supply is peaking before they are ready.

Some regions are harder hit than others. The Arctic has warmed faster than any other region over the last century, with some models predicting a further 5°C warming over the next 50 to 80 years. This brings significant habitat change, with boreal forests spreading northwards and tundra shrinking. Millions of migratory wildfowl and waders stand to lose breeding habitat.

Climate change is also disrupting marine ecosystems, and having an impact on seabirds. Vanishing prey has reduced breeding success in many species, from auks in the Atlantic to penguins in the Antarctic. Meanwhile, low-lying oceanic islands are threatened by sea-level rise, putting at risk coastal species such as the Critically Endangered Orange-bellied Parrot (*Neophema chrysogaster*) of southern Australia.

Despite worldwide consensus on the need to curb global warming, greenhouse gas emissions continue to rise. According to one study, between 15 and 37 percent of extant bird species will be "committed to extinction" by 2050. Birds are not the only victims, however, and as indicators they can play a vital role in combatting the threat.

Range reduction

The fate of endemic bird species in Australia's montane tropical rainforests depends upon the rate at which global warming reduces their habitat. A temperature rise of just 1°C will reduce their range by over 30%. A rise off more than 2°C will increase this loss – and the number of extinctions. A rise of 5.8°C, which some climate change models have projected for the end of this century, would mean extinction for almost all species.

▼ Australia's montane tropical rainforests
Impact of temperature increase on 13 endemic bird species

— percentage of range remaining
— number of extinctions
▭ range of temperature increase predicted for 21st century

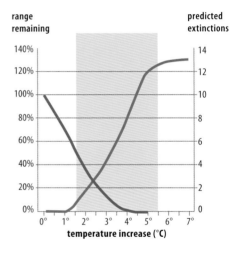

▼ Cape Longclaw

 current range
projected range by 2070–99

The Cape Longclaw (*Macronyx capensi*) is a grassland species endemic to southern Africa. At present it is a fairly common breeding resident, found from the coast to the highlands, but in a warmer climate its range is likely to shrink considerably. This would leave it restricted to the upland regions of South Africa.

▼ IMPACTS OF CLIMATE CHANGE

Disappearing shearwaters

The non-breeding population of Sooty Shearwaters off the west coast of North America (*Puffinus griseus*) fell by 90% from 1987 to 1994. Changes in ocean currents and surface temperatures, associated with climate change, have been held responsible for this decline.

The late bird

In 2009, the Common Cuckoo (*Cuculus canorus*) joined the UK Red List, its population having halved in the previous 25 years. One explanation for this dramatic decline lies in global warming. The cuckoo – a brood parasite that lays its eggs in the nests of host birds – has evolved to synchronize its annual arrival from Africa with the breeding of its hosts. With the UK spring now coming on average 5.1 days earlier than 50 years ago, many of its host species are arriving earlier, leaving the cuckoo too late to find suitable nests.

Threatened tundra

The Dunlin (*Calidris alpina*) is among a number of Arctic species threatened by the shrinking of their tundra breeding grounds. At current rates of global warming, this diminutive wader is projected to lose up to 58% of its breeding habitat if CO_2 levels double by 2090, as some models predict. Such species, which live at the polar edges of continents, have little scope for finding new areas of suitable habitat and so are especially vulnerable to climate change.

Toucan mountaineer

The Keel-billed Toucan (*Ramphastos sulfuratu*) is one of many lowland forest species in Costa Rica to have extended its range higher up mountain slopes between 1979 and 1998. A rise in the cloud-base level, attributed to climate change, has now made suitable habitat available for this species up to a height of at least 1,540 metres (5,050 ft).

Pied butcherbird

The Pied Butcherbird (*Cracticus nigrogulari*) is one of numerous Australian land birds that have extended their range south by as much as 300 km (185 miles) in just two decades. This range expansion has come to light in comparisons between Australian bird atlases from 1977–81 and 1998–2006. The fact that it has not been matched by a corresponding northward shift suggests that the explanation lies in global warming rather than some other environmental factor.

Krill crisis

Warming surface temperatures and shrinking sea-ice have reduced plankton biomass in Antarctic waters, with repercussions up the food chain. A shortage of krill (*Euphausia superba*), in particular, has been implicated in the decline of several populations of seabirds that depend upon this key prey species. For instance, Emperor Penguins (*Aptenodytes forsteri*) in one colony declined by 50% when abnormally warm temperatures led to poor krill production.

Copyright © Myriad Editions

Part Seven

PROTECTING BIRDS

Today, an ever-expanding conservation movement is making strenuous efforts to protect birds and their habitats, with the BirdLife International partnership reaching into almost every corner of the globe. International conventions aim to safeguard the Earth's biodiversity, of which birds are a vital component. Meanwhile, the public plays a significant role, through campaigning, volunteering, and simply by watching and enjoying birds. Conservation education is helping build skills and awareness in developing countries, where there is a growing realization of how important birds are to the economy and natural heritage. Feeding garden birds has made an important contribution to their welfare in many urban areas.

BirdLife International

Birds are very important to humankind. They are a key component of biodiversity, which is of incalculable value in terms of the ecological services it provides the planet. Birds also provide us with economic, cultural, and spiritual benefits. Our incentive to protect them, and to tackle the threats they face, is therefore huge, and birds have an energetic and expanding global conservation community on their side.

The number of people who belong to bird conservation societies is increasing year on year. In the UK, for instance, more than a million people are members of the Royal Society for the Protection of Birds (RSPB) – that's more than the combined membership of the three largest political parties. In New Zealand, 40,000 people people – roughly one in a 100 – belong to Forest and Bird, and in the USA, the National Audubon Society (now known simply as Audubon) has over 500 local chapters.

These organizations, and many others, fall under the umbrella of BirdLife International, a global partnership of NGOs that oversees bird conservation worldwide. BirdLife is the world's largest partnership of conservation organizations. It aims to maintain and, where possible, improve the conservation status of all bird species. It also looks beyond birds to conserve biodiversity in general, and to improve the quality of people's lives by integrating bird conservation into their livelihoods and communities.

Fundamental to BirdLife's mission has been the creation of its worldwide Important Bird Areas programme, which has identified the key sites and habitats for birds in every region of the world. BirdLife also sets action plans for individual threatened species, and initiates specific conservation action for all species in decline.

Today, BirdLife partners represent BirdLife in over 100 countries and territories. Each is an independent, membership-based NGO that can draw on local knowledge and experience to document and protect species and habitats, and can promote local interest and involvement through public campaigning and education. BirdLife partners often collaborate on broader programmes across their region.

All BirdLife partners place a strong emphasis on working with people. It is people, after all, who control resources and who therefore need encouragement to manage them sustainably – both for their own benefit and for that of biodiversity. Conservation initiatives, including the IBAs programme, aim to involve local people as much as possible. Meanwhile, international festivals and other events – for example, World Birdwatch, when over 180,000 people in more than 90 countries go birdwatching during one weekend – bring people together and raise the profile of bird conservation. A greater interest from the general public can often prove to be a decisive influence on those drafting policies and making decisions at a local, national, and international level.

Asociacion Armonía, Bolivia
Founded: 1992
Members: 256
Staff: 23
Key activities and recent achievements
- National campaign against the illegal bird trade
- Four conservation programmes combining indigenous community support
- Conservation of seven Critically Endangered birds
- Lodge created to support conservation of endemic Red-fronted Macaw (*Ara rubrogenys*) and Blue-throated Macaw (*Ara glaucogularis*)

Red-fronted Macaw (*Ara rubrogenys*)

▼ The Royal Society for the Protection of Birds (RSPB)

The RSPB is the BirdLife Partner for the UK. Founded in 1889, it is the world's largest bird conservation organization, with a membership of over 1 million. Driven by such significant public support, a large team of skilled staff and dedicated volunteers, and a nationwide chain of reserves, the RSPB has proved a powerful force for conservation in the UK, influencing government conservation policy, pioneering sustainable land management in agriculture, and even helping shape the National Curriculum in England and Wales.

In 2010 the RSPB reported:
- over **1 million members**, including over 195,000 youth members
- over **12,200 volunteers**; at least nine for every paid member of staff
- **200 nature reserves** covering almost 143,200 hectares (552 sq miles), which are home to 80% of the UK's most threatened birds
- **£78.6 million** had been available for charitable purposes in 2007
- **12 offices** nationwide, including UK HQ in Sandy
- **175 local groups** and more than 110 youth groups

BirdLife Finland

Founded: 1973
Members: 11,000
Staff: 10

Key activities and recent achievements
- Annual Bird of the Year project to collect information on threatened species
- Identifying bird areas important at county level
- Work on saving natural peat lands from mining industry
- Biodiversity guides for Finnish farmers

▼ BIRDLIFE INTERNATIONAL

Countries and territories with one or more partner or affiliate
2010

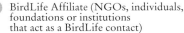

   BirdLife partner

   BirdLife Affiliate (NGOs, individuals, foundations or institutions that act as a BirdLife contact)

   BirdLife programme underway

The BirdLife Global Partnership has:

4,000+ staff working for conservation
2.5 million+ members worldwide
1 million+ hectares owned or managed

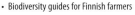

GREENLAND

ICELAND   FAROE IS.

NORWAY

FINLAND

RUSSIA

IRELAND   UK   DENMARK   SWEDEN   ESTONIA   LATVIA   LITHUANIA   BELARUS

NETH.   GERMANY   POLAND   UKRAINE

BEL.   LUX.   CZECH   AUS.   H.   ROM.

FRANCE   SWITZ.   ITALY   BUL.

KAZAKHSTAN

ANDORRA   GEORGIA   UZBEKISTAN   KYRGYZSTAN

PORTUGAL   SPAIN   MAC.   GREECE   TURKEY   AZERBAIJAN   TURKMENISTAN

GIBRALTAR   CYPRUS   LEB.   SYRIA   IRAQ

MOROCCO   MALTA   TUNISIA   ISRAEL   JORDAN   KUWAIT

WESTERN SAHARA   PALESTINIAN TERRITORIES   BAHRAIN   QATAR

EGYPT   SAUDI ARABIA   NEPAL

CHINA

JAPAN

Hong Kong SAR   TAIWAN

INDIA   BURMA   LAOS

YEMEN   THAILAND   VIETNAM   PHILIPPINES

BURKINA FASO   DJIBOUTI   CAMBODIA

SIERRA LEONE   CÔTE D'IVOIRE   GHANA   NIGERIA   ETHIOPIA   SRI LANKA

LIBERIA   CAMEROON   MALAYSIA

UGANDA   SINGAPORE

RWANDA   KENYA

BURUNDI   SEYCHELLES   INDONESIA

TANZANIA

MALAWI   MADAGASCAR

ZAMBIA

ZIMBABWE

BOTSWANA   AUSTRALIA

SOUTH AFRICA

NEW ZEALAND

Malaysian Nature Society (MNS)

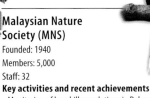
Rhinoceros Hornbill
(Buceros rhinoceros)

Founded: 1940
Members: 5,000
Staff: 32

Key activities and recent achievements
- Monitoring of hornbill populations in Belum-Temengor Forest Reserve
- Published *Blueprint for Conservation in Malaysia*
- Has published *Malayan Nature Journal* since 1940
- School Nature Club programme reaching 10,000 school children

PALAU   MARSHALL IS.

SAMOA   FRENCH POLYNESIA

NEW CALEDONIA   FIJI   COOK IS.

Fairy Tern
(Sterna nereis)

Spot-breasted Plover
(Vanellus melanocephalus)

Ethiopian Wildlife and Natural History Society (EWNHS)

Founded: 1966
Members: 449
Staff: 17

Key activities and recent achievements
- Planting of indigenous tree species
- Establishing school nature clubs
- Discovering important site for endemic Spot-breasted Plover (*Vanellus melanocephalus*)
- Regional workshop on the Vulnerable Harwood's Francolin (*Francolinus harwoodi*)
- Improving management practices at the Weserbi and Berga wetlands, the only known breeding sites for White-winged Flufftail (*Sarothrura ayresi*)

Eastern Imperial Eagle
(Aquila heliaca)

Royal Society for the Conservation of Nature (RSCN), Jordan

Founded: 1966
Members: 2,000
Staff: 165

Key activities and recent achievements
- Prevention of copper mining in the Dana Nature Reserve
- Solar-powered eco-lodge in Wadi Feynan, Dana Nature Reserve
- Reserve in Dibeen Forest
- 1,300 patrols by RSCN rangers; 251 violators apprehended, and 38 illegally caught animals released
- Integrated ecosystem management in Jordan Rift Valley Project creating important ecological corridor and migratory flyway

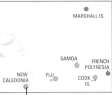

Société Calédonienne d'Ornithologie (SCO)

Founded: 1965
Members: 81
Staff: 4

Key activities and recent achievements
- Baiting of three islets (for rats) in the Northern Lagoon IBA, to help secure breeding habitats for seabirds, including the nationally threatened Fairy Tern (*Sterna nereis*)
- Conducts environmental impact assessment and acts as environmental watchdog
- Publishes quarterly newsletter, *Le Cagou*
- IBA identification process, funded by the European Commission
- Hosts the Kagu Recovery Plan (KRP)

Copyright © Myriad Editions

—Campaigns & Conventions—

B ird conservation operates at many levels, from planting trees in a park to lobbying for global political change. Success can depend as much upon raising awareness as upon raising funds. Numerous local campaigns are achieving positive results, while international conventions aim to safeguard biodiversity and the environment through legally binding treaties.

All conservation starts with research, with scientists and field workers gathering the evidence on which a case for action can be made. Next comes the groundwork. Dedicated conservationists, many of them volunteers, do their bit at a local level, whether clearing invasive flora, leading youth groups or safeguarding breeding sites.

Getting the message across is vital, and conservation campaigns prioritize education, whether producing materials for schools, or managing high-profile publicity campaigns. All this costs money, and NGOs raise funds by every means possible, from high-street collecting tins to internet campaigns. Without government funding, every penny counts.

Buoyed by public support, conservation groups can lobby for change. At a national level, conservation campaigns may target specific threats, such as proposed development projects. In recent years, such campaigns have successfully halted plans to develop a new airport in the UK's Thames Estuary, and shelved, pending further review, a proposed soda ash plant on Tanzania's Lake Natron that would devastate the world's largest breeding colony of Lesser Flamingos (*Phoenicopterus minor*).

BirdLife International also runs broader campaigns on issues that affect birds worldwide. The Born to Travel Campaign, for instance, aims to create more awareness about migrants of the African–Eurasian flyways and secure them better protection. The Forests of Hope Programme aims to bring together all BirdLife's forest conservation programmes worldwide, to prevent deforestation and restore at least 5 million hectares of tropical forest by 2015.

The ultimate aim of conservation NGOs such as BirdLife is to influence or secure legally binding international agreements within which conservation groups can act. There are more than 500 such treaties that concern the environment, including the Convention on Biological Diversity (1992), the Convention on International Trade in Endangered Species (1973), and the Ramsar Convention on Wetlands (1971).

Agreements to conserve biodiversity do not always translate into reliable action, especially in developing countries, where the threats birds face are often most severe but the capacity to tackle them most limited. Conservation groups boost this capacity by building awareness and involvement among local communities. BirdLife has teamed up with other organizations to create The Conservation Leadership Programme (CLP), which offers training to conservation professionals in the developing world. This programme has already supported nearly 3,000 individuals, laying the foundations for future generations of bird conservationists.

▼ Save the Albatross

Albatrosses are declining faster than any other bird family: 18 of the 22 species are globally threatened. The main cause is accidental bycatch in fisheries: longline fishing drowns around 100,000 albatrosses every year, while many more die in trawling and gillnet fisheries. The seas around New Zealand, southern Africa, and South America are particular black spots.

BirdLife's Save the Albatross Campaign advocates international agreements and a range of measures that benefit both bird and fisherman. Meanwhile, the RSPB (BirdLife's UK partner) manages the Albatross Task Force (ATF), a team of dedicated instructors who work with fishermen to put these measures into practice.

 countries in which Albatross Task Force has operated *2006–10*

 range of albatrosses in Southern Ocean

South of Chile
The incidental capture of seabirds was reduced from over 1,500 birds to zero through the use of modified fishing gear.

Brazil
The voluntary adoption of simple bird-scaring lines has helped reduce incidental capture of seabirds by 56%.

South African waters
For every 100 albatrosses being killed in 2006, 85 are now being saved.

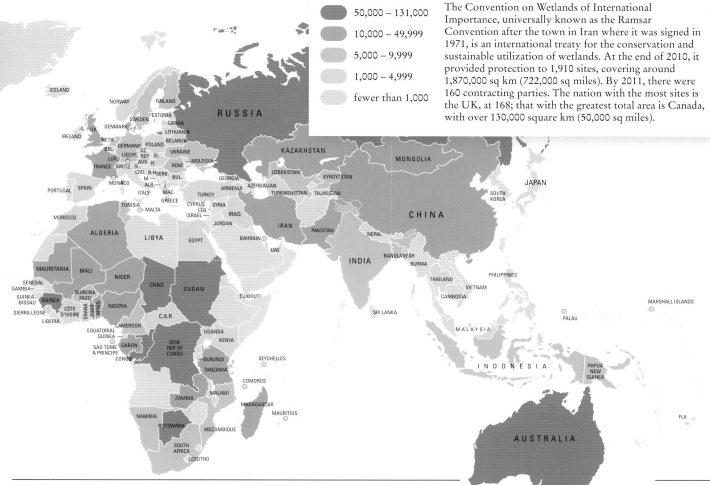

▼ RAMSAR SITES

Area of protected wetland in countries that are signatories
to Ramsar Convention *end 2010*

- 50,000 – 131,000
- 10,000 – 49,999
- 5,000 – 9,999
- 1,000 – 4,999
- fewer than 1,000

The Convention on Wetlands of International
Importance, universally known as the Ramsar
Convention after the town in Iran where it was signed in
1971, is an international treaty for the conservation and
sustainable utilization of wetlands. At the end of 2010, it
provided protection to 1,910 sites, covering around
1,870,000 sq km (722,000 sq miles). By 2011, there were
160 contracting parties. The nation with the most sites is
the UK, at 168; that with the greatest total area is Canada,
with over 130,000 square km (50,000 sq miles).

▼ Conservation action around the world

Airport anger

In 2002–05, the RSPB successfully opposed a proposed airport
at Cliffe, in the Thames Estuary. This region is used by 300,000
migratory birds and is home to one of Europe's largest groups of
internationally protected habitats. Development would not only
have meant massive environmental damage, but would also
have posed a risk to aircraft through bird strikes. More than
150,000 RSPB members wrote to the government demanding
that plans be shelved. After a lengthy investigation the
government concluded that this airport was not a viable option.

Going private

The corporate sector often gets a bad press in conservation
circles. However, some businesses recognize that they can help
protect biodiversity while still achieving business goals. Rio
Tinto, a multinational mining company, works in partnership
with BirdLife International at Important Bird Areas near its
businesses. In Namibia, for instance, Rössing Uranium has
collaborated with local businesses, the Ministry of Environment
and Tourism, and a local NGO, to safeguard seabird breeding
sites, including those of the Near Threatened Damara Tern
(*Sterna damarensis*), and make them accessible to birdwatchers.

Winning the rat race

The small island of Vatu-i-Ra in Fiji is an IBA supporting more
than 10,000 pairs of breeding seabirds of six species. The local
community was keen to protect this colony and to develop
low-impact tourist visits, but the high rat population posed a
serious threat to the eggs and chicks. An alien eradication
programme got underway in 2006. Community members
received training in rat eradication, seabird identification, and
methods for preventing the re-establishment of alien species.
In 2008, the island was declared rat free. The landowners have
since adopted quarantine measures to prevent any accidental
reintroduction of invasive species, and these are being
promoted among all communities associated with the island.

Copyright © Myriad Editions

Saving Species

BirdLife estimates that at least two-thirds of threatened bird species have received some form of conservation action since 2000. Much of this work has addressed broad issues, such as restoring habitats, and thus embraces many species. Sometimes, however, the problems facing individual species are so specific that more targeted action is required.

In the case of Critically Endangered species there is often no time to wait for long-term environmental solutions if the bird is to be saved from extinction. Emergency conservation measures can prove very successful. BirdLife estimates that 16 species would have become extinct between 1994 and 2004 had it not been for targeted conservation programmes. During this same period, conservation action targeting 49 Critically Endangered species (28 percent of the total) managed to slow the rate of decline in 24 and improve the status of the others.

Targeted action takes many forms. The first step may be to tackle immediate threats on the ground – for example, by eradicating invasive predators that threaten a breeding colony or by mounting a surveillance operation on a nest site. For birds in less immediate danger, work may start with research to understand the problem and then the formulation of strategies to tackle it. Studies of the decline of European farmland birds such as the Corncrake (*Crex crex*), for instance, have identified specific agricultural practices as the cause, and have thus been able to recommend sustainable solutions.

Sometimes, conservationists may have to intervene at the level of the individual bird. Such actions range from the capture and rehabilitation of oiled African Penguins (*Spheniscus demersus*) after a spill off the coast of South Africa, to the removal of the few remaining Kakapos (*Strigops habroptila*) from their predator-infested islands off New Zealand to new islands that had been cleared of predators.

Captive breeding, followed by reintroduction to the wild, has saved a number of birds from extinction, such as the Hawaiian Goose (*Branta sandvicensis*). Such operations are complex and expensive stop-gap measures, however, and only practical with certain species. Meanwhile, the underlying causes, such as habitat destruction, must be addressed to secure the species' longer-term survival.

Some rescue operations for Critically Endangered species have been touch-and-go. The Mauritius Kestrel (*Falco punctatus*) population had reached an all-time low of only four individuals by 1974, when conservationists decided to remove eggs from the remaining nests and rear the hatchlings in incubators before re-release. Slowly, the population increased. Today, there are more than 800 mature birds in the wild, and the captive breeding centre founded by the programme has become a pioneering research institution for raptor conservation.

BirdLife has launched an initiative specifically aimed at saving individual endangered species, called the Preventing Extinctions Programme. This targets the conservation needs of 190 Critically Endangered species. For each one it solicits funding from supportive companies, institutions, or individuals, known as "Species Champions", and appoints organizations or individuals known as "Species Guardians", who manage conservation work on the ground.

The cost of condors

By 1985, there were only nine California Condors (*Gymnogyps californianus*) left in the wild. A combination of threats had caused their catastrophic decline, notably poisoning by ingesting lead ammunition from carcasses. In 1987, in a pioneering effort to save the species, these last individuals were captured for a captive-breeding programme.

The species remains Critically Endangered, with its wild population still not regarded as self-sustaining. Released birds have continued to die from lead poisoning – or from collisions with power lines. Many have shown behavioural problems as a result of over-familiarity with humans. However, these problems are being addressed, and legislation has now been passed banning the use of lead ammunition within the species' range.

This has been the most expensive species conservation project ever undertaken in the USA, costing over $35 million to date, including $20 million in federal and state funding. Some conservationists argue that such large sums would have been better spent on initiatives that benefited a broader biodiversity. However, such high-profile projects involving large, charismatic species, can play a vital ambassadorial role for conservation in general.

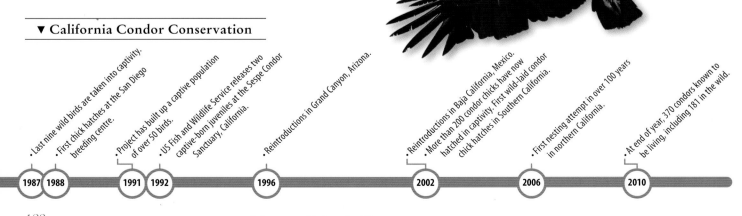

▼ California Condor Conservation

- **1987** · Last nine wild birds are taken into captivity.
- **1988** · First chick hatches at the San Diego breeding centre.
- **1991** · Project has built up a captive population of over 50 birds.
- **1992** · US Fish and Wildlife Service releases two captive-born juveniles at the Sespe Condor Sanctuary, California.
- **1996** · Reintroductions in Grand Canyon, Arizona.
- **2002** · Reintroductions in Baja California, Mexico. · More than 200 condor chicks have now hatched in captivity. First wild-laid condor chick hatches in Southern California.
- **2006** · First nesting attempt in over 100 years in northern California.
- **2010** · At end of year, 370 condors known to be living, including 181 in the wild.

▼ SPECIES-SPECIFIC CONSERVATION PROJECTS

Bustards boosted

The RSPB is working to restore to the UK countryside a number of species that have been driven to extinction in recent times. In 2010, The Great Bustard Project was awarded a grant of €2.2million from the European Union. This project, which aims to return the Great Bustard (*Otis tarda*) to its former habitat on Salisbury Plain in southern England, is a collaboration between the Great Bustard Group, the RSPB, the University of Bath, and Natural England. The grant will allow the project more security and a greater capacity to gather vital information: 16 of the birds have now been fitted with GPS satellite transmitters to provide data on their movements and ecology. The bustards – the world's heaviest flying birds – were reared from eggs rescued in southern Russia, and 2009 saw the first chicks to hatch in the wild in the UK since 1832. This project also aims to support other wildlife at risk associated with this threatened landscape.

Ibis alliance

One of Asia's most threatened birds, the Crested Ibis (*Nipponia nippon*), owes its recovery to close collaboration between China and Japan. A programme of captive breeding and release has succeeded in returning the species to much of its former range, and the population has increased from just a handful of individuals in 1982 to more than 500 wild birds in 2010. The two nations' commitment was highlighted at a historic meeting in 2007 of the countries' Prime Ministers to discuss the ongoing conservation effort. Both China and Japan maintain successful breeding programmes. China has donated a number of ibises to its neighbour, and plans are afoot to reintroduce the birds to Sado Island in Japan.

Rapid response

Europe's rarest seabird, Zino's Petrel (*Pterodroma madeira*), nests only on the Portuguese island of Madeira. Forest fires in the summer of 2010 ravaged its breeding cliffs. More than 65% of chicks died and, with the vegetation cover burned away, many burrows collapsed. A swift BirdLife appeal drew a generous response, allowing staff from the Parque Natural da Madeira (PNM), with support from SPEA (BirdLife's partner in Portugal), to take immediate emergency action. They shored up soil erosion, installed artificial fireproof burrows, and planted native flora to restore vegetation cover in time for the petrels' return in spring.

Parakeet recovery

By 1986, the world population of Mauritius Parakeet (*Psittacula eques echo*) had been reduced to fewer than a dozen birds, including just three females, and had not bred for nearly a decade. This decline was due largely to alien invasive species, including habitat destruction caused by deer and feral pigs, and competition for nest holes from other birds. An ambitious rescue programme, including captive breeding and release, control of invasive predators, provision of artificial nest cavities and brood manipulations, increased the wild population to 343 birds by 2007. The species has now been down-listed from Critically Endangered to Endangered.

Vulture restaurants

In Nepal, numbers of White-rumped Vulture (*Gyps bengalensis*) have dropped by more than 90% since 1990 due to exposure to the veterinary drug diclofenac, with similar declines recorded in two other vulture species. The Nepalese Government and Bird Conservation Nepal (BCN) have made strenuous efforts to save these birds. In 2006, a ban was introduced on the veterinary use of diclofenac, since when its use has declined by 90% in large areas. In 2007, BCN established the first community-managed Vulture Safe Zone at Pithauli in Nawalparasi district, where diclofenac-free carrion is provided at feeding stations. There has been a steady increase in the number of vultures visiting these "vulture restaurants" – and in the number of nesting White-rumped Vultures nearby. A new viewing area helps generate tourism revenue for the community.

Robin rescue

The Black Robin (*Petroica traversi*) is endemic to the Chatham Islands. When humans arrived, bringing marauding cats and rats, and degrading the forests, the species spiralled into decline. In 1976, there were only seven birds left. These were relocated to nearby Mangere Island, where thousands of trees had been planted to provide suitable habitat. Through a combination of nest protection, supplementary feeding and cross-fostering with the closely related Tomtit (*P. macrocephala*), conservationists brought about a steady recovery. Individuals were later introduced to South East Island. By the late 1990s, the population had reached its carrying capacity of 250 birds.

Copyright © Myriad Editions

Protecting Places

Despite many individual success stories, bird conservation cannot succeed on a species-by-species basis alone. The most significant threats to birds are from broad-scale environmental factors, such as deforestation, which affect many species simultaneously. Thus, effective long-term bird conservation targets the places that are most important for birds.

Many important places for birds already receive protection, for example as a national park or Ramsar site. The BirdLife programme of Important Bird Areas has identified more than 10,000 key sites for birds worldwide, and can thus help governments prioritize areas in need of protection. In Africa, for example, Ethiopia Wildlife Natural History Society and Nature Uganda (both BirdLife partners) have used their national IBA directories to influence the designation of Ramsar sites, while BirdLife South Africa has provided key information to wildlife authorities for the creation of trans-frontier parks.

Protected areas, however, are not the only solution. Broader threats persist beyond their boundaries. Migratory birds pose a particular challenge in this respect. Protecting a migratory species requires coordinated action along the entire length of its flyway. Safeguarding its breeding grounds is ineffective if, for instance, its wintering habitats are being degraded or the population is heavily hunted during its passage. By identifying key migration routes, conservation authorities can thus propose networks of protected areas that provide safe corridors for migrants.

Corridors are also an important concept when it comes to forests. Deforestation in many regions of outstanding biodiversity, from Madagascar to Sumatra, has reduced indigenous forest to small isolated pockets. It is seldom possible to restore entire forests, especially with increasing pressure on land, but the creation of narrow forest corridors, which link these pockets and thus allow movement in bird populations, can provide a huge boost to the conservation of birds and biodiversity in general.

Today, few true wilderness areas remain. Human pressures have transformed many landscapes completely, and compromised the biodiversity of most others. However, anthropogenic habitats such as farmland and urban areas need not be ecological deserts. With a little help – such as the provision of wildlife-friendly field margins, or the preservation of indigenous trees among plantations – many bird species can flourish in landscapes modified to suit human needs.

This raises a fundamental choice of conservation strategy. One approach is to pursue a policy of sustainable land-use, which means developing practices that preserve and encourage biodiversity. The other is "land sparing", which means setting aside habitat for protection. With the hungry human population set to reach 9 billion by 2050, this latter approach requires making already cultivated land much more productive.

On a local scale, modified land that has been freed from production can still be improved for biodiversity. Europe provides some good examples of projects – such as restoring heathland in the UK and wetlands in the Netherlands – where habitats surrounded by development have been made into havens for birds.

▼ Conservation requirements

Of globally threatened bird species
2008

- broad-scale action alone <1%
- 3% insufficiently known
- conservation of IBAs and broad-scale action 18%
- conservation of single IBAs 23%
- conservation of a network of IBAs 56%

Western Meadowlark (*Sturnella neglecta*)

▼ Services from birds

As conservationists encourage landowners to adopt more bird-friendly farming practices, birds in turn continue to do their bit for farmers. Many tropical species play an important role as seed dispersers, while others are key pollinators. Insect-eating birds make a huge contribution to pest control. In California's Sacramento Valley, Western Meadowlarks (*Sturnella neglecta*) alone are estimated to consume 193 tons of insects daily during the breeding season. During outbreaks of the destructive western spruce budworm during the 1980s, the Evening Grosbeak (*Coccothraustes vespertinus*) provided biological control services estimated to be worth $1,820 per square kilometer. Meanwhile, across the Atlantic, the European Pied Flycatcher (*Ficedula hypoleuca*) helps control insects in forestry plantations, taking significant quantities of moths and caterpillars. Plantation owners often provide nest boxes to encourage insect-eating flycatchers and tits.

Copyright © Myriad Editions

Arctic agenda

December 2010 saw the 50th anniversary of the Arctic National Wildlife Refuge. This vast reserve, covering some 78,050 square km (30,135 sq miles) protects huge numbers of migratory and breeding waterbirds, as well as polar bears and the world's largest caribou herd, but has long been dogged by controversial plans for oil exploration. Leading scientists, conservationists, and natural resource managers across the USA and Canada, including Audubon, marked the anniversary by sending a joint letter to US President Obama, urging him to safeguard this vast area from exploitation. High-profile lobbying of this kind helps ensure that the fate of valuable habitats and their biodiversity remains at the top of both the public and political agendas.

Building buffers

The biggest threat to habitats worldwide may be climate change. Low-lying countries, such as the Netherlands, are especially vulnerable to sea-level rise caused by global warming. Vogelbescherming Nederland (BirdLife Netherlands) is a partner in the Ooijpolder "climate buffer" project. This project aims to restore natural wetland processes and habitats to the Gelderse Poort IBA, which supports wintering White-fronted Goose (*Anser albifrons*) as well as breeding Great Bittern (*Botaurus stellaris*), see below, and Corncrake (*Crex crex*). It also provides an important buffer against the effects of climate change, by restoring enhanced natural wetland drainage systems.

Farming by example

The continuing intensification of agricultural practices across Europe, driven by the EU's Common Agricultural Policy, has led to a dramatic decline in many farmland bird species, including the Eurasian Skylark (*Alauda arvensis*). In 1999, the RSPB purchased Hope Farm in Cambridgeshire, UK, in order to develop and demonstrate farming techniques that benefit wildlife. In 2000, there were 10 pairs of Skylarks on the 180-hectare farm; by the summer of 2003, in the same pattern of crops there were 27. Numbers of other declining farmland birds have also since tripled. Most importantly, if this is to be a model for modern agriculture, the farm's agricultural yield has also increased.

African investigations

Many Afro-Palearctic migrant species, such as the Turtle Dove (*Streptopelia turtur*), Wood Warbler (*Phylloscopus sibilatrix*), and Whinchat (*Saxicola rubetra*) are declining rapidly. While these birds have been extensively studied on their European breeding grounds, little is known about what happens to them in Africa. Migrants in Africa is a collaboration between the Ghana Wildlife Society, Naturama (the BirdLife Partner in Burkina Faso), the British Trust for Ornithology, and the RSPB, which is investigating how changes in land-use are affecting populations of these birds. It forms part of a larger investigation into their status all along their migration flyway, and will help inform conservation strategies in all countries concerned.

War-torn wetlands

The marshlands of southern Iraq supported numerous breeding and migrant birds, but in the 1990s Saddam Hussein drained them to drive out the Marsh Arabs, who had risen against him after the first Gulf War. Within months, the marshes were reduced to a tenth of their original size, devastating both local communities and wildlife. Since the fall of Saddam, however, the pioneering conservation group Nature Iraq has restored large sections, and wildlife has rapidly returned. In winter 2010, some 46,000 Marbled Teal (*Marmaronetta angustirostris*) were counted, around twice the previous estimate of the entire global population. Nature Iraq is now addressing the problem of salination, building an embankment to raise the level of the Euphrates and increase the flooded area, and shutting down one of Saddam's drainage canals.

Forest corridors

Logging, palm oil plantations, and other uncontrolled forms of exploitation have reduced Sumatra's rainforests by more than 95% since 1900. This has taken a heavy toll on birds and other species, including the Sumatran tiger. In 2006, a joint project involving Burung Indonesia (BirdLife) and the RSPB took over the management of one forest patch, Harapan. The plan is to plant 1 million trees to create a wildlife corridor that links existing areas of rainforest. With help from more than 200 local people, seeds from 57 fast-growing local tree species have been collected, and the RSPB's "One million tree appeal" is raising funds to pay for a replanting programme that will restore the forest to its former glory.

People Power

While governments, scientists, and NGOs work to protect the world's birds, they can achieve little without the support of ordinary people. Thankfully, public interest in birds continues to increase, as does appreciation of the benefits that protecting birds can bring. Ultimately, it is how we use the Earth's resources that will make the difference in securing its birdlife for generations to come.

Many householders in developed countries already make a significant contribution to bird conservation. Simply by providing food, water, and nest boxes, and by gardening in a wildlife-friendly way – for instance, planting indigenous shrubs and setting aside wild patches – they can transform urban and suburban environments into bird-rich habitats, helping compensate for the loss of such habitats in the wider countryside.

Elsewhere, developing communities are becoming increasingly involved in bird conservation. In southern Turkey, religious leaders have helped generate local support for a project to restore wetlands around Lake Burdur, a crucial site for wintering White-headed Duck (*Oxyura leucocephala*). And in Nepal, local villagers have helped develop an ecotourism project to bolster the preservation of Phulchowki Mountain Forest.

These efforts bring rewards. In poor, rural communities, bird conservation can bring tangible benefits – especially where people's livelihoods depend directly upon harvesting natural resources in a sustainable way. In the industrialized world, birdwatching is now a multi-billion dollar industry. Meanwhile, conservation enhances physical and psychological wellbeing – especially for those living in urban environments, where green space is in short supply. Numerous studies illustrate how nature helps people recover from stress and depression-related illness, and enhances the physical, emotional, and psychological development of children.

As birds and birdwatching become ever more popular, so the public is amassing a huge body of potentially important information – whether through formal records or simple ad hoc observations. Conservation groups have devised "citizen science" schemes, such as the Big Garden Birdwatch (UK) and the Christmas Bird Count (USA), which harness this public energy for research purposes. WorldBirds allows people around the world to submit their records via a national online recording system, and conservationists in many developing countries are training community members to conduct their own research – thus harnessing indigenous knowledge, while helping build a local conservation capacity.

Ultimately, everybody has a part to play in bird conservation. The way in which each of us lives is inextricably linked to the patterns of production and consumption that are depleting the Earth's natural resources and biodiversity. Conservation groups emphasize how our everyday choices – such as the way in which we consume energy and water, and what we do with our waste – have a cumulative global impact. Much of their work, therefore, is to teach and encourage ways of living more sustainably.

The big picture

BirdTrack was launched in 2004 by the British Trust for Ornithology (BTO) in partnership with other bird conservation organizations in Britain and Ireland. It invites members of the public to submit details of any birds they have seen, including more unusual visitors to the region, such as this Iceland Gull (*Larus glaucoides*). This helps expand the BTO's knowledge of the populations, distribution, and movements of birds, which in turn informs conservation strategy. In 2010, Birdtrack added to its database the archive from BirdGuides, a birdwatching information service, uploading in the process a massive 1 million records from over 15,000 sites across Britain and Ireland. All these data are published in the Bird Atlas 2007–11, helping paint the most complete picture yet of bird distribution and movement in Britain and Ireland. It also makes its data available to the WorldBirds project.

Great Backyard Bird Count

The Great Backyard Bird Count (GBBC) is an annual four-day event organized in the USA and Canada – including Hawaii – by Audubon. Birdwatchers of all ages and levels of experience count birds for as little as 15 minutes on one or more days of the event, and report their sightings online at www.birdcount.org. All checklists are submitted to researchers at the Cornell Lab of Ornithology, who analyze the data to learn more about the status of birds and how to protect them. In 2010, the GBBC set a new record by submitting more than 97,200 checklists, recording 602 species from every corner of the USA and Canada.

Bullock's Oriole (Icterus bullockii) at bird feeder.

▼ Fair returns

Amount raised by Birdfair for conservation projects *1989–2009*

1989–98 A total of £310,000 was raised to support projects that included conservation of wetlands in Poland, Spain, and Morocco, and forests in Vietnam and Ecuador.

1998	globally threatened birds	£120,000
1999	Atlantic forests, Brazil	£130,000
2000	global seabirds	£125,000
2001	Eastern Cuba	£135,000
2002	Sumatran rainforests	£147,000
2003	Madagascan wetlands	£157,000
2004	Peruvian dry forests	£164,000
2005	Saving Gurney's pitta	£200,000
2006	Pacific parrots	£215,000
2007	Preventing Extinctions	£226,000
2008	Preventing Extinctions	£265,000
2009	Preventing Extinctions	£263,000

The British Birdwatching Fair, known as Birdfair, is the world's largest bird conservation event, and attracts over 20,000 visitors and 330 exhibitors annually. Held in Rutland, Cambridgeshire, it brings together conservation groups and commercial operators, and has, as of 2010, raised more than £2.5 million. Visitors find everything from bird clubs and tour groups, to books, binoculars, and bird-food sellers, and enjoy talks, auctions, and other events.

The funds raised support conservation issues, proposed and managed by the BirdLife International partnership, and have led to the creation of several new national parks. Birdfair is the main sponsor of BirdLife's Preventing Extinctions Programme.

Copyright © Myriad Editions

Big Garden Birdwatch

Each year, on a set weekend in January, around 400,000 people in the UK give up an hour of their time to record the birds they see in their garden for the RSPB's Big Garden Birdwatch at www.rspb.org.uk/birdwatch. Participants simply record the highest number of each bird species seen in their garden or local park during their allotted hour, and then submit the results. These provide conservationists with an important annual snap-shot of how well different species are faring.

▼ Top ten
Average number of birds reported in Big Garden Birdwatch
2010

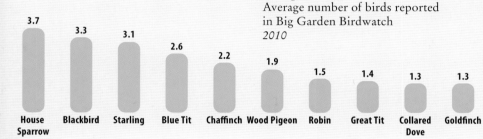

3.7	3.3	3.1	2.6	2.2	1.9	1.5	1.4	1.3	1.3
House Sparrow	Blackbird	Starling	Blue Tit	Chaffinch	Wood Pigeon	Robin	Great Tit	Collared Dove	Goldfinch

▼ WORLD BIRDS

participating countries with recording system *2010*

The WorldBirds project is a joint initiative of BirdLife International, the RSPB (UK), and Audubon (USA). It aims to collect birdwatchers' records for conservation use, as well as to provide a way for all participants to store, manage, and share their data.

Research looks local

Scientists who conduct biodiversity surveys in developing countries are often foreign to the region in which they are working. This does not always encourage local involvement in conservation. In Nepal, more than 14,000 local forest associations manage roughly 1.2 million hectares of forest, including 12 of Nepal's 27 IBAs. Conservationists are training local forest-users in biodiversity monitoring techniques, including transect walks, focus group discussions, resource mapping, and fixed-point photography. Participants also receive bird identification material, and learn bird identification skills. Initiatives of this kind both build local conservation capacity and make the research findings more directly relevant to the needs of local people.

Friends of the forest

Arabuko-Sokoke Forest in Kenya has a rich biodiversity, including a number of endemic or near-endemic birds, such as the Endangered Sokoke Scops Owl (*Otus ireneae*), but has suffered from unsustainable exploitation. BirdLife, working with Nature Kenya, has pioneered management schemes that allow local people to harvest the forest's resources sustainably, and have encouraged the establishment of various income-generating activities, including honey production, butterfly farming, mushroom farming, and ecotourism. The sale of butterfly pupae from 1994 to 2005 alone earned the community more than $750,000. The community has received environmental education and training in business skills and ecotourism, which have fostered a greater appreciation of the forest's importance, and rallied local support for its conservation.

Part Eight

BIRD TABLE

Statistics about birds – such as how
many species are found in each country,
and which are endangered – vary from one
source to another, and are subject to constant
change. Nonetheless, the data presented here provide
an interesting audit of the state of the world's birds today.

	1 Human population 1,000s 2010	2 Land area sq km 2010	3 Agricultural land as % of total area 2008	4 Length of coastline km 2010	5 Fisheries capture tonnes 2008	6 CO_2 emissions tonnes CO_2e per person 2005
Afghanistan	29,117	652,230	58%	0	1,000	0.5
Albania	3,169	28,748	43%	362	5,510	2.9
Algeria	35,423	2,381,741	17%	998	138,833	4.0
American Samoa	69	199	25%	116	4,451	–
Andorra	87	468	55%	0	–	–
Angola	18,993	1,246,700	46%	1,600	317,262	8.0
Antigua and Barbuda	89	443	30%	153	3,521	5.6
Argentina	40,666	2,780,400	49%	4,989	995,083	8.4
Armenia	3,090	29,743	61%	0	3,700	2.4
Aruba	107	180	11%	69	151	–
Australia	21,512	7,741,220	54%	25,760	178,576	27.3
Austria	8,387	83,871	38%	0	350	11.1
Azerbaijan	8,934	86,600	58%	0	1,517	5.7
Bahamas	346	13,880	1%	3,542	9,117	7.2
Bahrain	807	760	11%	161	14,177	29.0
Bangladesh	164,425	143,998	71%	580	1,557,754	0.9
Barbados	257	430	44%	97	3,551	5.7
Belarus	9,588	207,600	44%	0	900	8.5
Belgium	10,698	30,528	45%	67	22,609	13.3
Belize	313	22,966	7%	386	4,621	2.4
Benin	9,212	112,622	31%	121	37,495	1.4
Bermuda	65	54	15%	103	400	–
Bhutan	708	38,394	15%	0	180	2.8
Bolivia	10,031	1,098,581	34%	0	6,797	6.7
Bosnia & Herzegovina	3,760	51,197	42%	20	2,005	5.2
Botswana	1,978	581,730	46%	0	86	6.4
Brazil	195,423	8,514,877	31%	7,491	775,000	5.4
British Virgin Islands	23	151	47%	80	1,200	33.1
Brunei	407	5,765	2%	161	2,358	8.6
Bulgaria	7,497	110,879	48%	354	8,861	1.3
Burkina Faso	16,287	274,200	45%	0	10,600	0.3
Burma	50,496	676,578	18%	1,930	2,493,750	2.2
Burundi	8,519	27,830	85%	0	17,766	–
Cambodia	15,053	181,035	31%	443	431,000	1.6
Cameroon	19,958	475,440	19%	402	138,000	2.1
Canada	33,890	9,984,670	7%	202,080	937,370	22.9
Cape Verde	513	4,033	23%	965	21,910	1.0
Cayman Islands	57	264	–	160	125	–
Central African Republic	4,506	622,984	8%	0	15,000	14.9
Chad	11,506	1,284,000	39%	0	40,000	2.1
Chile	17,135	756,102	21%	6,435	3,554,814	5.4
China	1,354,146	9,596,961	56%	14,500	14,791,163	5.5
China, Hong Kong SAR	7,069	1,104	–	733	158,126	–
China, Macao SAR	548	28	–	41	1,500	–
Colombia	46,300	1,138,910	38%	3,208	135,000	4.0
Comoros	691	2,235	81%	340	16,000	0.6
Congo	3,759	342,000	31%	169	54,104	4.9
Congo, Dem. Rep.	67,827	2,344,858	10%	37	236,000	1.6
Cook Islands	20	236	13%	120	3,000	3.2
Costa Rica	4,640	51,100	35%	1,290	21,750	2.3
Côte d'Ivoire	21,571	322,463	64%	515	58,000	1.6
Croatia	4,410	56,594	23%	5,835	49,024	6.9
Cuba	11,204	110,860	62%	3,735	27,856	3.7
Cyprus	880	9,251	13%	648	2,011	10.5
Czech Republic	10,411	78,867	55%	0	4,164	13.8
Denmark	5,481	43,094	63%	7,314	690,202	11.7

7 Bird species number 2004	8 Endemic bird species as % of number 2004	9 Threatened bird species number 2010	10 Ramsar sites		11 CITES* party to 2010	
			number 2010	area sq km 2010		
434	0.7%	13	–	–	√	Afghanistan
303	0%	6	3	831	√	Albania
372	0.3%	11	47	29,812	√	Algeria
36	6%	8	–	–		American Samoa
119	0%	–	–	–		Andorra
930	2%	21	–	–		Angola
178	2%	1	1	36	√	Antigua and Barbuda
1,038	4%	50	19	53,184	√	Argentina
302	0.3%	10	2	4,922	√	Armenia
88	0%	1	–	–		Aruba
851	45%	52	65	75,102	√	Australia
412	0.7%	8	19	1,200	√	Austria
364	0.5%	15	2	996	√	Azerbaijan
316	5%	5	1	326	√	Bahamas
196	1%	4	2	68		Bahrain
604	1%	29	2	6,112	√	Bangladesh
223	1%	1	1	0	√	Barbados
226	0%	4	9	3,710	√	Belarus
427	0.7%	2	9	429	√	Belgium
544	2%	4	2	236	√	Belize
485	0%	5	4	11,794	√	Benin
235	1%	1	–	–		Bermuda
625	0.8%	17	–	–	√	Bhutan
1,414	1%	33	8	78,945	√	Bolivia
312	0.3%	6	3	568	√	Bosnia & Herzegovina
570	0.5%	9	1	55,374	√	Botswana
1,712	12%	123	11	65,684	√	Brazil
125	0.8%	1	–	–		British Virgin Islands
455	2%	19	–	–	√	Brunei
379	0.3%	12	10	203	√	Bulgaria
452	0%	6	15	6,525	√	Burkina Faso
1,047	2%	41	1	3	√	Burma
597	0.7%	10	1	10	√	Burundi
521	1%	24	3	546	√	Cambodia
936	1%	16	5	7,841	√	Cameroon
472	1%	12	37	130,667	√	Canada
160	3%	4	3	–	√	Cape Verde
209	2%	1	–	–		Cayman Islands
702	0.1%	7	2	3,763	√	Central African Republic
663	0%	9	6	124,051	√	Chad
531	6%	34	12	3,590	√	Chile
445	21%	85	37	31,685	√	China
306	6%	17	–	–		China, Hong Kong SAR
56	4%	4	–	–		China, Macao SAR
1,221	7%	91	5	4,585	√	Colombia
1,821	1%	8	3	160	√	Comoros
138	0.7%	3	7	84,543	√	Congo
597	4%	34	3	74,356	√	Congo, Dem. Rep.
1,148	0.9%	15	–	–		Cook Islands
35	49%	19	12	5,697	√	Costa Rica
838	0%	14	6	1,273	√	Côte d'Ivoire
365	0.5%	10	4	866	√	Croatia
358	9%	17	6	11,884	√	Cuba
349	0.9%	5	1	11	√	Cyprus
386	0.8%	6	12	547	√	Czech Republic
427	0.9%	2	38	20,788	√	Denmark

* Convention on International Trade in Endangered
Species of Wild Fauna and Flora (1973)

	1 Human population 1,000s 2010	2 Land area sq km 2010	3 Agricultural land as % of total area 2008	4 Length of coastline km 2010	5 Fisheries capture tonnes 2008	6 CO_2 emissions tonnes CO_2e per person 2005
Djibouti	879	23,200	73%	314	450	1.5
Dominica	67	751	31%	148	694	2.3
Dominican Republic	10,225	48,670	52%	1,288	15,424	2.8
East Timor	1,171	14,874	25%	706	3,125	–
Ecuador	13,775	283,561	30%	2,237	434,239	3.3
Egypt	84,474	1,001,450	4%	2,450	373,815	2.9
El Salvador	6,194	21,041	75%	307	48,000	1.8
Equatorial Guinea	693	28,051	11%	296	5,400	18.0
Eritrea	5,224	117,600	75%	2,234	1,665	0.9
Estonia	1,339	45,228	19%	3,794	101,037	14.5
Ethiopia	84,976	1,104,300	35%	0	16,770	1.0
Falkland Islands (Malvinas)	3	12,173	–	1,288	81,708	–
Faroe Islands	50	1,393	–	1,117	495,348	–
Fiji	854	18,274	23%	1,129	48,453	3.3
Finland	5,346	338,145	8%	1,250	158,399	13.0
France	62,637	643,427	53%	3,427	457,127	9.0
French Guiana	231		0%	378	3,957	–
French Polynesia	272	4,167	12%	2,525	11,909	–
Gabon	1,501	267,667	20%	885	30,000	10.2
Gambia	1,751	11,295	66%	80	42,645	0.9
Georgia	4,219	69,700	36%	310	26,512	2.0
Germany	82,057	357,022	49%	2,389	229,499	11.9
Ghana	24,333	238,533	69%	539	349,831	1.0
Gibraltar	31	7	–	12	–	–
Greece	11,183	131,957	36%	13,676	88,971	11.5
Greenland	57	2,166,086	1%	44,087	233,754	–
Grenada	104	344	35%	121	2,384	2.7
Guadeloupe	467	1,629	26%	306	10,100	–
Guam	180	541	35%	126	302	–
Guatemala	14,377	108,889	39%	400	22,826	2.2
Guinea	10,324	245,857	56%	320	74,000	2.1
Guinea-Bissau	1,647	36,125	58%	350	6,750	1.3
Guyana	761	214,969	9%	459	42,168	7.0
Haiti	10,188	27,750	65%	1,771	10,000	0.8
Honduras	7,616	112,090	28%	820	12,904	2.2
Hungary	9,973	93,028	64%	0	7,394	8.2
Iceland	329	103,000	23%	4,970	1,284,034	11.1
India	1,214,464	3,287,263	60%	7,000	4,104,877	1.7
Indonesia	232,517	1,904,569	27%	54,716	4,957,098	2.7
Iran	75,078	1,648,195	30%	2,440	407,842	8.1
Iraq	31,467	438,317	22%	58	34,472	4.3
Ireland	4,589	70,273	61%	1,448	205,342	16.8
Israel	7,285	22,072	23%	273	3,435	11.7
Italy	60,098	301,340	46%	7,600	235,785	9.6
Jamaica	2,730	10,991	43%	1,022	13,175	4.8
Japan	126,995	377,915	13%	29,751	4,248,697	10.5
Jordan	6,472	89,342	11%	26	500	4.2
Kazakhstan	15,753	2,724,900	77%	0	55,581	13.4
Kenya	40,863	580,367	48%	536	133,286	1.2
Kiribati	100	811	42%	1,143	34,300	0.5
Korea, North	23,991	120,538	24%	2,495	205,000	5.0
Korea, south	48,501	99,720	19%	2,413	1,943,870	11.8
Kuwait	3,051	17,818	8%	499	4,373	34.8
Kyrgyzstan	5,550	199,951	56%	0	8	1.9
Laos	6,436	236,800	10%	0	26,925	3.0
Latvia	2,240	64,589	29%	498	157,934	4.7

7 Bird species number 2004	8 Endemic bird species as % of number 2004	9 Threatened bird species number 2010	10 Ramsar sites		11 CITES* party to 2010	
			number 2010	area sq km 2010		
312	0.6%	6	1	30	√	Djibouti
164	2%	3	–	–	√	Dominica
224	4%	14	1	200	√	Dominican Republic
1	100%	7	–	–		East Timor
1,515	4%	71	13	2,011	√	Ecuador
481	0.8%	10	2	1,057	√	Egypt
434	1%	5	5	1,435	√	El Salvador
418	1%	5	3	1,360	√	Equatorial Guinea
537	0.6%	10	–	–	√	Eritrea
267	0%	3	12	2,260	√	Estonia
839	3%	23	–	–	√	Ethiopia
203	6%	10	–	–	√	Falkland Islands (Malvinas)
251	0.4%		–	–		Faroe Islands
112	29%	13	1	6		Fiji
421	1%	4	49	7,995	√	Finland
517	1%	7	36	33,143	√	France
644	0.2%	0	–	–		French Guiana
116	36%	32	–	–		French Polynesia
632	0%	5	9	28,185	√	Gabon
535	0%	6	3	312	√	Gambia
268	0%	10	2	345	√	Georgia
487	1%	6	34	8,682	√	Germany
729	0%	9	6	1,784	√	Ghana
270	0%	3		–		Gibraltar
412	0.7%	11	10	1,635	√	Greece
133	0.8%	0	–	–		Greenland
148	2%	1	–	–	√	Grenada
189	4%	1	–	–		Guadeloupe
61	15%	14	–	–		Guam
684	2%	10	7	6,286	√	Guatemala
640	0%	13	16	64,224	√	Guinea
459	0%	3	1	391	√	Guinea-Bissau
786	0.5%	3	–	–	√	Guyana
271	4%	13	–	–		Haiti
699	1%	9	6	2,233	√	Honduras
367	0.5%	9	28	2,354	√	Hungary
305	0.3%	0	3	590	√	Iceland
1,180	6%	78	25	6,771	√	India
1,604	28%	119	3	6,565	√	Indonesia
498	0.8%	21	22	14,838	√	Iran
396	0.3%	18	1	1,377		Iraq
408	1%	1	45	670	√	Ireland
534	1%	13	2	4	√	Israel
478	0.6%	8	52	602	√	Italy
298	12%	10	3	378	√	Jamaica
592	9%	40	37	1,310	√	Japan
397	0.8%	10	1	74	√	Jordan
497	1%	21	7	16,268	√	Kazakhstan
1,103	2%	30	5	1,018	√	Kenya
50	16%	6	–	–		Kiribati
369	4%	22	–	–		Korea, North
423	5%	30	13	98	√	Korea, south
358	0.3%	9	–	–	√	Kuwait
207	0%	12	2	6,397	√	Kyrgyzstan
704	1%	22	2	–	√	Laos
325	0.3%	3	6	1,487	√	Latvia

	1 Human population 1,000s 2010	2 Land area sq km 2010	3 Agricultural land as % of total area 2008	4 Length of coastline km 2010	5 Fisheries capture tonnes 2008	6 CO_2 emissions tonnes CO_2e per person 2005
Lebanon	4,255	10,400	67%	225	3,811	4.8
Lesotho	2,084	30,355	78%	0	50	0.8
Liberia	4,102	111,369	27%	579	7,890	0.6
Libya	6,546	1,759,540	9%	1,770	47,645	11.5
Liechtenstein	36	160	38%	0	–	–
Lithuania	3,255	65,300	43%	90	182,763	5.7
Luxembourg	492	2,586	50%	0	–	26.7
Macedonia	2,043	25,713	42%	0	122	5.8
Madagascar	20,146	587,041	70%	4,828	120,464	1.7
Malawi	15,692	118,484	58%	0	70,019	0.5
Malaysia	27,914	329,847	24%	4,675	1,395,942	9.2
Maldives	314	298	30%	644	133,086	2.5
Mali	13,323	1,240,192	32%	0	100,000	1.9
Malta	410	316	31%	197	1,279	7.2
Marshall Islands	63	181	72%	370	35,436	–
Martinique	406		26%	350	6,200	–
Mauritania	3,366	1,030,700	38%	754	195,328	3.0
Mauritius	1,297	2,040	48%	177	6,152	3.1
Mexico	110,645	1,964,375	53%	9,330	1,588,857	6.3
Micronesia (Fed. States of)	111	702	32%	6,112	21,699	–
Moldova	3,576	33,851	76%	0	1,407	3.3
Monaco	33	2	–	4	–	–
Mongolia	2,701	1,564,116	75%	0	88	11.9
Montenegro	626	13,812	38%	294	900	7.8
Morocco	32,381	446,550	67%	1,835	995,773	2.0
Mozambique	23,406	799,380	62%	2,470	119,645	1.2
Namibia	2,212	824,292	47%	1,572	372,822	5.7
Nauru	10	21	20%	30	39	11.2
Nepal	29,853	147,181	29%	0	21,500	1.5
Netherlands	16,653	41,543	57%	451	416,748	13.7
Netherlands Antilles	201	800		364	16,698	–
New Caledonia	254	18,575	14%	2,254	3,719	–
New Zealand	4,303	267,710	43%	15,134	451,052	19.1
Nicaragua	5,822	130,370	43%	910	29,810	2.5
Niger	15,891	1,267,000	34%	0	29,960	0.5
Nigeria	158,259	923,768	86%	853	541,368	2.1
Niue	1	260	19%	64	200	2.2
Northern Mariana Islands	88	464	7%	1,482	292	–
Norway	4,855	323,802	3%	25,148	2,430,842	10.9
Oman	2,905	309,500	6%	2,092	145,631	18.9
Pakistan	184,753	796,095	34%	1,046	451,414	1.5
Palau	21	459	11%	1,519	1,007	9.9
Panama	3,508	75,420	30%	2,490	222,508	3.3
Papua New Guinea	6,888	462,840	2%	5,152	223,631	1.4
Paraguay	6,460	406,752	51%	0	20,000	4.8
Peru	29,496	1,285,216	17%	2,414	7,362,907	2.7
Philippines	93,617	300,000	40%	36,289	2,561,192	1.6
Poland	38,038	312,685	53%	440	142,496	9.8
Portugal	10,732	92,090	38%	1,793	240,192	7.8
Puerto Rico	3,998	13,790	21%	501	1,793	–
Qatar	1,508	11,586	6%	563	17,688	68.9
Réunion	837	2,510	19%	207	2,905	–
Romania	21,190	238,391	59%	225	5,410	6.1
Russian Federation	140,367	17,098,242	13%	37,653	3,383,724	13.7
Rwanda	10,277	26,338	82%	0	9,050	0.4
St. Helena	4	308	–	60	794	–

7 Bird species number 2004	8 Endemic bird species as % of number 2004	9 Threatened bird species number 2010	10 Ramsar sites number 2010	area sq km 2010	11 CITES* party to 2010	
377	0.5%	7	4	11		Lebanon
311	1%	7	1	4	√	Lesotho
576	0.2%	11	5	959	√	Liberia
326	0%	4	2	1	√	Libya
241	0%	0	1	1	√	Liechtenstein
227	0%	4	5	511	√	Lithuania
284	0%	0	2	172	√	Luxembourg
291	0%	10	2	216	√	Macedonia
262	42%	35	7	11,461	√	Madagascar
658	0.5%	14	1	2,248	√	Malawi
746	3%	45	6	1,342	√	Malaysia
166	0.6%	0	–	–		Maldives
624	0.2%	7	1	41,195	√	Mali
357	0.3%	3	2	0	√	Malta
57	11%	4	1	690		Marshall Islands
168	2%	2	–	–		Martinique
521	0%	9	4	12,406	√	Mauritania
137	31%	11	2	4	√	Mauritius
1,026	12%	55	119	82,255	√	Mexico
97	26%	10	–	–		Micronesia (Fed. States of)
203	0%	9	3	947	√	Moldova
12	0%		1	0	√	Monaco
387	2%	21	11	14,395	√	Mongolia
–	–	11	1	200	√	Montenegro
430	0.2%	10	24	2,720	√	Morocco
685	0.3%	23	1	6,880	√	Mozambique
619	0.8%	24	4	6,296	√	Namibia
13	31%	2	–	–		Nauru
864	0.9%	33	9	345	√	Nepal
444	1%	2	49	8,189	√	Netherlands
259	2%	1	–	–		Netherlands Antilles
150	19%	15	–	–		New Caledonia
351	36%	70	6	555	√	New Zealand
632	1%	11	8	4,057	√	Nicaragua
493	0%	6	12	43,179	√	Niger
899	0.4%	13	11	10,767	√	Nigeria
21	10%	8	–	–		Niue
93	11%	15	–	–		Northern Mariana Islands
442	1%	2	37	1,164	√	Norway
483	0.8%	10	–	–	√	Oman
625	1%	26	19	13,436	√	Pakistan
112	15%	4	1	5	√	Palau
904	2%	17	5	1,840	√	Panama
720	16%	37	2	5,949	√	Papua New Guinea
696	1%	27	6	7,860	√	Paraguay
1,781	7%	96	13	67,840	√	Peru
590	35%	72	4	1,320	√	Philippines
424	0.5%	6	13	1,451	√	Poland
501	0.8%	9	28	866	√	Portugal
310	7%	8	–	–		Puerto Rico
151	0%	5	–	–	√	Qatar
73	29%	6	–	–		Réunion
365	0.3%	12	5	6,836	√	Romania
645	4%	18	35	103,238	√	Russian Federation
665	0.3%	12	1	–	√	Rwanda
128	16%	19	–	–		St. Helena

	1 Human population 1,000s 2010	2 Land area sq km 2010	3 Agricultural land as % of total area 2008	4 Length of coastline km 2010	5 Fisheries capture tonnes 2008	6 CO_2 emissions tonnes CO_2e per person 2005
St. Kitts and Nevis	52	261	20%	135	450	5.9
St. Lucia	174	616	18%	158	1,713	2.6
St. Pierre and Miquelon	6	242	–	120	–	–
St. Vincent and the Grenadines	109	389	26%	84	3,828	2.3
Samoa	179	2,831	23%	403	3,800	1.8
San Marino	31	61	–	0	0	–
São Tomé and Príncipe	165	964	57%	209	4,250	1.1
Saudi Arabia	26,246	2,149,690	81%	2,640	68,000	16.3
Senegal	12,861	196,722	48%	531	447,754	1.9
Serbia	9,856	77,474	57%	0	3,197	7.8
Seychelles	85	455	9%	491	69,172	8.8
Sierra Leone	5,836	71,740	58%	402	203,582	0.8
Singapore	4,837	697	1%	193	1,623	11.4
Slovakia	5,412	49,035	40%	0	1,655	9.3
Slovenia	2,025	20,273	25%	47	869	10.1
Solomon Islands	536	28,896	3%	5,313	26,235	8.9
Somalia	9,359	637,657	70%	3,025	30,000	–
South Africa	50,492	1,219,090	82%	2,798	643,686	9.0
Spain	45,317	505,370	56%	4,964	917,188	10.1
Sri Lanka	20,410	65,610	42%	1,340	327,575	1.3
Sudan	43,192	2,505,813	58%	853	65,500	3.2
Suriname	524	163,820	0%	386	23,811	7.3
Swaziland	1,202	17,364	71%	0	70	2.4
Sweden	9,293	450,295	8%	3,218	231,336	7.4
Switzerland	7,595	41,277	39%	0	1,582	7.2
Syrian Arab Republic	22,505	185,180	76%	193	6,996	3.6
Taiwan	22,900	35,980	–	1,566	1,016,390	12.4
Tajikistan	7,075	143,100	34%	0	146	1.5
Tanzania	45,040	947,300	39%	1,424	325,476	1.5
Thailand	68,139	513,120	38%	3,219	2,457,184	5.3
Togo	6,780	56,785	67%	56	20,000	1.0
Tonga	104	747	43%	419	2,141	2.5
Trinidad and Tobago	1,344	5,128	11%	362	13,833	27.4
Tunisia	10,374	163,610	64%	1,148	100,241	3.3
Turkey	75,705	783,562	51%	7,200	494,124	5.5
Turkmenistan	5,177	488,100	69%	0	15,000	18.9
Turks and Caicos Islands	33	948	1%	389	6,133	–
Uganda	33,796	241,038	66%	0	450,000	1.1
Ukraine	45,433	603,550	71%	2,782	195,449	10.5
United Arab Emirates	4,707	83,600	7%	1,318	74,075	39.0
United Kingdom	61,899	243,610	73%	12,429	596,004	10.7
United States of America	317,641	9,826,675	45%	19,924	4,349,853	23.4
Uruguay	3,372	176,215	85%	660	110,691	12.7
Uzbekistan	27,794	447,400	63%	0	2,800	6.9
Vanuatu	246	12,189	15%	2,528	60,881	2.1
Venezuela	29,044	912,050	24%	2,800	295,364	9.8
Vietnam	89,029	331,210	32%	3,444	2,087,500	2.2
Virgin Islands (US)	109	1,910	11%	188	1,065	–
Western Sahara	530	266,000	19%	1,110	–	–
Yemen	24,256	527,968	45%	1,906	127,132	1.4
Zambia	13,257	752,618	30%	0	79,403	4.4
Zimbabwe	12,644	390,757	41%	0	10,500	2.1

7 Bird species number 2004	8 Endemic bird species as % of number 2004	9 Threatened bird species number 2010	10 Ramsar sites		11 CITES* party to 2010	
			number 2010	area sq km 2010		
132	0.8%	1	–		√	St. Kitts and Nevis
162	4%	5	2	1	√	St. Lucia
308	0.6%	1	–	–		St. Pierre and Miquelon
153	3%	2	–	–	√	St. Vincent and the Grenadines
49	22%	7	1	–	√	Samoa
6	0%	0	–	–	√	San Marino
112	24%	10	1	0	√	São Tomé and Príncipe
433	0.7%	14	–	–	√	Saudi Arabia
612	0.2%	9	4	997	√	Senegal
381	0.5%	11	9	556	√	Serbia
238	9%	10	3	440	√	Seychelles
626	0%	10	1	2,950	√	Sierra Leone
400	4%	17	–	–	√	Singapore
332	0.3%	7	14	407	√	Slovakia
350	0.3%	4	3	82	√	Slovenia
248	21%	20	–	–	√	Solomon Islands
642	2%	11	–	–	√	Somalia
829	3%	39	20	5,532	√	South Africa
515	2%	15	68	2,852	√	Spain
381	8%	14	4	134	√	Sri Lanka
952	0.3%	14	4	81,896	√	Sudan
674	0.1%	0	1	120	√	Suriname
490	0.8%	9	–	–	√	Swaziland
457	0.7%	3	51	5,147	√	Sweden
382	0%	2	11	87	√	Switzerland
350	0.3%	13	1	100	√	Syrian Arab Republic
392	8%	24	–	–		Taiwan
351	0%	9	5	946		Tajikistan
1,056	3%	42	4	48,684	√	Tanzania
971	2%	45	11	3,728	√	Thailand
565	0%	11	4	12,104	√	Togo
46	13%	4	–	–		Tonga
435	0.7%	2	3	159	√	Trinidad and Tobago
360	0%	7	20	7,265	√	Tunisia
436	0.7%	15	13	1,799	√	Turkey
318	0.9%	15	1	2,671		Turkmenistan
186	2%	2	–	–		Turks and Caicos Islands
1,015	0.7%	22	12	4,543	√	Uganda
325	0.6%	12	33	7,447	√	Ukraine
268	0%	10	1	6	√	United Arab Emirates
557	2%	2	168	12,743	√	United Kingdom
888	14%	37	28	14,410	√	United States of America
414	1%	23	2	4,249	√	Uruguay
343	0.9%	15	2	5,584	√	Uzbekistan
108	14%	7	–	–	√	Vanuatu
1,392	3%	27	5	2,636	√	Venezuela
837	3%	40	2	258	√	Vietnam
223	2%	1	–	–		Virgin Islands (US)
163	0%	1	–	–		Western Sahara
385	3%	14	1	–	√	Yemen
770	0.6%	9	8	40,305	√	Zambia
661	0%	9	–	–	√	Zimbabwe

Sources

14–15 Bird Beginnings
LM Chiappe, Downsized Dinosaurs: The
Evolutionary Transition to Modern Birds.
Evolution: Education and Outreach, vol. 2, no.
2; 2009. pp.248–56.

16–17 Fit for Purpose
The beating heart
A bird's heart and blood. www.earthlife.net

18–19 Feathers
The wonder of bird feathers. www.earthlife.net

22–23 Bird Habitats
Forest bird species
Habitat
State of the World's Birds. BirdLife International;
2004. p.20.
Terrestrial Biomes
Map by Sten Porse, available under GNU
License from Wikimedia Commons.

24–25 Country Counts
Biogeographic distribution
State of the World's Birds. BirdLife International;
2004. p.7
Country distribution
World Conservation Monitoring Centre of the
United Nations Environment Programme
(UNEP-WCMC); 2004. earthtrends.wri.org

26–27 Endemic Birds
Endemic Bird Areas
Island endemics
BirdLife International, Most Endemic Bird
Areas are in the tropics and important for other
biodiversity too. www.birdlife.org
Endemic bird species
World Conservation Monitoring Centre of the
United Nations Environment Programme
(UNEP-WCMC); 2004. earthtrends.wri.org

28–29 Important Bird Areas
IBAs in Turkey
State of the World's Birds. BirdLife International;
2004. p29.
32% of Europe's IBAs
BirdLife International, Agricultural
intensification threatens Important Bird Areas
in Europe. www.birdlife.org
IBAs by region
BirdLife International data zone, global
summary;16 March 2010. www.birdlife.org
BirdLife World IBAs
Map kindly supplied by BirdLife International.
Sudan–Guinea savanna biome
LDC Fishpool and MI Evans (eds), *Important
Bird Areas in Africa and associated islands:
priority sites for conservation*. Newbury and
Cambridge, UK: Pisces Publications and
BirdLife International; 2001.
BirdLife International, Important Bird Areas in
biomes: an example from north-central Africa.
www.biodiversityinfo.org

30–31 Europe
Corncrake conservation
Des Callaghan, Corncrakes in Important Bird

Areas in Europe, in N Schäffer and U Mammen
(eds.), *Proceedings International Corncrake
Workshop 1998*. Hilpoltstein/Germany; 2001.
www.corncrake.net
Important Bird Areas
Map kindly supplied by BirdLife International.
Europe's most bird-rich countries
BirdLife International, Europe Important Bird
Areas. www.birdlife.org

32–33 Asia & the Middle East
Collared dove goes west
L Svensson, *Collins Bird Guide*, 2nd edition.
HarperCollins Publishers Ltd; 2009.
Important Bird Areas
Birdlife International, Asian Important Bird
Areas. www.birdlife.org
Map kindly supplied by BirdLife International.

34–35 Africa
IBA protection status
BirdLife International, *Strategy for the
conservation and sustainable management of
IBAs in Africa: 2005–15*. p5. www.birdlife.org
Importance of IBA networks
LDC Fishpool and MI Evans (eds), *Important
Bird Areas in Africa and associated islands:
priority sites for conservation*. Newbury and
Cambridge, UK: Pisces Publications and
BirdLife International; 2001.
BirdLife International, Important bird areas for
globally threatened species: Blue Swallow.
www.biodiversityinfo.org
Important Bird Areas
Map kindly supplied by BirdLife International.
Africa's most bird-rich countries
BirdLife International, Africa Important Bird
Areas. www.birdlife.org

36–37 The Americas
Species diversity in North America
H Berlanga, et al., *Saving Our Shared Birds:
Partners in Flight Tri-National Vision for
Landbird Conservation*. Cornell Lab of
Ornithology: Ithaca, NY; 2010.
www.savingoursharedbirds.org
Important Bird Areas
Map kindly supplied by BirdLife International
South America's most bird-rich countries
BirdLife International, South America's
Important Bird Areas. www.birdlife.org

38–39 Australia
Australian IBAs
IBA Results, Reviewing maps and database; May
2008. www.birdsaustralia.com.au
Important Bird Areas
Map kindly supplied by BirdLife International

40–41 Antarctica, Oceans & Islands
Threatened seabirds in the Southern Ocean
Map kindly supplied by BirdLife International.
The southern oceans are important for
threatened seabirds. www.birdlife.org
Important Bird Areas
Map kindly supplied by BirdLife International
Back from the brink
Nene. www.wwt.org.uk

44–61 Birds in Order
CG Sibley and BL Monroe, *Distribution
and Taxonomy of Birds of the World*. Yale
University Press; 1990
CM Perrins, et al., *Birds of the Western Palearctic*.
Oxford University Press; 1998.
British Trust For Ornithology (BTO), Bird
Families of the World. www.bto.org
The Internet Bird Collection. ibc.lynxeds.com

64–65 Taking to the Air
Winged record breakers
Stephen Moss, *Everything you always wanted to
know about birds*. Christopher Helm; 2005
Wing loading
SM Carr, Wing loading ratios in bats and birds.
www.mun.ca

66–67 By Land & Water
Plumbing the depths
Stephen Moss, *Everything you always wanted to
know about birds*. Christopher Helm; 2005.
Record dive…
B Wienecke, G Robertson, R Kirkwood and
K Lawton, Extreme dives by free-ranging
emperor penguins. *Polar Biology*, vol 30, No 2,
133–142. www.springerlink.com

68–69 Finding Food
What birds eat Author calculations.

70–71 Sense & Sensitivity
Exploring Bird Intelligence. www.birdminds.com

72–73 Showing Off
Personal space
M Unwin, *RSPB Guide to Birdwatching: a Step-
by-Step Approach*. A&C Black; 2008

74–75 From Egg to Adult
Extreme nests
Stephen Moss, *Everything you always wanted to
know about birds*. Christopher Helm; 2005
Hatching calendar
M Unwin, *RSPB Guide to Birdwatching: a Step-
by-Step Approach*. A&C Black; 2008

76–77 Living Together
Gannet Colonies in southern Africa
RJ M Crawford, et al., Trends in numbers of
Cape gannets (Morus capensis), 1956/1957–
2005/2006, with a consideration of the influence
of food and other factors. *ICES Journal of
Marine Science*; November 2, 2006.

78–79 Birds on the Move
Barn Swallow migration routes
Born to Travel campaign.
www.borntotravelcampaign.com
Migration Altitude
M Unwin, *RSPB Guide to Birdwatching: a Step-
by-Step Approach*. A&C Black; 2008

80–81 Flyways
Veracruz migration
Pronatura Veracruz.
www.pronaturaveracruz.org
Hawk Mountain. www.hawkmountain.org

82–83 Different Journeys
Satellite assistance
Finnish Museum of Natural History, Male Osprey M-47346 Harri. www.luomus.fi
Looping the Loop
The incredible journey of sooty shearwater from New Zealand to the north Pacific for an endless summer; 23 April 2007. http://terranature.org
Globe-trotters
The author
Irruption
Great Backyard Bird Count. www.birdsource.org

86–87 Birds on the Menu
Turkeys and ducks
EarthTrends database, WDI online indicators, Livestock. http://earthtrends.wri.org
From jungle to battery farm
National Agricultural Statistics Service, US Department of Agriculture, especially Livestock Track Records; September 2004. United Egg Producers. www.unitedegg.org British Egg Information Service. www.briteggg.co.uk
UK pheasants in figures
P Canning (ADAS), *The UK Game Bird Industry – a short study*. Prepared for DEFRA. www.defra.gov.uk

88–89 Putting Birds to Use
How birds are used
SHM Butchart, *Red List indices to measure the sustainability of species use and impacts of invasive alien species*. Bird Conservation International; 2008. www.birdlife.org
Multipurpose fowl
BBC Follow your dream. www.bbc.co.uk/wales
Precious plumes
RE Allen, *Birds of the Caribbean*. New York: Viking Press; 1961.

90–91 Birds in Culture
Shakespeare's top 20 birds
P Acobas, Shakespeare's Ornithology. www.acobas.net
Artistic gold
NJ Collar, A J Robles, P Gil, and J Rojo, *Birds and people: bonds in a timeless journey*. Mexico City: CEMEX; 2007.

92–93 Learning from Birds
Eastern US peregrines
Chesapeake Bay Field Office, Peregrine falcon, A success story. www.fws.gov

94–95 Conflicts with Birds
Collision course
B Dedman, Bird strikes becoming a more serious threat; 16 Jan 2009. www.msnbc.msn.com
Impact of H5N1
H5N1 totals
Cumulative number of confirmed human cases of Avian Influenza A/(H5N1) reported to WHO; 2 February 2011. www.who.int
Feed the birdie
D Haag-Wackernagel and H Moch, *Health hazards posed by feral pigeons*. Institute of Anatomy, University of Basel, Basel, Switzerland. www.ncbi.nlm.nih.gov
Crops lost to Quelea
CCH Elliott, Quelea Management in Eastern and Southern Africa. http://icosamp.ecoport.org Botswana Ministry of Agriculture, Arable Agriculture Statistics; April 2009. www.gov.bw

96–97 Birds for Pleasure
Stephen Moss, Foreword on birding past, present and future – a global view. In: J del Hoyo, A Elliott, DA Christie (eds), *Handbook of the Birds of the World*. vol.14, Lynx Edicions; 2009.
Number of birdwatchers worldwide
Stephen Moss, Foreword on birding past, present and future – a global view. Op. cit.
Feeding the birds in the UK
We spend £200 million a year on wild bird food; Dec 2006. www.bto.org
Birdwatching in the USA
E Carver, *Birding in the US – A demographic and economic analysis*. US Fish and Wildlife Service; June 2009, amended July 2009. p.8. http://library.fws.gov
The value of birdwatching tourism
CH Sekercioglu, *Impacts of birdwatching on human and avian communities*. Center for Conservation Biology, Department of Biological Sciences, Stanford University, Stanford; 2002
Bird watching to contribute 10% of tourism revenue. *New Times*, Rwanda; 2009. www.newtimes.co.rw

100–01 Extinction
News release from Dukes University, Birds face extinction risk due to human activities; 5 July 2006. news.mongabay.com
Continents and Islands
BirdLife International, We have lost over 150 bird species since 1500. www.birdlife.org
Types of threat
BirdLife International, Invasive alien species have been implicated in nearly half of recent bird extinctions. www.birdlife.org
Exctinctions
Extinct Birds. en.wikipedia.org
Polly gone?
BirdLife International, Spix's Macaw, Species factsheet. www.birdlife.org

102–03 Birds under Threat
Threatened Birds
BirdLife International, Birds on the IUCN Red List. www.birdlife.org
IUCN Red List, Summary statistics, Table 5. www.redlist.org
BirdLife International, Some countries are particularly important for threatened birds. www.birdlife.org
Parrot pressures
BirdLife International, Yellow-eared Parrot, Species factsheet. www.birdlife.org
Widespread but threatened
BirdLife International, Lesser Kestrel, Species factsheet. www.birdlife.org

Endangered ibis
BirdLife International, Asian Crested Ibis, Species factsheet. www.birdlife.org
Scarce sandpiper
BirdLife International, Spoon-billed Sandpiper, Species factsheet. www.birdlife.org
85% of albatross species are threatened…
RSPB, Save the albatross. www.rspb.org

104–05 Losing Land
Major tropical crops
FAOStat [Accessed 7 Dec 2010]. http://faostat.fao.org
Rainforest loss
Earthtrends database, WDI online indicators [Accessed 7 Dec 2010]. http://earthtrends.wri.org
Agricultural land
FAOStat [Accessed 7 Dec 2010]. http://faostat.fao.org
Forest on fire
BirdLife International, In Indonesia, human-initiated fires are responsible for massive losses of rainforest. www.birdlife.org

106–07 Infrastructure & Pollution
Disrupted wetlands
BirdLife International, Large dams and barrages are an increasing threat to wetland-dependent birds. www.birdlife.org
Development Threats
BirdLife International, Threatened birds indicate the consequences of unchecked infrastructure development. www.birdlife.org
Mine every mountain
BirdLife International, Mountaintop mining in the Appalachians is causing a decline in Cerulean Warblers. www.birdlife.org
Declining numbers
BirdLife International, Vultures are under threat from the veterinary drug diclofenac. www.birdlife.org
V Prakash, Recent changes in populations of resident *Gyps* vultures in India. *Journal of the Bombay Natural History Society*; May–Aug 2007,104 (2). www.bnhs.org

108–10 Birds Wanted: Dead or Alive
Overexploited families
BirdLife International, Overexploitation is a threat to many large and conspicuous bird species. www.birdlife.org
Harrying the harrier
RSPB, Wild Birds and the Law 2010. www.rspb.org.uk
Illegal killings
RSPB, Illegal killings of birds of prey in Scotland 2009. www.rspb.org.uk
Hunter's haven
BirdLife International, International action to stop illegal hunting in Malta; 18 Jan 2010. www.birdlife.org
Parrot prison
BirdLife International, The illegal parrot trade remains a problem in South America. www.birdlife.org
Fly Free. www.parrots.org

Trapping trade
Overexploitation at its worst
BirdLife International, Unsustainable
 exploitation of birds is most prevalent in Asia.
 www.birdlife.org

110–11 Alien Invasion
The Global Invasive Species Database (GISD).
 www.issg.org
More than 50% of known bird extinctions...
The biggest killers
BirdLife International, Invasive alien species have
 been implicated in nearly half of recent bird
 extinctions. www.birdlife.org
Globe-trotting sparrow
Map based on data from: UN Glutz von
 Blotzheim and KM Bauer: *Handbuch der Vögel
 Mitteleuropas*. Band 14-I, Passeriformes (5.
 Teil), AULA-Verlag; 1997.
Going viral
BirdLife International, West Nile Virus is
 spreading throughout the Western Hemisphere.
 www.birdlife.org
Killer kitty
RSPB, Are cats causing bird declines?
 www.rspb.org.uk
Plummeting petrel
BirdLife International, Galapagos petrel, Species
 factsheet. www.birdlife.org
Invasive species affect 75%...
BirdLife International, Small island birds are
 most at risk from invasive alien species.
 www.birdlife.org

112–13 All at Sea
BirdLife International, Longline fishing effort
 overlaps with foraging hotspots for seabirds;
 Gillnets pose a significant threat to some
 seabird populations; Seabirds suffer from eating
 "junk". www.birdlife.org
Fish production
FAO Yearbook of Fishery Statistics, Summary
 tables: World fisheries production by capture &
 aquaculture by country 2008.
 www.fao.org/fishery
Fish stocks
FAO, *World review of fisheries and aquaculture
 2008*. p.30.
Deadly tangle
BirdLife International, Trawl fisheries cause
 significant mortality to albatrosses along the
 west coast of southern Africa.
 www.birdlife.org
Hard to swallow
DM Fry, SI Fefer and L Sileo, Ingestion of plastic
 debris by Laysan Albatrosses and Wedge-tailed
 Shearwaters in the Hawaiian Islands. *Marine
 Pollution Bulletin*, vol 18, Issue 6, Supplement
 2; June 1987. pp.339–343.
Oil: the silent killer
Deepwater Horizon oil spill; 5 Dec 2010.
 www.eoearth.org

114–15 Warming UP
BirdLife International, The world's climate has
 changed significantly over recent decades, and
 larger changes are predicted. www.birdlife.org

Australia's montane tropical rainforests
BirdLife International, The number of montane
 endemic birds that go extinct in Australia
 depends on the degree of warming.
 www.birdlife.org
Cape Longclaw
BirdLife International, In southern Africa, the
 range of Cape Longclaw is predicted to retreat
 to upland areas. www.birdlife.org
The late bird
BirdLife International, Climate change is already
 documented as having impacted many bird
 species. www.birdlife.org
Threatened tundra
BirdLife International, In the Arctic tundra,
 climate change will cause dramatic losses in
 waterbird breeding habitat. www.birdlife.org
Krill crisis
BirdLife International, Seabird communities are
 declining in the Southern Californian Current
 System. www.birdlife.org
Pied butcherbird
A Silcocks and C Sanderson, Volunteers
 monitoring change: the atlas of Australian
 birds. In P Olsen (ed.) *The state of Australia's
 birds 2007: birds in a changing climate*.
 Wingspan 14 (Suppl); 2007. p.10.

118–19 BirdLife International
BirdLife International
BirdLife Partners. www.birdlife.org
**The Royal Society for the Protection of Birds
 (RSPB)**
RSPB, Facts and figures. www.rspb.org.uk

120–21 Campaigns & Conventions
Ramsar Sites
Contracting parties to the Convention [Accessed
 Jan 2010]. www.ramsar.org
Airport anger
RSPB. www.rspb.org.uk
Going private
BirdLife International, Business needs to take
 biodiversity on board. www.birdlife.org
Winning the rat race
BirdLife International, The Magnificent Seven
 (Rat-free Fijian Islands). www.birdlife.org
Save the Albatross
Save the Albatross, A global campaign by
 BirdLife International. www.rspb.org.uk

122–23 Saving Species
California Condor Conservation
Birds: California Condor, San Diego Zoo.
 www.sandiegozoo.org
Bustards boosted
Chick success for Great Bustard Project; 2 June
 2009. www.rspb.org
Rapid Response
BirdLife International, Zino's Petrel, Species
 factsheet. www.birdlife.org
Parakeet recovery
BirdLife International, Mauritius parakeet,
 Species factsheet. www.birdlife.org
Vulture restaurants
BirdLife International, Supplementary feeding
 for vultures in Nepal. www.birdlife.org

Ibis alliance
BirdLife International, Asian Crested Ibis,
 Species factsheet. www.birdlife.org
Robin rescue
BirdLife International, Black Robin, Species
 factsheet. www.birdlife.org

124–25 Protecting Places
Conservation requirements
BirdLife International, Broad-scale conservation
 is needed alongside site-scale approaches to
 conserve threatened birds. www.birdlife.org
Services from Birds
BirdLife Data Zone. www.birdlife.org
Arctic agenda
National Audubon Society, Arctic national
 wildlife refuge. policy.audubon.org
Building buffers
BirdLife International Data. www.birdlife.org
Farming by example
RSPB, Hope Farm. www.rspb.org.uk
African investigations
RSPB, Saving our migrant birds – new research
 work in West Africa on Afro-Palearctic
 migrants. www.rspb.org.uk
War-torn wetlands
BirdLife International, Miracle in the marshes of
 Iraq. www.birdlife.org
Forest corridors
RSPB, Save the Sumatran rainforest.
 www.rspb.org.uk

126–27 People Power
Fair returns
Birdfair. www.birdfair.org.uk
The big picture
BirdTrack. www.bto.org
BirdGuides. www.birdguides.com
Big Garden Birdwatch
RSPB. www.rspb.org.uk
Wildlife Extra. www.wildlifeextra.com
Research looks local
BirdLife International, Involving local
 communities in the assessment and monitoring
 of biodiversity. www.birdlife.org
Friends of the forest
BirdLife International, Improved livelihoods at
 Arabuko–Sokoke Forest in Kenya.
 www.birdlife.org

130–137 Table
1 UN Population Division. World population
 prospects: the 2008 revision.
2 CIA Factbook. www.cia.gov
 www.worldatlas.com
3 FAOStat [Accessed 7 Dec 2010]
4 Earthtrends. WRI. www.wri.org and
 CIA World Factbook www.cia.gov
5 The State of the World's Fisheries and
 Aquaculture, 2008. ftp.fao.org
6 Climate Analysis Indicators Tool
 www.cait.wri.org
7, 8 World Conservation Monitoring Centre
 (UNEP-WCMC), 2004.
 http://earthtrends.wri.org
9 IUCN Red List. Summary statistics. Table 5.
 www.redlist.org
10 www.ramsar.org [Accessed Jan 2011]
11 www.cites.org [Accessed 14 Feb 2011]

Bird Index